MANAGING HUMAN RESOURCES FOR NONPROFITS

The core resources and capabilities of any nonprofit organization lie in their human capital; their knowledge, skills and behaviors are critical to the achievement of the organization's mission and performance. Thus, effective management of this key resource is integral to the nonprofit organization's success.

This book focuses on the unique characteristics, challenges and contributions of human resource management to the strategic objectives of the nonprofit. It explores contemporary issues that place the management of people at the intersection between the mission, strategy and performance of the organization. The book:

- Uses the latest theories to build models that explain the determinants and dimensions of strategic HRM within the nonprofit sector
- Examines the core HRM functions in the context of the nonprofit sector to provide insights into how nonprofits can optimize HRM contributions to performance
- Provides a step-by-step process to develop, implement and manage HR practices that are aligned with the strategy of the nonprofit organization
- Demonstrates how to integrate volunteer management into Strategic HRM, using examples from around the world, as well as cases to facilitate learning.

This book is ideal for students and professionals interested in strategic human resource management, and nonprofit management.

Kunle Akingbola is an Associate Professor in the Faculty of Business Administration at Lakehead University, Canada. His intellectual interests focus on complex interactions in HRM and strategic management in nonprofit and healthcare organizations. He is a certified HR professional with industry experience and a consultant to nonprofit organizations.

Managing Human Resources for Nonprofits

Kunle Akingbola

Routledge
Taylor & Francis Group

NEW YORK AND LONDON

First published 2015
by Routledge
711 Third Avenue, New York, NY 10017

and by Routledge
2 Park Square, Milton Park, Abingdon, Oxon OX14 4RN

Routledge is an imprint of the Taylor & Francis Group, an informa business

Library of Congress Cataloging-in-Publication Data
Akingbola, Kunle.
Managing human resources for nonprofits / by Kunle
Akingbola. —First Edition.
pages cm
Includes bibliographical references and index.
1. Nonprofit organizations. 2. Personnel management. I. Title.
HD62.6.A425 2015
658.3—dc23
2014035436

ISBN: 978-0-415-84067-5
ISBN: 978-0-415-84069-9
ISBN: 978-0-203-76703-0

Typeset in Bembo Std
by Swales & Willis Ltd, Exeter, Devon, UK

Printed and bound in the United States of America by Publishers Graphics,
LLC on sustainably sourced paper.

Dedicated to the memories of
Olawale Adebayo and Omotayo Olowoyo

CONTENTS

FIGURES

TABLES

BOXES

FOREWORD

Nonprofit organizations are vital to our aspirations for a vibrant economy and an engaged society. They represent the problem-solving capacity of a community because they take on challenges that governments and (or) the for-profit enterprises are unable or unwilling to address. From local to national and from national to international settings, nonprofit organizations are helping us pursue values and ideals that are important to society.

The ability of nonprofit organizations in achieving their mandate and being effective within their context, is largely dependent on a key asset: its human resources. The importance of human resource management in nonprofit organizations, is now at the centre of discourse among practitioners, managers and researchers. This book makes a significant contribution to the understudied, and often misunderstood, role of human resource management in nonprofit organizations. It is one of the few publications that provides a comprehensive and holistic treatment of the issues that every nonprofit organization must address in order to mobilize their human resources in pursuit of their core mission and strategic objectives.

In this book, Kunle Akingbola encapsulates the essential body of knowledge for managers, practitioners and students of nonprofit management. He has combined his knowledge gained through research and work experience in nonprofit human resource management to put together an excellent treatment of the subject for policymakers, students and researchers alike. It provides managers and other practitioners with a comprehensive overview of the concepts, issues and practices that they would need to effectively lead and inspire their team. The context for nonprofit organizations is changing and evolving continuously. It requires nonprofit professionals to constantly update their knowledge and adjust practices such as attracting new talent, motivating them, and combining them in effective teams with volunteers. This book is an essential reading for nonprofit managers and workers as they join hands to navigate the ever-changing environment.

For students of nonprofit management, the comprehensive material covered in this book is a valuable resource for learning. It enables students to gain an in-depth understanding of the systems and processes that attract, motivate and retain talent in nonprofit organizations. The distinctive contribution of this book lies in its ability to relate important theoretical perspectives to policy development through illustrative examples.

This book is also an excellent starting point for researchers who are launching their own studies of nonprofit HRM. What they would find useful and intriguing, as I did myself, is that the book provokes thought by explaining what we do know and highlighting areas where more work needs to be done to advance our knowledge of the field.

Anil Verma, *Professor,*
Rotman School of Management,
Director, Centre for Industrial Relations
& Human Resources University of Toronto

ACKNOWLEDGMENTS

I would like to express my heartfelt thanks to Professor Jack Quarter at the University of Toronto for his tremendous support including feedback on some of the chapters. In addition to encouraging and fostering scholarship, he exemplifies many of the values that characterize the core ideals of nonprofits. I thank Professor Agnes Meinhard of Ryerson University for her comments on the initial proposal for this book. I'm also grateful to Dr. Natalya Brown of Nipissing University for her comments on some chapters in the book. I am also thankful, to Ms. Bonnie Horton for her editorial support.

A number of individuals who were participants in the HR Certificate workshops at the Social Economy Centre of the University of Toronto and members of the Nonprofit HR Network provided information that contributed to the cases and examples. I extend my gratitude to everyone. I am indebted to my family, especially Olayinka for her support and understanding.

1

OVERVIEW OF NONPROFIT ORGANIZATIONS

Learning Objectives

After studying this chapter, you should understand:

1. A sampling of the different definitions that have been used to describe nonprofit organizations.
2. What type of organizations are categorized as nonprofit and non-governmental organizations.
3. The broad objectives and characteristics of nonprofit organizations.
4. The type of services that are offered by nonprofit organizations.
5. Theories that explain why nonprofit organizations are established.
6. Examples of the sizes of nonprofit and non-governmental sectors in selected countries.

TechSoup Global and Easter Seals of Nebraska

With the assistance of TechSoup Global, a nonprofit that receives and distributes software donated by top manufacturers, Easter Seals Nebraska introduced Nebraska Mobility. The program developed with Microsoft MapPoint, improved route, saved time and money for the clients of Easter Seals who are people with disabilities and special needs.[1]

Oxfam

Oxfam, an international non-governmental organization with a mission to work with others to end poverty, injustice and respond to emergencies, has been at the forefront of delivering food programs, providing clean water, sanitation and general protection to the thousands of people who have escaped the violence in Goma, Congo.[2]

Introduction

Before one can understand or even start to discuss the management of human resources in nonprofit organizations, it is important to explain what type of organizations are being considered and why they deserve to be studied differently from other types of organizations. Accordingly, this chapter offers a cogent introduction to nonprofit organizations. It offers an overview of how nonprofit organizations have been defined and the broad categories of organizations that are included and excluded in such definitions. It also outlines the type of services and products that these organizations provide and the scope of their role in society. The chapter briefly examines the theories that have been offered to explain why nonprofit organizations are established.

Naming a Sector

The term nonprofit organization means something different to different people. As illustrated in the brief overview of the web of activities of TechSoup Global and the direct humanitarian support that Oxfam provides to internally displaced people in the Democratic Republic of Congo, nonprofits connect with people and organizations in diverse ways. For that reason, the terminology used to describe these organizations is different depending on the context, country and often the academic orientation of the researcher. Since this book recognizes that terms such as third sector, non-governmental organizations (NGOs), voluntary and nonprofit sector are relevant and each offers a unique standpoint for describing and conceptualizing the broader sector, the chapter briefly discusses some of the labels before exploring the definitions of nonprofit.

Third sector. The term third sector is used to describe organizations that are focused on serving the economic and social needs of people and cannot be considered to be entirely part of the public or private sector.[3] Originally proposed by Etzioni, the 'third sector' is a big umbrella terminology that attempts to capture various organizations that are not driven either primarily by the market or the state. Therefore, the 'third sector' is used by some to describe a wide spectrum of organizations including nonprofits, non-governmental organizations, co-operatives, social enterprise, social clubs and others.[4] From the example, TechSoup Global, Easter Seals of Nebraska and Oxfam are part of the third sector.

Voluntary sector. This label is an indication of the dependence of nonprofit organizations on volunteers to provide their services.[5] The use of the term 'voluntary' ties the identity of these organizations to the unpaid labor that support their activities. However, it does not suggest that the organizations are run entirely by volunteers.[6] More importantly, it is a terminology of civil participation and engagement. It recognizes that people freely volunteer in organizations that are established to achieve a social mission. The voluntary sector is used commonly in the UK and to some extent in Canada. It includes organizations that one would typically consider to be part of the third sector.

Social economy: This is perhaps the broadest of the terms that are used to describe organizations with a social mission. Although social economy is commonly used in France, it is increasingly being adopted by academics in North America and Europe. It denotes organizations that are characterized by social mission, demonstrate social purpose in their practices and make some kind of economic contribution.[7] Social economy organizations such as cooperatives may have clear economic goals while others make an important contribution to the economy through their activities. Quarter, Mook, and Armstrong[8] suggest that there are four broad groupings of social economy organization: social economy businesses, community economic development, public sector nonprofits, and civil society organizations.

As evidenced in the terms social economy, third sector and voluntary sector, each terminology seems to be aimed at identifying these organizations as different from the business and public sectors. This is also true for other terms that are sometimes used to describe nonprofits such as charitable sector and civil society organizations. This notion is perhaps most obvious with the terms nonprofit and non-governmental, both of which are discussed below. In this book, the term nonprofit is used as a generic terminology to describe organizations in the sector including international non-governmental agencies.

It is relevant to note that in order to address the supposed shortcoming of the varied terms used to describe nonprofit organizations, some authors have opted to use the term voluntary nonprofit sector. However, regardless of the term used to describe these organizations, their functions, characteristics and the services they provide offer the all-important context for the understanding of human resource management in the sector. The definitions are the starting point for clarifying what the organizations are about and how the varied terminologies describe organizations such as TechSoup Global, Easter Seals of Nebraska and Oxfam.

Definitions

The definition of nonprofit organizations can be as varied as the terms that are used to describe the sector. A logical starting point for defining such organizations is to identify two important features of nonprofits that are explicit in most definitions. First and foremost, social mission is the core purpose of nonprofits.[9] This means that nonprofits can simply be defined as organizations that are set up with the primary goal of achieving a social mission. Irrespective of the services, goods and activities of the organization, what should be paramount in the minds of managers and employees of nonprofits is how to deliver on the social mission of the organization. For TechSoup Global, which was established in 1987, that social mission is about technology resources and knowledge for every nonprofit and NGO (see Box 1.1).

BOX 1.1 TECHSOUP GLOBAL

TechSoup Global is working toward a time when every nonprofit and NGO on the planet has the technology, resources and knowledge they need to operate at their full potential.

Second, nonprofits do not generally have stock and do not distribute their net earnings to officers, members or directors of the organization.[10] Since nonprofits do not have shareholders or owners, any net earnings generated by the organization basically belong to the organization. When a nonprofit is a corporation, it is a corporation without stocks.[11] But regardless of the incorporation status of a nonprofit, the point is that it has a non-distribution constraint, that is, it is not able to distribute excess revenue or profit to owners or directors.[12] As will be discussed later in the chapter, although nonprofits sometimes offer similar services or products as the business sector and many regularly partner with businesses to achieve their social mission (for example TechSoup Global), the non-distribution constraint is one of the features that clearly identifies them as different from other business organizations.

While the two characteristics of social mission and non-distribution of net earnings are widely recognized, it is not to suggest that there are no blurry lines if one should dig deeper into the activities and characteristics of nonprofits. Following from this background understanding of the core characteristics of nonprofits, what is most relevant for the purpose of this book is that these features are embedded in the key definitions of nonprofits. Accordingly, one other useful way to understand nonprofits is to compare a few definitions of these organizations and what is emphasized in each. Although the definitions overlap, nonprofits seem to be defined in three ways.

A first approach to defining nonprofits is to describe the organizations simply in terms of their social mission and non-distribution characteristics, that is, the core characteristics discussed above. For example:

> Part of social order that is non-market, non-state and non-household, and whose net earnings are not distributed to owners or shareholders but are retained for the purpose of fulfilling organizational mandates.[13]

The United Nations adopted a not so dissimilar emphasis. The world body's System of National Accounts defined nonprofit institutions as:

> Entities created for the purpose of producing goods and service whose status does not permit them to be a source of income, profit, or other financial gain for the units that establish, control or finance them.[14]

A second approach to defining nonprofits takes a step further by highlighting what the organizations do or whom they serve. This approach succinctly explains the essence and characteristics of nonprofits and wants us to understand the organizations both in terms of what they are and what they are not. A good example of this approach can be found in Quarter who stressed that nonprofits are not entirely part of the government or the private business sector. But more importantly, he explained that:

> Nonprofits serve the public by providing humanitarian and social services or a defined membership by satisfying a mutual interest [.] (The organization) is created solely to provide a service for as long as there is financing and a need for the service.[15]

The centrality of service, financing and the need in the last sentence point to the fine balance between social mission, funding and responsiveness to the needs of the community as core defining characteristics of nonprofits. In addition to providing an important and relevant twist to the definition of nonprofits, it lays out what the goals of the organizations are centered upon, the drivers or factors that bring about the goals and the key resources they need to keep the goals alive.

The third approach to defining nonprofits is somewhat similar to the second above in that it includes the functional characteristics of the organizations. In addition, it also incorporates the operational features to provide a detailed description of what makes an organization a nonprofit. This approach developed by Salamon, Anheier and Associates noted that a nonprofit organization has the following characteristics:

- Organized. The organization must have some of formal structure.
- Private. The organization must be distinct from government and must not exercise government authority.
- Not profit-distributing. The organization must not distribute any profits to directors or owners.
- Self-governing. The organization must be able to control its own activities.
- Voluntary. The organization must have substantial volunteer participation either in its day-to-day operations and management or at the board of directors' level.[16]

In the *Handbook on Non-Profit Institutions in the System of National Accounts*, the United Nations clarified and elaborated on their 1993 definition of nonprofit institutions.[17] The world body acknowledged that the 1993 definition has ambiguities which may blur the lines between nonprofits and corporations and governments. As a result, it adopted a simplified structural-operational definition that defines the nonprofit sector to include units that are:

a) organizations

b) not-for-profit and non-profit-distributing

c) institutionally separate from government

d) self-governing

e) non-compulsory.

(p. 18)

To summarize this definition, a nonprofit is an organization that is self-governing, constitutionally independent of the state, does not distribute profits to shareholders and benefits to a significant degree from voluntarism.[18]

It is important to acknowledge that the application of the definitions excludes organizations which are sometimes considered to be nonprofit such as cooperatives with shareholders and mutual associations that are not incorporated but have a formal structure and fit the criteria, in that they fulfill a social mission without profit to shareholders. Moreover, beyond the general definition, the legal categorization of an organization as nonprofit is often different from country to country, similar to some of the terms used to describe the sector.[19] For example, many hospitals and universities are included in the sector in the US but similar organizations are considered not to be part of the nonprofit sector in Britain.[20] In Canada, hospitals and universities are part of the broader nonprofit sector but due to close affinity to the public sector, they are not considered to be in the "core nonprofit sector". This book recognizes the broader class of nonprofits with the exception of cooperatives. It uses examples from nonprofit organizations that provide services to the general public or to a membership, that are not directly controlled by the government, depend on volunteers to support staff in the provision of services and rely on revenues from such sources as private donors and government grants/contracts.

Legal Status

Despite the different terms and the different approaches to defining these organizations, nonprofits are well-defined under the legal provision of their respective countries. In the US, although there may be some exceptions, most nonprofits that have the characteristics outlined in the definitions are classified as public benefit organizations 501(c)(3) and social welfare or advocacy organizations 501(c)(4). Moreover, while almost all types of nonprofits have federal income tax exemption privileges, only nonprofits classified as public benefit organizations 501(c)(3) are mostly eligible for contribution deductions.[21]

Charitable, educational and religious are the most common types of 501(c)(3) organizations.[22] According to the Internal Revenue Service, in order to be eligible for the tax exempt status under 501(c)(3), a nonprofit must have three components: (1) be organized as a "corporation, trust, or unincorporated association"; (2) be operated not for the purpose of prohibited or restricted activities including distribution of earnings to any private shareholder or individual; (3) have one or more purposes recognized by the law that governs nonprofits in its organizing document.[23] Box 1.2 provides a detailed outline of the eligibility for 501(c)(3) designation.

BOX 1.2 ELIGIBILITY FOR 501(C)(3) STATUS, UNITED STATES

Who is eligible for 501(c)(3) status?

There are three key components for an organization to be exempt from federal income tax under section 501(c)(3) of the IRC. A not-for-profit (i.e., nonprofit) organization must be *organized* and *operated* exclusively for one or more *exempt purposes*.

Organized—A 501(c)(3) organization must be *organized* as a corporation, trust, or unincorporated association. An organization's organizing documents (articles of incorporation, trust documents, articles of association) must: limit its purposes to those described in section 501(c)(3) of the IRC; not expressly permit activities that do not further its exempt purpose(s), i.e., unrelated activities; and permanently dedicate its assets to exempt purposes.

Operated—Because a substantial portion of an organization's activities must further its exempt purpose(s), certain other activities are prohibited or restricted including, but not limited to, the following activities. A 501(c)(3) organization:

- must absolutely refrain from participating in the political campaigns of candidates for local, state, or federal office;
- must restrict its lobbying activities to an insubstantial part of its total activities;
- must ensure that its earnings do not inure to the benefit of any private shareholder or individual;
- must not operate for the benefit of private interests such as those of its founder, the founder's family, its shareholders or persons controlled by such interests;

(continued)

(continued)

- must not operate for the primary purpose of conducting a trade or business that is not related to its exempt purpose, such as a school's operation of a factory; and
- may not have purposes or activities that are illegal or violate fundamental public policy.

Exempt purpose—To be tax exempt, an organization must have one or more *exempt purposes*, stated in its organizing document. Section 501(c)(3) of the IRC lists the following exempt purposes: charitable, educational, religious, scientific, literary, fostering national or international sports competition, preventing cruelty to children or animals, and testing for public safety.

Source: Internal Revenue Service Tax Exempt and Government Entities Exempt Organizations: Applying for 501(c)(3) Tax-Exempt Status. http://www.irs.gov/pub/irs-pdf/p4220.pdf

Nonprofits in Canada may opt to formally register as charitable organizations with the Canada Revenue Agency. The agency recognizes the following activities as charitable: (1) relief of poverty; (2) advancement of education; (3) advancement of religion; (4) certain other purposes that benefit the community in a way the courts have said is charitable.[24] The charitable status allows a nonprofit to issue tax receipts for donations. It is estimated that about half of all incorporated nonprofits in Canada are registered as charitable organizations.[25] The registered charity status is further classified into two main categories: charitable organization; and charitable foundation. A charitable foundation does not necessarily provide the actual charitable services but "operates as a corporation or a trust solely for charitable purpose".[26] Charitable foundations can be subdivided into two: (1) those that give from an endowment such as family and community foundations; (2) those that receive and transfer the funds they raise to an aligned or many aligned organizations such as university and hospital foundations. The charitable foundation can also issue receipts for donation. Although a charitable status is most often associated with nonprofits serving the public, some mutual nonprofits (e.g. religious congregation) are normally registered charities.

In the UK, the Charity Commission, the body that regulates charities in England and Wales, recognizes an organization to be a charity if its purposes are focused exclusively on charitable activities.[27] In other words, charities are not permitted to mix charitable activities with non-charitable activities. The commission's designation of charitable purpose is defined under the Charities Act 2011 which outlines 13 descriptions of purposes (Box 1.3). Very importantly, the Act stipulates that the purpose must be for public benefit. Similar to their

US and Canadian counterparts, registered charities in the UK do have special tax status under the law, which allows them to receive preferential tax treatment for contributions from persons or organizations.[28]

BOX 1.3 DESCRIPTION OF CHARITABLE PURPOSES, CHARITIES ACT 2011, UNITED KINGDOM

Descriptions of Purposes

(1) A purpose falls within this subsection if it falls within any of the following descriptions of purposes—

   (a) the prevention or relief of poverty;

   (b) the advancement of education;

   (c) the advancement of religion;

   (d) the advancement of health or the saving of lives;

   (e) the advancement of citizenship or community development;

   (f) the advancement of the arts, culture, heritage or science;

   (g) the advancement of amateur sport;

   (h) the advancement of human rights, conflict resolution or reconciliation or the promotion of religious or racial harmony or equality and diversity;

   (i) the advancement of environmental protection or improvement;

   (j) the relief of those in need because of youth, age, ill-health, disability, financial hardship or other disadvantage;

   (k) the advancement of animal welfare;

   (l) the promotion of the efficiency of the armed forces of the Crown or of the efficiency of the police, fire and rescue services or ambulance services;

   (m) any other purposes—

      (i) that are not within paragraphs (a) to (l) but are recognised as charitable purposes by virtue of section 5 (recreational and similar trusts, etc.) or under the old law,

      (ii) that may reasonably be regarded as analogous to, or within the spirit of, any purposes falling within any of paragraphs (a) to (l) or sub-paragraph (i), or

      (iii) that may reasonably be regarded as analogous to, or within the spirit of, any purposes which have been recognised, under the law relating to charities in England and Wales, as falling within sub-paragraph (ii) or this sub-paragraph.

Source: Charities Act, 2011. http://www.legislation.gov.uk/ukpga/2011/25

Theories of Nonprofits

Similar to the diverse take on the terms used to label nonprofit organizations and the definitions of the sector, scholars have attempted to explain why nonprofit organizations exist. They have proposed a number of theories that offer explanation and draw attention to the determining factors that are likely to contribute to the emergence of nonprofits. Although it is difficult to say that one factor or a set of factors are particularly more likely to influence the development of nonprofits than the others, each explanation offers a valuable insight into the economic, social and political rationale for the existence of nonprofit organizations. Moreover, while each explanation is unique, they tend to relate to and complement other explanations.[29] We will briefly review five dominant explanations of why nonprofits exist that have been suggested by scholars.[30]

Public Goods Theory

The public goods theory developed by the economist Burton Weisbrod provides an economic rationale for the existence of nonprofits. The foundation of the theory is based on two core ideas. First, there is limitation in the ability of the market to provide public goods or services, that is, goods that are available to all irrespective of contribution or payment.[31] This limitation, which economists call "market failure", means that public goods are within the domain of the government. Second, due to the diversity of opinion and competing priorities in terms of which public goods to provide, the government in a democracy will generally provide the public goods demanded by the median voter in order to help their re-election.[32] Anheier defines the median voter as the "largest segment of the demand for public and quasi-public goods within the electorate" (p. 121). This latter situation is called "government failure," the implication is that there will be significant unmet demand for public goods that are not provided at all or below the level of demand by the government. As a result of government failure, nonprofit organizations may step in to provide the public goods. In other words, people may establish nonprofits in order to provide public goods and services that are not provided at all, or for which supply by the government and the market is below the level of demand.

Entrepreneurship Theory

Unlike the public goods theory that underscores the demand for public goods, entrepreneurship theory emphasizes the supply-side to explain why nonprofits exist.[33] As noted by Anheier, the basic tenet of the entrepreneurship theory is based on the work of Estelle James, Susan Rose-Ackerman and Dennis Young.[34] From the perspective of the entrepreneurship theory, nonprofits are also established through the efforts of social entrepreneurs who match opportunities with innovative solutions by creating social mission organizations—i.e. nonprofits, to supply the goods. Entrepreneurs have been defined as "innovative, opportunity-oriented, resourceful, value-creating change agents."[35] According to Alvarez and Busenitz, people with entrepreneurial cognition have characteristics and decision styles that enable them to recognize opportunities.[36] They follow a nonlinear approach to assess opportunities and are able to see what others do not. In nonprofit organizations, the entrepreneurial cognition emphasizes the mission, goals and outputs over monetary returns.[37] The need to solve mutual or general interest needs drive social entrepreneurs to see issues as opportunities for the nonprofit to provide the goods and services.

Trust Theory

Trust theory is premised on the asymmetries in information between the provider and consumers for certain types of services. An upshot of the work of Hansmann, the theory suggests that there are situations in which, due to the nature of the service, how the service is purchased or other factors, consumers lack the information they need to assess the quality of the goods or services they are purchasing.[38] For example, it is difficult for parents to continuously assess the quality of the service provided by a day care.[39] Following from the information asymmetries, consumers will seek another factor upon which they will base their trust of the provider for the quality of the service they deliver. Since nonprofit organizations have non-distribution constraint, which means they do not allow the distribution of net earnings to officers, members or directors of the organization, consumers develop trust for nonprofits as organizations that are less likely to take advantage or profit from consumers.[40] In essence, nonprofits are established because consumers trust that their motivation is not to take advantage, and there is alignment of interests between nonprofit players, funders and the organization.[41]

Stakeholder Theory

Stakeholder theory builds on the key reasoning that underlies both the trust and entrepreneur theories discussed above. Based on the work of Avner Ben-Ner,[42] the theory acknowledges the position of trust theory which suggests that, due to the fact that consumers are not able to monitor market providers of certain public goods for the quality of the goods they provide, nonprofits are established to meet the demand for these trust goods.[43] The theory also recognizes that there are entrepreneurs and other players who opt to establish nonprofits because they are driven by profit motive. However, the central proposition of the stakeholder theory is that the entrepreneurs, consumers, religious leaders and other actors are stakeholders who are concerned about public goods and, as a result, establish nonprofits to have control over its production and delivery.[44] Through their concern for specific public goods, they give voice to groups of people who may also be concerned, or whose interests are not served by the government or private firms. In essence, they build social cohesion to facilitate the establishment of nonprofit organizations. They take control of the provision of the public goods in order to ensure the quality of service and protect against those who may not act in the best interests of the consumers.[45] A good example of stakeholder theory can be found in social purpose enterprises for and by people with psychiatric disabilities.

Interdependence Theory

The interdependence theory emphasizes the close partnership between nonprofits and the government. According to Salamon, it presupposes that the government and nonprofits are neither in a conflict nor a competitive relationship.[46] Rather, their relationship is characterized by mutual interdependence, support of nonprofit organizations by the government and partnership in the provision of public goods and services.[47] Through the support of the government, nonprofits are able to offer services that are derived from the purposes of the government and can make decisions about the spending of public funds. The relationship is developed through many channels. For example, nonprofits are attractive potential partners to the government because they are generally present in a service domain before the government and have expertise which the government can draw upon. Also, nonprofits can reach out to the government to gain political support for their service area. The latter point lays the foundation for nonprofits to have a role once the government has entered the service area. The second strand of the interdependence theory suggests that in addition to market failure and government failure, nonprofits also have their own limitations which can hinder their ability to address public problems. This concept, known as "voluntary failure", indicates that there are inherent factors that will constrain the ability of nonprofits to address public needs. Anheier[48] summarized the four major areas of the limitations of the voluntary sector as follows:

- *Philanthropic insufficiency* (resource inadequacy). This limitation or weakness suggests that, due to the population of people in need and the issue of free-rider, the resources that are required to address problems in modern society cannot be provided sufficiently and reliably by the goodwill and charity of a few. Anheier describes free-rider problem as a situation in which "those who benefit from voluntary action have little or no incentive to contribute" (p. 130).
- *Philanthropic particularism.* This limitation is explained from the perspective that voluntary organizations tend to help particular subgroups or clients and ignore others. In effect, only the needs of those in groups that have an agency or service dedicated to them are highlighted by voluntary organizations. In line with this thinking, there could be unnecessary duplication of services

for the "deserving" poor, with an emphasis on the preferences of those who control resources and lack of service for other groups.

- *Philanthropic paternalism.* In simple terms, philanthropic paternalism suggests that voluntary organizations may focus on activities, issues and needs that are important to donors but not necessarily the broader social needs in society. Hence, voluntary organizations may not be self-sufficient or have significant discretions to determine the services they offer on behalf of donors.
- *Philanthropic amateurism.* It emphasizes that voluntary organizations depend extremely on volunteers, who may not have the knowledge, skills and abilities to deal with social problems. The significant dependence on volunteers for specialized roles is due to the fact that often these organizations cannot afford to pay for professional teams of social workers, nurses, psychologists and others.

As a result of voluntary failure, the government may come to the aid of nonprofits to enhance its ability to meet the needs of the public by providing support to address their limitations.[49] The key point in interdependence theory is that the government and nonprofits collaborate. They work together to mitigate the limitations of each other and foster a partnership that strengthens them to go on doing what they do well. It is important to note that the theories overlap in many ways, as we have seen in the overview above. As Anheier noted, "to a large extent, the various theories are complementary rather than rival."[50]

The theories of nonprofits combine relevant theoretical perspectives to explain why nonprofit organizations are established, developed and contribute to the provision of public goods and services in society. Also, the theories offer a valuable insight into how the wide-ranging theoretical underpinnings could explain the diverse activities and interactions of nonprofits. For example, understanding who is involved in the governance, funding, service delivery and how these actors interact with the organization starts with the theories. Specifically for the purpose of this book, the key elements highlighted in the theories have an impact on how employees are attracted, motivated and retained in order to achieve the mission and strategic goals of nonprofits. The theories explain aspects of the context of strategic human resource management (SHRM) which we will discuss in subsequent chapters.

Functions of Nonprofits

Nonprofit organizations are critical to the effectiveness of the economic, political and social institutions in society. They play a particularly important role in the health and personal well-being of people. Hence, the roles of nonprofits are of significant value to the public.[51] Scholars have proposed two main categories of the roles of nonprofit organizations that illustrate how they impact people and the society at large. Gordon and Babchuk suggested that nonprofits, which they called voluntary associations, have both (a) expressive roles and (b) instrumental roles.[52] They explained that expressive functions are those activities based within the organizations that are aimed primarily at the individual participants, members or stakeholders in the organization. Examples of organizations that perform expressive roles include senior citizens clubs and recreation associations. Instrumental functions are activities that are focused on the external environment of the organization and aimed at purposes that benefit other people, not only members of the organization. Organizations such as the Red Cross and Easter Seals perform instrumental roles. Gordon and Babchuk also noted that many nonprofits perform both expressive and instrumental roles and their "members identify with the organization both for the fellowship it provides and for the special objectives it seeks" (p. 28). The Kiwanis and the Rotary Club are two examples of nonprofits that perform both roles.

Frumkin extended the expressive-instrumental classification of the roles of nonprofits by Gordon and Babchuk and proposed that nonprofits also engage in demand–supply activities.[53] The demand role of nonprofits relates to the unmet societal needs that these organizations help to address. In other words, the products and services that nonprofits provide were previously unavailable in society. The supply role is based on the activities of individuals and groups who establish nonprofit organizations to offer solutions and explore an opportunity in society. As in the typology proposed by Gordon and Babchuk, demand and supply roles of nonprofits may overlap. The same nonprofit may engage in both a demand role for specific societal needs and supply role for an opportunity in a related or unrelated need. For example, the Salvation Army in Canada provides homeless services, an unmet societal need. The organization also runs thrift stores across the country, which is an example of matching an opportunity. This approach to explaining the roles of nonprofits highlights the relevance of the theories of why nonprofits exist discussed above.

Perhaps a more extensive and inclusive outline of the roles of nonprofits is important to better understand the significant contribution of these organizations to the economic, social and health outcomes of society. Also, it provides a better insight into what nonprofits do without the broad categorization of the organizations based on their roles.[54] Drawing on previous work by scholars and practitioners, Moulton and Eckerd[55] proposed a list of six unique roles of nonprofit organizations:

- *Service delivery*. Nonprofits generally deliver services that the market or government neglects or fails to provide in areas such as education, health, social services and community economic development.[56] Often, nonprofits may complement services delivered by the government because what the government provides is inadequate to meet the demand or requirement of the society.[57]
- *Innovation*. Nonprofits do generally find new ways to solve existing social or public problems. It is suggested that due to this ability to match solutions

to existing problems, nonprofits may gain competitive advantage especially when resources are limited.[58]

- *Individual expression and specialization.* Nonprofits are generally seen as organizations that provide opportunities for individual expression.[59] They allow direct stakeholders such as employees, volunteers and donors to live their values and commitments through participation in the activities of the organization. The effect of this is that over time nonprofits develop specialization and diversify into activities that are consistent with the values of the employees, volunteers and donors

- *Political advocacy.* It is a widely held fact that nonprofits actively advocate, especially for the rights and needs of the vulnerable and the underrepresented in society. Thus, nonprofits play an important role in highlighting issues that affect society and their mission. Although there may be variation between countries in terms of the extent of the involvement of nonprofits in political advocacy, they engage in political advocacy in order to influence government policies.[60]

- *Social capital and community building.* Nonprofits are engines for social connection. They facilitate social capital which Putnam (2000, p. 19) defined as the "connections among individuals—social networks and the norms of reciprocity and trustworthiness that arise from them."[61] Social capital contributes to the ability of people to foster civic engagement or participation[62] the benefits of which are transferrable to other situations including business.[63] In essence, nonprofits contribute significantly to community building.

- *Citizen engagement and democratization.* Nonprofits connect people to the government system and as a result facilitate to the democratic process. Moulton and Eckerd noted that the citizen engagement role allows people to be involved directly in the political processes and may or may not involve the government. They suggested that this could be an alternative to nonprofits focusing on direct political advocacy.

The roles highlight the big picture contribution of nonprofits to the economic, social and political health of each country. They show the ways nonprofits add value to our everyday life, create employment, enhance social capital and promote democracy. These roles are actualized through the numerous activities of nonprofit organizations. In addition, the category of activities is another way nonprofits are classified. The next section offers a summary of the types of activities one can find in nonprofit organizations.

Nonprofit Activities

Several classification systems have been developed to group the activities of nonprofits.[64] The International Classification of Nonprofit Organizations (ICNPO) developed by the Johns Hopkins Comparative Nonprofit Sector Project[65] offers one of the most widely used categories of nonprofit activities.

It classifies nonprofits into 12 major activity groups that are based on the services or goods offered in each category (see Table 1.1).

In the US, the formal classification system that is generally used to categorize nonprofit activities is the Internal Revenue Service's (IRS) National Taxonomy of Exempt Entities (NTEE).[66] The classification system, which was originally developed by the National Center for Charitable Statistics of the Urban Institute in collaboration with nonprofit organizations, divides nonprofit activities into 10 major categories which are further sub-divided into 26 major groups.[67] The complete NTEE Core Codes classification system has about 600 service categories. The 10 major categories of the NTEE are:

- Arts, Culture and Humanities
- Education

TABLE 1.1 International Classification of Nonprofit Organizations (ICNPO) Classification

Major Activity Groups	*Subgroups*
1. Culture and Recreation	Culture and Arts
	Sports
	Other Recreation and Social Clubs
2. Education and Research	Primary and Secondary Education
	Higher Education
	Other Education
	Research
3. Health	Hospitals and Rehabilitation
	Nursing Homes
	Mental Health and Crisis Intervention
	Other Health Services
4. Social Services	Social Services
	Emergency and Relief
	Income Support and Maintenance
5. Environment	Environment
	Animal Protection
6. Development and Housing	Economic, Social and Community Development
	Housing
	Employment and Training
7. Law, Advocacy and Politics	Civic and Advocacy Organizations
	Law and Legal Services
	Political Organizations
8. Philanthropic Intermediaries and Voluntarism Promotion	
9. International	
10. Religion	
11. Business and Professional Associations, Unions	
12. Not Elsewhere Classified	

- Environment and Animals
- Health
- Human Services
- International, Foreign Affairs
- Public, Societal Benefit
- Religion Related
- Mutual/Membership Benefit
- Unknown, Unclassified.

The UK's National Council for Voluntary Organizations (NCVO) uses the ICNPO classification system to categorize registered charities in England and Wales. The multi-dimensional classification system employed by the Charity Commission, which incorporates the purpose of the organization, how it accomplishes the purpose and who the charity serves, is difficult for statistical purposes.[68] Statistics Canada also adopts the ICNPO classification system for its Satellite Account of Non-profit Institutions and Volunteering.

Revenue

Nonprofit organizations work to create and sustain social and economic value. In the context of nonprofits, value is the tangible and intangible worth of the goods and services of the sector. They create value through the translation of shared values and common concerns in the community to problem-solving activities.[69] Although the value created by nonprofits is also beneficial to other stakeholders such as employees, government, suppliers and funders, the primary beneficiary of the value nonprofits create are the clients.[70] As we will discuss in subsequent chapters, the value is the outcomes achieved for the clients and it is one of the core measures of the performance of nonprofits. Following from the centrality of outcomes for the consumer and as evidenced in the diverse activities that make up the goods and services provided by these organizations, there is no question that financial resources are important for the value creation process. It is therefore important for managers and stakeholders to understand the sources of revenue that constitute the financial input nonprofits deploy to create value. First, we will briefly clarify what we mean by revenue in nonprofit organizations.

Revenue in nonprofits includes all income generated by the organization. Similar to any other type of organization, revenue is inextricably linked with the cost of creating value.[71] Put differently, for consumers to benefit from the mission of the nonprofits, the organization must generate sufficient revenue to cover the cost of its operations. Revenue thus represents one of the core enablers to achieving the mission and the value creation goal of the nonprofit. The ability of the organization to generate revenue is an important competency. Since each source of revenue comes with its own ambiguity,[72] managers must not only understand the current and potential sources of revenue for their organization, they must also learn how to cultivate and sustain an effective relationship with the revenue sources, and how to effectively adapt the organization to changes in the sources of its revenue.

It is important to note that there are variations between the types and categories of nonprofits as well as variations across countries in terms of sources of revenue. In recent findings from the implementation of the *UN Nonprofit Handbook*, Salamon et al.[73] reconstructed the sources of nonprofits' revenue into three broad categories: (1) fees charged for the provision of goods and services, (2) government sources, and (3) philanthropic giving and donations. They noted the difference between the reconstructed sources of revenue and the standard government accounts which classifies nonprofit revenue sources into: (a) market sales, (b) property income, and (c) transfers. We will adopt a broad category of the sources of revenue for nonprofits that is similar to the one proposed by Salamon et al. in name, but which is different in content, especially in terms of what is included under government funding. Accordingly, for the purpose of this book, the three main sources of revenue for nonprofit organizations are:

1. Earned income
2. Government sources
3. Philanthropy.

Earned Income

Many nonprofits earn income through their various activities (see the example of YMCA of Greater New York in Box 1.4 and Figure 1.1). Such income includes fees for service, dues paid by members, proceeds from goods sold, property income, income from special events, business and investment income. Earned income often contributes a significant percentage of the revenue of nonprofits in the categories of recreation, arts and culture, where membership fees and service fees are common.[74] Similarly, private foundations rely on income from their investments to provide the revenue to sustain their grant-making mission. To increase earned income, some nonprofits develop revenue generating promotional initiatives which may require a licence from the government. A special lottery is one example of this type of earned income in Canada.[75]

BOX 1.4 YMCA OF GREATER NEW YORK

The YMCA of Greater New York has three areas of focus: youth development; healthy living; and social responsibility. The organization generated 59 percent of its total revenue and support in 2011 from membership dues and program fees. The 150-years-old organization also generated another 18 percent of its revenue from residence and related services. This suggests that close to 80 percent of its revenue comes from earned income.

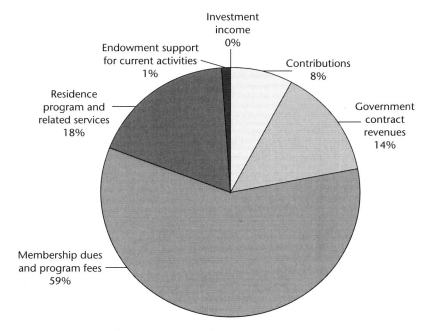

FIGURE 1.1 YMCA of Greater New York: Revenue & Support, 2013

Source: Chart based on financials in YMCA of Greater New York 2013 Annual Report, http://www. ymcanyc.org/association/pages/2013-annual-report. Retrieved August 28, 2014.

In response to the challenges of and competition for revenue from other sources, nonprofits have increasingly pursued a strategy that increases their earned income.[76] The strategy is an important step in the direction to pursue an increased and diverse source of revenue.[77] Studies have found that nonprofits use income from revenue-generating services to develop services required by low-paying clients.[78] This strategy is especially critical in order to ensure that each organization will have some resemblance of financial stability, overcome the substantial challenges in funding and adapt to the new reality of the funding environment. However, there is a risk that must be considered by managers and the board of directors of nonprofits, especially those in which fees and charges are not easily aligned to their services. Essentially, such organizations may experience a tendency to discount their original mission and goals to create value for the exigencies of following the money.[79]

For the US, earned income and investment income as defined above represent the largest percentage of total revenue—78 percent of the $1.59 trillion generated by nonprofit organizations that were classified as 501(c)(3) public charities in 2011.[80] A further breakdown of the data show that earned income includes fees for services and goods from private sources and fees paid by government sources for the contracted services delivered by the nonprofit organizations (see Figure 1.2).[81]

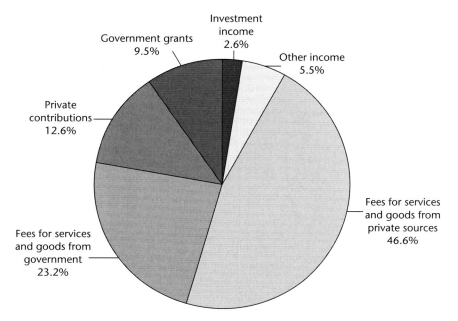

FIGURE 1.2   USA Revenue Sources for Reporting Public Charities, 2011

Sources: Pettijohn, S (2013). The Nonprofit Sector in Brief: Public Charities, Giving, and Volunteering, 2013. The Urban Institute.

Although it could be classified otherwise, the latter is consi⸳red as earned income due to the fact that it includes fees paid for a variety of p⸳lic services such as Medicare and Medicaid and *business-like* contracts which ar⸳ ⸳mewhat different from government grants. Another importan⸳ point to not⸳ ⸳ere is that, unlike the UK and Canada, large nonprofit hospita⸳⸳ and universiti⸳⸳ are included in the 501(c)(3) public charities in the US. Hence⸳ ⸳his category o⸳ ⸳onprofit organization provides a significant source of earned ⸳⸳come due to tu⸳⸳ion payments and hospital patient revenues.

As noted previously there is variation in revenue sources b⸳⸳ween countries. This is evident in the UK where voluntary o⸳ganizations gene⸳⸳ted £21.2 billion from earned income and £2.7 billion from investment income in 2010–2012.[82] These numbers represent 54 percent of the total income of £39.2 billion generated by voluntary organizations in the fiscal year (Figure 1.3). However, it is important to clarify that some of the revenue sources included under earned income are specific to the UK voluntary sector environment. Earned income includes: fees and payments from individuals, including rent; fees and payments from statutory (government) sources; services provided under contract from the voluntary sector; payment from the private sector: and internally generated income, including investments.

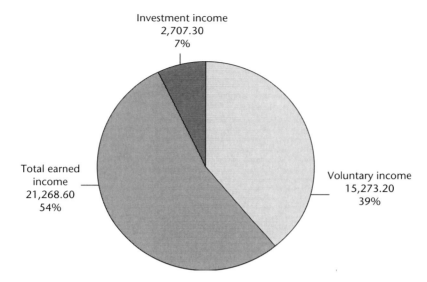

FIGURE 1.3 United Kingdom Overview of Voluntary Sector, 2011/12

Source: Chart based on data from NCVO *UK Civil Society Almanac*: Voluntary sector income by size of organization, 2011/12 (£ millions), http://data.ncvo.org.uk/a/almanac14/income-3/ Retrieved July, 2014.

Although to a lesser extent than the US and the UK, the core nonprofit organizations in Canada generate most of their revenue through earned income and investment income. This classification of nonprofits excludes public hospitals and colleges and universities, which are classified as part of the overall nonprofit sector. In 2007, earned income from sales of goods and services represented $35.4 billion or 45.6 percent, while investment income accounted for $3.8 billion or 4.9 percent of the total revenue of $77.9 billion.[83] Another form of earned income, membership fees, contributed $12.4 or 15.9 percent of the total revenue in 2007 (Figure 1.4). The relatively not too disproportionate distribution of revenue across few categories of the core nonprofit sector appears to suggest that the contribution of earned income to the total revenue is not limited to the recreational, art and culture areas of activity.[84] Further analysis of the revenue of the core nonprofit organizations by Statistics Canada shows that the sector has increased the share of its revenue from sales of goods and services to over 45 percent during the decade. Earned income retained its position as the largest source of revenue. A recent survey of nonprofit leaders in Canada indicates that an almost equal percentage of nonprofits experienced an increase (23 percent) as those who experienced a decrease (24 percent) in revenue between 2012 and 2013.[85]

The question of earned income is a challenge for many nonprofit organizations. For one, it may be inconsistent with their mission to do "public good" and the goal to create value for their clients.[86] As we have noted, the quest for earned

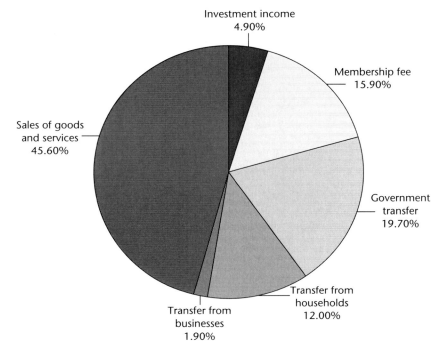

FIGURE 1.4 Canada Revenue by Source: Core Nonprofit Sector, 2007

Source: Satellite Account of Non-profit Institutions and Volunteering 2007. Statistics Canada (Catalogue no. 13-015-X, ISSN 1710-9264).

income may overshadow the needs of the clients or, at the least, introduce fees which they cannot afford. However, it is not all bad news. Research has shown that the need for earned income can bring about the diversification of nonprofit services, revenue sources and grant the organization more control of their activities.[87] With this in mind, we next discuss the other sources of revenue for nonprofit organizations.

Government

Either directly or indirectly, the government has always been a source of revenue for nonprofit organizations in many developed countries.[88] What is relatively new is the level of revenue generated from government sources and the type of relationship between the government and nonprofit organizations.[89] There is extensive research on how the relationship has evolved and the current interaction between government and nonprofits. We will examine the key dimensions of the relationship in Chapter 3. For now, the important point is that government is a major source of revenue for nonprofits. Revenue from government sources comes in different forms and varies significantly between countries. The reconstructed sources of revenue for nonprofits that was proposed from the findings on the implementation of the *UN Nonprofit Handbook* classified government contracts or reimbursements for services provided (vouchers) and government grants under revenue from government. However, since fees/reimbursement generated from the government is considered to be market sales (earned income) under standard national accounts, it is recognized as such here. Again, for the purpose of this book, there are three broad revenue categories from government sources: (1) fees and reimbursements, (2) grants, and (3) contracts.[90]

- *Fees and reimbursements* are payments to a nonprofit organization for a specified good or service supplied by the organization. Basically, it is the purchase of a good or service by the government from the nonprofit organization. In some countries, the competition process to determine the supplier of the good or service generally emphasizes priority for a nonprofit organization to be the supplier and involves detailed eligibility criteria.[91] As a result, it is not generally an open competition process that both for-profit and nonprofit organizations can participate in. Regardless, fees and reimbursements are considered to be a form of earned income for nonprofit organizations in many countries.
- *Contracts* are agreements between a contracting government source and a nonprofit organization to provide a good or service.[92] One key difference between contracts and fees is that the nonprofit is providing the good or performing the service on behalf of the government. It is therefore subject to the performance goals and outcomes defined by the government. The nonprofit organization may also be required to participate in a government audit. Contracts are generally considered to be a form of government funding.
- *Grants* are transfer payments provided by a government source to support the mission, operation or organizational capacity of a nonprofit. It is generally intended to aid the organization to provide a good or service that is outlined in its mission and for which there is no other or a very limited source of funding.[93] In addition to services, grants can also support specified organizational capacity such as human resources and information technology. Grants are considered to be the traditional form of government funding that has been changed into contracts over the past three decades.

Following from these three sources of revenue for nonprofits from the government, Figure 1.2 shows that nonprofit organizations that are classified as 501(c)(3) public charities in 2011 in the US generated 9.5 percent of their revenue from government grants. As noted under earned income, the larger percentage of revenue in the US is generated through fees paid by government sources for the contracted services delivered by the nonprofit organizations.[94] In all, either combined with grants or separated as fees, government is the second largest source of revenue for nonprofit organizations in the US.

The picture of revenue from government sources which is labelled as statutory sources in the UK is somewhat different. Voluntary sector organizations in the UK generated £11.02 billion from fees and payments for contracted services by government sources, another £2.5 billion from grants and £70.3 million from fundraising in the public sector in 2011–2012.[95] Although the fees and payments for contracted services to government are designated as earned income, they are also included in the total revenue from government sources. The total voluntary sector revenue from government sources in 2011–2012 was £13.6 billion, which represents 35 percent of the total revenue of the sector. However, without the fees and payments for contracted services, government grants only accounted for 6.6 percent of the revenue of voluntary organizations in the UK in 2011–2012. As in many developed countries, the percentage of voluntary sector revenue from government grants has decreased correspondingly with the increase in fees and payments for contracted services over the past decade.

Revenue from government transfers constitutes the second largest source of income for nonprofit organizations in Canada. In 2007, this stream generated $15.3 billion or 19.7 percent of the total revenue of the sector, second only to sales of goods and services.[96] The core nonprofit sector generated significantly less percentage of their revenue from government than universities, colleges and hospitals, which received about 75 percent from government transfers. Unlike the US and the UK, there is no indication that payments for contracted services from government sources are either included in earned income or designated under government transfers.

Irrespective of how income from government sources is designated in each country, it constitutes an important source of revenue for nonprofit organizations. As evidenced in the summary numbers from the US, the UK and Canada, this revenue stream highlights the pivotal connection between government and nonprofit organizations, a point we will return to in Chapter 3.

Philanthropy

The third major category of source of revenue for nonprofit organizations is even more diverse than earned income and the government. Philanthropy encompasses different forms of donations, gifts and support that are freely given to nonprofit organizations, generally with no expectations of benefits to the individual or organization doing the philanthropic act. This description echoes how the *UK Civil Society Almanac* outlines this revenue stream and emphasizes two key characteristics of philanthropy as a source of revenue for nonprofits. First, it is based on altruism, that is, charitable undertaking by individuals and organizations. The nonprofit is generally not expected to provide a good or perform a service for the donor in return. Second, it is private. It does not generally involve the government. However, due to the complexity of the revenue generation process in the nonprofit sector, the reality of these two characteristics may overlap with either earned income or revenue from government sources or both. For example, a private foundation may receive a government grant which will help it to support nonprofit organizations.

To make sense of the diverse types of philanthropy as sources of revenue for nonprofits, we shall group them into three main categories: (1) individuals, (2) corporations, and (3) foundations and agencies.

Individual philanthropy includes all forms of donations and gifts from an individual to a nonprofit organization. This source of revenue could depend on the fundraising ability of the organization and the profile of the cause to attract the attention of the public, especially the wealthy and connected members of the public.[97] This suggests that individual philanthropy is a particularly difficult and expensive source of revenue to depend on.[98] Again, there is variation between countries in terms of the contribution of individual philanthropy to the revenue of nonprofits. As Anheier noted, the US has a well-developed system of individual philanthropy.[99] Individuals donated $228.93 billion to public charities in the US in 2012, with a significant percentage of the contributions going to religious organizations, educational institutions and human services organizations.[100] Individual philanthropy contributed £8.9 billion to the revenue of voluntary organizations in the UK in 2011–2012. In addition to donations, £8.4 billion was raised through membership subscriptions paid by individuals and fundraising where benefits are received in return.[101] The NCVO *UK Civil Society Almanac* shows that, with the exception of international sub-sector of the UK's voluntary sector, religious organizations generated the most revenue from what is classified as voluntary sources (of which individual philanthropy makes up approximately half). In Canada, individual philanthropy, which is categorized as transfers from households, contributed $9.3 billion (25 percent) of the $77.9 billion revenue of the core nonprofit sector in 2007 (see Figure 1.7). Although the breakdown of individual philanthropy is not provided, previous data would suggest that contribution to religious organizations is likely to be a significant share of the total.[102]

Corporations also engage in philanthropy through donations, gifts and sponsorship of nonprofit organizations. Although small in comparison to the other sources of revenue, corporations contribute to the financial capacity of nonprofit organizations. However, it has been suggested that corporations appear to prefer small and short-term project-based donations for large visible nonprofit organizations rather than longer-term funding commitments.[103] Researchers have noted that the pattern highlights the difficulty for nonprofit organizations to rely on corporate philanthropy as an alternative to revenue from government sources. Nonetheless, the revenue from corporations helps nonprofits to sustain their operations. Estimates from Giving USA indicate that corporations contributed $14.10 billion (4 percent) of the private contributions revenue of public charities in 2009.[104] In a survey, most of the public charities reported that corporations often account for less than 10 percent of their revenue.[105] This pattern is similar in the UK and Canada. Corporations contributed £933 million to charity organizations in the UK in 2011–2012 and $1.4 billion to nonprofit organizations in Canada in 2007. However, it is important to note that the NCVO *UK Civil Society Almanac* categorizes nonprofit revenue of £393 million from sponsorship and £496 million from corporations in the form of research and royalties as earned income. In total, the revenue of the UK voluntary sector from corporations in 2011–2012 was £1.8 billion. In essence, revenue from corporations accounts for about 4 percent of the total revenue of the voluntary sector in the UK in 2011–2012 and 1.9 percent of the revenue of the core nonprofit sector in Canada in 2007.

Foundations and agencies include revenue generated from charitable foundations, trusts and intermediary agencies such as the United Way. Foundations are established either to use the income from their endowments for specific causes or to raise and distribute funds for nonprofit organizations.[106] Also, as noted by Scott,[107] foundations are either private, in that they are responsible for the disbursement of funds from private sources to support the activities of nonprofits, or public foundations that solicit for and combine assets from group of people to build endowments which they use to support charities. Although they are not foundations per se, intermediary community fundraising organizations such as the United Way are more or less similar to public foundations. Many public foundations and the United Way are important revenue sources for nonprofit organizations. More importantly, they often provide revenue that is aligned to the charitable mission of the organization and to sustaining the nonprofit than other sources of revenue.[108] However, funding from foundations contributes a significantly smaller percentage to the total revenue of nonprofits than government. It is estimated that grant-making foundations contributed $38.44 billion (13 percent) of the private contributions revenue of public charities in the US in 2009.[109] UK charity organizations received £2.3 billion in the form of grants and £686 million for services provided under contract to foundations and trusts in 2011–2012.[110]

Ultimately, philanthropy represents an important source of revenue to nonprofits not only because it contributes to the financial capacity of each organization but, more importantly, it signifies the buy-in of the community to the mission of the organization and is a potential indicator of the social alignment between the organization and its stakeholders.[111] This connection is the basis of the social legitimacy a nonprofit must attain in order to survive and sustain its activities.[112] Although revenue from philanthropy is smaller than those from government and earned income, its connection to the grassroots plays a crucial role in the vibrancy and size of the sector.

Size

The previous sections highlight the scope of activities and the revenue streams of nonprofit organizations, drawing on examples from the US, UK and Canada. While these provide some insights into the general situation of nonprofits, to complete the picture, we need to understand the overall size of the sector and its contribution to the economy, especially in light of the significant growth of nonprofits in many developed countries over the past decades.

In 2012 the nonprofit sector in the US was estimated to have 2.3 million organizations operating in diverse areas of activity. About 1.4 million of the organizations in the sector were reported to be registered as 501(c)(3) public non-profit charities, highlighting an increase of 42 percent over the decade.[113] As the single largest cohort, public charities generated three-quarters of the total revenue of the US nonprofit sector.[114] According to the recent findings on the implementation of the *UN Nonprofit Handbook*, the US nonprofit sector is a major employer. The sector as a whole employs 10.2 percent of the total workforce, of which 7.7 percent are part of the paid workforce and 2.5 percent are volunteers.[115] It contributed 6.6 percent to the gross domestic product (GDP) of the country.

The NCVO *UK Civil Society Almanac* shows that there were over 161,266 voluntary organizations in 2011–2012.[116] Consistent with the significant growth of the nonprofit sector in developed countries, the UK's voluntary sector has experienced a steady influx of new voluntary organizations since the 1960s.[117] The statistics indicate that the sector employs about 2.7 percent of the UK workforce, which is the culmination of a constant increase over the past decade. It is estimated that voluntary organizations employed 765,000 people in 2010. Using the gross value added (GVA), which is similar to the GDP, to estimate the production or output of the sector, the NCVO *Almanac* also estimates that the voluntary sector contributes £11.7 billion to UK gross value added.

In relative terms, Canada has a very vibrant nonprofit sector. The estimated 165,000 nonprofits in Canada contributed $35.6 billion or 2.5 percent to the GDP of the country in 2007. With colleges, universities and hospitals in the mix, the overall nonprofit sector contributed $100.7 billion or 7.1 percent of the GDP in 2007. If volunteer labor is added, nonprofits account for 8.1 percent of the GDP, placing Canada at the top of the 16 country average in the recent findings on the implementation of the *UN Nonprofit Handbook*. One other keynote about the statistics for Canada is the average 7.1 percent growth of the core nonprofit sector over the 11-year period. In short, the nonprofit sector in Canada has seen significant growth.

All in all, nonprofit organizations in many countries have experienced rapid and significant change over the past few decades. To some extent, this transformation could be attributed to changes in the social needs of communities, demographic factors and economic forces. However, government policies seem to have played the most significant role in the transformation of the sector in developed countries.[118] The increased size and scope of the sector has further accentuated the strategic significance of nonprofit organizations to the social well-being of the people and their contribution to the economic and political institutions of these countries.

Summary

Managing human resources in nonprofit organizations requires an in-depth understanding of what nonprofit organizations are about. This chapter has summarized a great deal of essential knowledge about the sector to provide not only a definition of nonprofits but also to provide important insights about theories, the scope of activities, size and the sources of revenue of these organizations. In the process, the chapter has set the stage for many of the themes and issues that are relevant in the subsequent chapters of the book. For example, how a revenue source plays out in the design and implementation of an HR system is a constant question that will be evidenced in subsequent chapters.

Also, given the big picture of the goods and services of nonprofit organizations discussed in this chapter, the importance of employees and volunteers as stakeholders is undeniable. As a result, the question of how to attract, motivate and retain them as well as establish an effective system to align HR practices to the organization's strategy cannot be overemphasized. As we will discuss in the subsequent chapters, managing these critical human assets of nonprofit organizations is intertwined with the strategies each organization adopts to adapt to change in the external environment. Put differently, if a nonprofit can effectively manage its human capital, it will stand a better chance of adapting and succeeding in a constantly turbulent operating environment.

Discussion Questions

1. Identify a definition of nonprofit in this chapter that makes the most sense to you and explain why.
2. Pick a nonprofit organization that you are familiar with, review the mission and core values of the nonprofit. What are the services of the nonprofit and who are the primary clients of the organization?
3. Of the functions of nonprofits discussed in this chapter, which one is most important to you and why?
4. Based on the ideas presented in this chapter about nonprofits, what is it about nonprofits that interest you the most?

Notes

1 *Easter Seals Nebraska Moves People and Information with Microsoft MapPoint,* http://www. techsoupglobal.org/local-impact-map#2. Retrieved January 22, 2013.
2 *Conflict in the Democratic Republic of the Congo,* http://www.oxfam.org/en/drc-conflict. Retrieved January 22, 2013.
3 Etzioni, A. (1973) "The third sector and domestic missions," *Public Administration Review,* 33(4): 314–323.
4 Corry, O. (2010). "Defining and theorizing the third sector," in R. Taylor, *Third Sector Research,* pp. 11–20. New York: Springer.

5   Quarter, J., Mook, L., & Richmond, B. J. (2003) *What Counts: Social Accounting for Nonprofits and Cooperatives*, Chapter 2. Upper Saddle River, NJ: Prentice Hall.

6   Hall, M., & Banting, K. (2000). "The nonprofit sector in Canada: An introduction," in K. Banting (Ed.), *The Nonprofit Sector in Canada: Roles and Relationships*, pp. 1–28. Kingston, ON: Queen's University School of Policy Studies.

7   Quarter, J., Mook, L., & Ryan, S. (Eds.) (2010) *Researching the Social Economy*. Toronto: University of Toronto Press.

8   Quarter, J., Mook, L., & Armstrong, A. (2009) *Understanding the Social Economy: A Canadian Perspective*. Toronto: University of Toronto Press.

9   Quarter, J. (1992). *Canada's Social Economy: Co-operatives, Nonprofits and Other Community Enterprises*. Toronto: James Lorimer & Company; Drucker, P. F. (1992). *Managing the Nonprofit Organization: Principles and Practices*. New York: Harper.

10 Quarter, *Canada's Social Economy*; Hansmann, H. B. (1980) "The role of nonprofit enterprise," *The Yale Law Journal*, 89(5): 835–901.

11 Quarter, *Canada's Social Economy*; Drucker, *Managing the Nonprofit Organization*.

12 Quarter, *Canada's Social Economy*; Hansmann, H. B. (1980). "The role of nonprofit enterprise," *The Yale Law Journal*, 89(5): 835–901.

13 Phillips, S. D. (1995, November) "Redefining government relationships with the voluntary sector: On great expectations and sense and sensibility." Paper presented at the Voluntary Sector Roundtable, Ottawa, Ontario, Canada, in A. R. Febbraro, M. H. Hall, & M. Parmegiani (1996), *Developing a Typology of the Voluntary Health Sector in Canada: Definitions and Classification Issues*. Ottawa: Canadian Centre for Philanthropy, Canadian Policy Research Networks, Coalition of National Voluntary Organizations, Health Canada.

14 United Nations (UN) (1993) *System of National Accounts*. New York: United Nations, http://unstats.un.org/unsd/nationalaccount/docs/1993sna.pdf.

15 Quarter, *Canada's Social Economy*; Drucker, *Managing the Nonprofit Organization*.

16 Salamon, L., Anheier, H., et al. (1998). *The Emerging Sector Revisited: A Summary, Initial Estimates*. Baltimore, MD: The Johns Hopkins University, Institute for Policy Studies, Center for Civil Society Studies.

17 United Nations Department of Economic and Social Affairs Statistics Division (2003) *Handbook on Nonprofit Institutions in the System of National Accounts*. New York: United Nations Statistics Division.

18 Salamon, L. M., & Anheier, H. K. (Eds.) (1997) *Defining the Nonprofit Sector: A Cross-National Analysis*. Manchester: Manchester University Press.

19 Courtney, R. (2002) *Strategic Management for Voluntary Nonprofit Organizations*. London: Routledge.

20 Ibid.

21 Salamon, L. M., & Flaherty, S. L. (1996) "Nonprofit law: Ten issues in search of resolution." Working Papers of the Johns Hopkins Comparative Nonprofit Sector Project, no. 20, edited by Salamon, L. M., & Anheier, H. K., Baltimore, MD: The Johns Hopkins Institute for Policy Studies.

22 Internal Revenue Service Tax Exempt and Government Entities Exempt Organizations: Applying for 501(c)(3) Tax-Exempt Status. http://www.irs.gov/pub/irs-pdf/p4220.pdf. Retrieved February 24, 2013.

23 Ibid.

24 "What is charitable?" http://www.cra-arc.gc.ca/chrts-gvng/chrts/pplyng/cpc/wtc-eng.html. Retrieved February 25, 2013.

25 Hall, M. H. (2006) "The Canadian nonprofit and voluntary sector in perspective," in V. Murray (Ed.), *Management of Nonprofit and Charitable Organizations in Canada* (pp. 25–50). Markham: LexisNexis.

26 Day, K., & Devlin, R. A. (1997) *The Canadian Nonprofit Sector*. Ottawa: Canadian Policy Research Networks.

27 Guidance on Charitable Purposes. http://www.charitycommission.gov.uk/Charity_requirements_guidance/Charity_essentials/Public_benefit/charitable_purposes.aspx. Retrieved February 25, 2013.

28 Salamon & Flaherty, "Nonprofit law."

29 Anheier, H. (2005) *Nonprofit Organizations: Theory Management Policy*. London: Routledge.

30 The primary sources for the overview in this section are: Anheier, *Nonprofit Organizations*; and Salamon & Anheier (1998) "Social origins of civil society: Explaining the nonprofit sector cross-nationally," *Voluntas*, 9(3): 213–248.

31 Salamon & Anheier, "Social origins of civil society."

32 Anheier, *Nonprofit Organizations*; Salamon & Anheier, "Social origins of civil society."

33 Anheier, *Nonprofit Organizations*.

34 James, E. (1987) "The non-profit sector in comparative perspective," in W. W. Powell (Ed.), *The Non-Profit Sector: A Research Handbook*. New Haven, CT: Yale University Press; Rose-Ackerman, S. (1996). "Altruism, nonprofits and economic theory," *Journal of Economic Literature*, 34: 701–728; Young, D. (1983) *If Not for Profit, for What? A Behavioural Theory of the Nonprofit Sector Based on Entreprenuership*. Lexington, KY: Lexington Books; Anheier, *Nonprofit Organizations*.

35 Dees, J. G., Emerson, J., & Economy, P. (2001) *Enterprising Nonprofits*. New York: John Wiley & Sons; Anheier, *Nonprofit Organizations*.

36 Alvarez, S., & Busenitz, L. (2001) "The entrepreneurship of resource-based theory," *Journal of Management*, 27(6): 755–775. DOI: 10.1177/014920630102700609.

37 Anheier, *Nonprofit Organizations*.

38 Anheier, *Nonprofit Organizations;* Salamon & Anheier, "Social origins of civil society."

39 Salamon & Anheier, "Social origins of civil society."

40 Hansmann, H. (1987) "Economic theories of nonprofit organizations," in W. W. Powell (Ed.), *The Non-Profit Sector: A Research Handbook*. New Haven, CT: Yale University Press; Quarter, *Canada's Social Economy*; Hansmann, H. B. (1980) "The role of nonprofit enterprise." Also cited in 39, 45.

41 Anheier, *Nonprofit Organizations*.

42 Ben-Ner, A., & Van Hoomissen, T. (1993) "Nonprofit organizations in the mixed economy: A demand and supply analysis," in A. Ben-Ner & B. Gui (Eds.), *The Nonprofit Sector in the Mixed Economy*. Ann Arbor, MI: University of Michigan Press. Ben-Ner, A., & Van Hoomissen, T. (1991) "Nonprofit organizations in the mixed economy: A demand and supply analysis," *Annals of Public and Cooperative Economics*, 62(4): 519–550. Cited in 39.

43 Anheier, *Nonprofit Organizations*.

44 Ibid.

45 Ibid.

46 Salamon, L. M. (1995) *Partners in Public Service: Government-Nonprofit Relations in the Modem Welfare State*. Baltimore, MD: The Johns Hopkins University Press.

47 Anheier, *Nonprofit Organizations;* Salamon & Anheier, "Social origins of civil society."

48 See Anheier, *Nonprofit Organizations*, pp. 130–131.

49   Salamon, L. M. (1995) *Partners in Public Service: Government-Nonprofit Relations in the Modern Welfare State*, Baltimore, MD: The Johns Hopkins University Press, pp. 29, 30.

50   Anheier, *Nonprofit Organizations*.

51   Moulton, S., & Eckerd, A. (2012) "Preserving the publicness of the nonprofit sector: Resources, roles, and public values," *Nonprofit and Voluntary Sector Quarterly* (August 2012), 41 (4): 656–685.

52   Gordon, C. W., & Babchuk, N. (1959) "A typology of voluntary associations," *American Sociological Review*, 24: 22–29.

53   Frumkin, P. (2002) *On Being Nonprofit: A Conceptual and Policy Primer*. Cambridge, MA: Harvard University Press. Cited in Salamon & Flaherty, "Nonprofit law."

54   Moulton, S., & Eckerd, A. (2012) "Preserving the publicness of the nonprofit sector."

55   Ibid., pp. 661–664

56   Salamon, L. M., Hems, L. C., & Chinnock, K. (2000). "The nonprofit sector: For what and for whom?" Working papers of the Johns Hopkins Comparative Nonprofit Sector Project No. 37. Baltimore, MD: The Johns Hopkins Center for Civil Society Studies.

57   Salamon, L. M. (1987) "Of market failure, voluntary failure, and third-party government: Toward a theory of government–nonprofit relations in the modern welfare state," *Nonprofit and Voluntary Sector Quarterly*, 16: 29–49; Salamon, L. M. (1995) *Partners in Public Service: Government Nonprofit Relations in the Modern Welfare State*. Baltimore, MD: Johns Hopkins University Press.

58   Dart, R. (2004) "Being 'business-like' in a nonprofit organization: A grounded and inductive typology," *Nonprofit and Voluntary Sector Quarterly*, 33: 290–310.

59   Frumkin, P., & Andre-Clark, A. (2000) "When missions, markets, and politics collide: Values and strategy in the nonprofit human services," *Nonprofit and Voluntary Sector Quarterly*, 29(1): 141–163; Jeavons, T. (1992). "When the management is the message: Relating values to management practice in nonprofit organizations," *Nonprofit Management and Leadership*, 2: 403–417.

60   Salamon, Hems, & Chinnock, "The nonprofit sector."

61   Putnam, R. (2000) *Bowling Alone: The Collapse and Revival of American Community*. New York: Simon & Schuster.

62   Frumkin, *On Being Nonprofit*.

63   Anheier, H. K. (2009) "What kind of nonprofit sector, what kind of society? Comparative policy reflections," *American Behavioral Scientist*, 52: 1082–1094.

64   Anheier, *Nonprofit Organizations*.

65   Salamon, L. M., & Helmut H. K. (1996) "The international classification of nonprofit organizations: ICNPO-revision 1, 1996." Working Papers of the Johns Hopkins Comparative Nonprofit Sector Project, no. 19. Baltimore, MD: The Johns Hopkins Institute for Policy Studies.

66   Salamon & Flaherty, "Nonprofit law."

67   National Center for Charitable Statistics. http://nccs.urban.org/classification/NTEE.cfm. Retrieved March 4, 2013.

68   NCVO UK Civil Society Almanac. http://data.ncvo-vol.org.uk/datastore/datasets/dataset-4-icnpo-classification-of-charities/. Retrieved March 5, 2013.

69   Smith, R., & Lipsky, M. (1993) *Nonprofits for Hire: The Welfare State in the Age of Contracting*. Cambridge, MA: Harvard University Press.

70   For a discussion of value in healthcare, see Porter, M. E. (2010) "What is value in health care?" *The New England Journal of Medicine*, 363(26), 2477–2481. For a discussion

of value in business, see Grant, R. M. (2012) *Contemporary Strategy Analysis*, 7th Edition. Chichester, West Sussex: Wiley.

71 Porter, "What is value in health care?"

72 Weisbrod, B. A. (1998) "Modeling the nonprofit organization as a multiproduct firm: A framework for choice," in B. A. Weisbrod (Ed.), *To Profit or Not to Profit: The Commercial Transformation of the Nonprofit Sector*. Cambridge and New York: Cambridge University Press.

73 Salamon, L. M., Sokolowski, S. W., Haddock, M. A., & Tice, H. S. (2013) "The state of global civil society and volunteering: Latest findings from the implementation of the UN Nonprofit Handbook." Working Paper No. 49. Baltimore, MD: Johns Hopkins Center for Civil Society Studies.

74 Hall & Banting, "The nonprofit sector in Canada."

75 Eakin, L. (2001) An Overview of the Funding of Canada's Nonprofit Sector: Voluntary Sector Initiative Working Group on Financing. Ottawa: Voluntary Sector Initiative Secretariat, September 2001.

76 Alexander, J. (2000) "Adaptive strategies of nonprofit human service organizations in the era of devolution and new public management," *Nonprofit Management and Leadership*, 10(3): 287–303.

77 Scott, K. (2003) *Funding Matters: The Impact of Canada's Funding Regime on Nonprofit and Voluntary Organizations*. Ottawa: Canadian Council on Social Development.

78 Alexander, J. (2000) "Adaptive strategies of nonprofit human service organizations"; Scott, *Funding Matters.*

79 Scott, *Funding Matters.*

80 National Center for Charitable Statistics. Quick Facts about Nonprofits http://nccs. urban.org/statistics/quickfacts.cfm. Retrieved April, 2014.

81 Blackwood, A. S., Roeger, K. L., & Pettijohn, S. L. (2012) *The Nonprofit Sector in Brief: Public Charities, Giving, and Volunteering, 2012*. Urban Institute. http://www.urban. org/UploadedPDF/412674-The-Nonprofit-Sector-in-Brief.pdf

82 NCVO UK Civil Society Almanac http://data.ncvo-vol.org.uk/almanac/about-the-almanac/fast-facts/. Retrieved March 23, 2013.

83 Statistics Canada, "Satellite Account of Non-profit Institutions and Volunteering 2007." (Catalogue no. 13-015-X, ISSN 1710-9264).

84 Ibid.

85 Lasby, D., & Barr, C. (2014). "Sector monitor," *Imagine Canada*, 4(1): n.p.

86 Scott, *Funding Matters.*

87 Weisbrod, "Modeling the nonprofit organization as a multiproduct firm"; Alexander, "Adaptive strategies of nonprofit human service organizations."

88 Martin, S. (1985) *An Essential Grace*. Toronto: McCllelland and Stewart. Also see Salamon, Sokolowski, Haddock, & Tice, "The state of global civil society and volunteering," and YMCA of Greater New York 2013 Annual Report.

89 Smith & Lipsky, *Nonprofits for Hire.*

90 These are adapted from the three main types of government funding in Scott, *Funding Matters.*

91 Martin, *An Essential Grace*, p. 74.

92 Scott, *Funding Matters.*

93 Ibid.

94 Blackwood, Roeger, & Pettijohn, *The Nonprofit Sector in Brief.*

95 NCVO UK Civil Society Almanac, http://data.ncvo-vol.org.uk/almanac/voluntary-sector/income-in-focus/what-are-the-main-trends-in-statutory-funding/. Retrieved March 23, 2013.

96 Statistics Canada, "Satellite Account of Non-profit Institutions and Volunteering 2007."

97 Hall & Banting, "The nonprofit sector in Canada."

98 Scott, *Funding Matters.*

99 Anheier, "What kind of nonprofit sector, what kind of society?"

100 Charitable Giving. "Giving USA 2012." Cited in National Center for Charitable Statistics. Quick Facts about Nonprofits, http://nccs.urban.org/statistics/quickfacts.cfm. Retrieved July, 2014.

101 NCVO UK Civil Society Almanac, http://data.ncvo-vol.org.uk/almanac/voluntary-sector/finance-the-big-picture/how-is-the-voluntary-sectors-income-distributed/. Retrieved March 23, 2013.

102 Hall & Banting, "The nonprofit sector in Canada."

103 Leat, D. (1995) "Funding matters," in J. Davis, C. R. Smith & R. Hedley (Eds.), *An Introduction to the Voluntary Sector.* New York: Routledge. Cited in Alexander, "Adaptive strategies of nonprofit human service organizations."

104 National Center for Charitable Statistics. "Frequently asked questions." http://nccs.urban.org/FAQ/. Retrieved March 23, 2013.

105 The 2010 Nonprofit Fundraising Survey. "Funds raised in 2010 compared to 2009." The Nonprofit Research Collaborative http://www.urban.org/uploadedpdf/1001529-2010-Nonprofit-Fundraising-Survey.pdf. Retrieved March 23, 2013.

106 Scott, *Funding Matters.*

107 Ibid.

108 Eakin, An Overview of the Funding of Canada's Nonprofit Sector.

109 Leat, "Funding matters."

110 NCVO UK Civil Society Almanac. http://data.ncvo.org.uk/a/almanac14/what-are-the-sectors-different-sources-and-types-of-income-3/. Retrieved July, 2014.

111 Akingbola, K. (2012) "Context and Nonprofit Human Resource Management." *Administration & Society.* DOI: 10.1177/0095399712451887.

112 DiMaggio, P. J., & Anheier, H. K. (1990) "The sociology of nonprofit organizations and sectors," *Annual Review of Sociology,* 16: 137–159.

113 Blackwood, Roeger, & Pettijohn, *The Nonprofit Sector in Brief.*

114 Ibid.

115 Salamon, Sokolowski, Haddock, & Tice, "The state of global civil society and volunteering."

116 NCVO UK Civil Society Almanc http://data.ncvo.org.uk/a/almanac14/how-many-voluntary-organisations-are-active-in-the-uk-3/. Retrieved July, 2014.

117 NCVO UK Civil Society Almanac http://data.ncvo-vol.org.uk/almanac/voluntary-sector/scope/is-the-number-of-voluntary-organisations-increasing/. Retrieved March 23, 2013.

118 Smith & Lipsky, *Nonprofits for Hire.*

2

THEORIES OF STRATEGIC HUMAN RESOURCE MANAGEMENT

Learning Objectives

After studying this chapter, you should understand:

1. Basic knowledge of the variety of perspectives in organizational theory that have been used to examine the essential questions of strategic human resource management (SHRM).
2. How some of the theoretical perspectives might play out in the context of nonprofit organizations.

Donations and Aging Population in Canada[1]

Donations to charities are bouncing back after two years of recession, but the weight of philanthropic giving still rests on the shoulders of older Canadians. Statistics Canada data released Monday show that tax filers claimed donations of just under $8.3 billion in 2010, up 6.5 percent from 2009. At the same time, the number of donors increased 2.2 percent to just over 5.7 million Canadians, but the average age of donors remains 53—a figure that has remained relatively the same for the past decade.

While the rebound in giving is positive news, analysts say there is not cause for celebration just yet. "For the last 20 years, the percentage of tax filers claiming donations has been steadily going down from about [traditionally] 30 percent", said Marcel Lauzière, the president and CEO of Imagine Canada, an umbrella organization for charities.

This year, the figure climbed back slightly to 23.4 percent, up from the all-time low of 23.1 percent in 2009, but Mr. Lauzière fears the overall downward trend, coupled with effects of the recession, might have nudged Canadians out of the habit of donating.

Introduction

One conclusion you might have reached after reading Chapter 1 is that non-profits are not simple organizations. They are uniquely complex organizations that play a pivotal role in the social, economic and political well-being of the society. In order to perform the essential roles that we outlined in Chapter 1 and achieve the mission of the organization, they must attract, retain and motivate employees and volunteers. They must effectively interact with stakeholders and adapt to the environment. This means that the knowledge, skills and behavior of employees and volunteers (HR) are of utmost importance in the performance of a nonprofit. Essentially, they must develop and deploy strategic human resource management (SHRM) in order to align how they manage people with the overall strategy of the organization. However, to properly understand this process in non-profits, it is essential to understand the theoretical foundation of SHRM.

Strategic Human Resource Management

SHRM has been defined as "the pattern of planned human resource deployments and activities intended to enable the firm to achieve its goals."[2] Scholars have noted that the basic idea of SHRM is based on the critical importance of how people are managed, the link to the overall strategy of the organization and its capability to adapt to change. Basically, SHRM suggests that an emphasis must be placed on how HR aligns with the current and changing goals of the organization. In other words, the external environment and organizational factors influence HRM, strategy, and structure of the organization. Trends and issues in the external environment including economic, demographic and political factors play an important role in shaping the HR practices of organizations.

In Chapter 3, we will go into detail on the general and industry factors in the external environment of nonprofits and how they impact the operations and HR practices of organizations in the sector. This is followed by a discussion of the SHRM process in Chapter 4. In the meantime, the opening news report and two other examples from the media help to illustrate the point about how the economic, political and demographic environment could impact nonprofits (Boxes 2.1 and 2.2). The importance of the external environment is emphasized in most of the theories we review in this chapter.

BOX 2.1 GOVERNMENT AND CHARITABLE DEDUCTION IN THE US

Congressman Calls for Hearing on Charitable Deduction

NonProfit Times – February 6, 2013

The charitable deduction is in congressional crosshairs again as Rep. Dave Camp (R-MI) called for a hearing on the topic on Feb. 14. Camp, the chairman of the House Ways and Means Committee, announced Tuesday that he wants representatives from the charitable sector to testify to the Committee about how limits to the charitable deduction would impact nonprofits. Organizations have fought changes to the deduction in the past, and the hearing by the House Ways and Means Committee will give representatives from the sector another chance to explain why they believe it's a bad idea to limit the deduction.

"Because of the critical role that charities play, the Committee must hear directly from the charitable community before considering any proposals as part of comprehensive tax reform that might impact their ability to obtain the resources they need to fulfill their missions," said Camp in a statement. Examples of efforts to limit the charitable deduction in the past include limiting the tax rate against which contributions may be deducted; a dollar cap on total itemized deductions; a floor below which contributions may not be deducted; and the replacement of the deduction with a tax credit available regardless of whether the taxpayer itemizes.

Although Congress averted part of the so-called "fiscal cliff" by avoiding across the board tax-increases for all Americans, the deal reached only delayed the sequester—automatic budget cuts to domestic and defense spending—until March 1. The White House and many members of Congress would like to replace it with new, more targeted spending cuts, but Democrats and President Barack Obama are insisting that any deal must include revenue from tax reform. Presumably, some of this revenue would come from limiting the charitable deduction which, under Section 170 of the Internal Revenue Code, provides a deduction to the nearly one-third of taxpayers who itemize their deductions for charitable contributions.

In a statement published Tuesday, Washington, D.C.-based Independent Sector urged the White House not to cap the charitable deduction at 28 percent. "Even though the Administration has expressed a commitment to ensuring that the cuts do not fall disproportionately on those least able to bear them," the statement read, "this action to cap the charitable deduction does not penalize those taxpayers who claim it, but the millions of individuals, families, and communities who rely on the programs and services provided by America's nonprofit and philanthropic sector." The statement from

Independent Sector noted that experts believe that a cap on the charitable deduction, when marginal tax rates for the wealthy were at 35 percent, would have reduced giving by $7 billion a year.

With rates now at 39.6 for Americans earning more than $400,000 a year, that number is expected to be even larger. The House Ways and Means Committee hearing will begin on Thursday, Feb. 14 at 9:30 AM in Room 1100 of the Longworth House Office Building. Individuals from the charitable sector who are interested in testifying can contact the committee by phone (202-225-5522) or at tax.reform@mail.house.gov using the subject line "charitable deduction." Individuals who are not able to make the hearing are encouraged to submit written statements. Requests must be submitted by Thursday, Feb. 7.

Source: www.thenonprofittimes.com/news-articles/congressman-calls-for-hearing-on-charitable-deduction/

BOX 2.2 ECONOMY, GOVERNMENT AND VOLUNTEER CENTERS IN ENGLAND

Half of volunteer centres in England lost more than a quarter of their income last year

By Ian Griggs, Third Sector Online, 14 May 2013

National Council for Voluntary Organisations' survey shows average annual income was the lowest since 2008, but Justin Davis Smith says the picture is "not universally bleak". Nearly half of all volunteer centres in England lost more than a quarter of their income in 2011/12 compared with the previous year, a survey has shown. The Annual Return for Volunteer Centres 2011/12, a survey of volunteer centres by the National Council for Voluntary Organisations, also shows that one in five saw their income halved in the same period.

But a quarter of the 160 volunteer centres that responded to the survey said their income had increased on the previous financial year. Overall, the average annual income for volunteer centres was £52,500, a fall of £3,932 from the previous year and the lowest average annual income since the recession began in 2008. The report shows a shift away from central government funding with only 7 per cent of volunteer centres saying that they received funding from this source, compared with 24 per cent the previous year.

The NCVO said this was because of various national programmes supporting infrastructure programmes coming to an end. By comparison,

(continued)

(continued)

83 per cent of volunteer centres said they received some funding from local government—an average of £32,000 per centre. The survey also found that a third of all enquiries about volunteering opportunities were from people who were unemployed and seeking work.

"We know that volunteer centres can be the start of a journey back into employment for many people who need to find ways to gain skills—something that is particularly important as the economy remains challenging," said Justin Davis Smith, executive director for volunteering at the NCVO.

"The picture is not universally bleak—some volunteer centres had success in developing new work and sources of income in this year. However, it is crucial that all volunteer centres have the chance to develop new ways of working and income sources, and sudden and sharp funding cuts make this harder to achieve."

Source: www.thirdsector.co.uk/news/1182174/Half-volunteer-centres-England-lost-quarter-income-last-year/

One perspective that continues to dominate SHRM research and practice is the notion of contingency and fit.[3] Contingencies are factors or variables that make up the environment and characteristics of organizations.[4] Contingencies are within and outside of the organization. There are three main contingencies—the environment, organizational size and strategy.[5] Internal contingencies include size, task uncertainty and task interdependence. The characteristics of the external environment of the organization such as government policy, economic and social factors are examples of external contingencies.[6] Fit has been defined as "the degree to which the needs, demands, goals, objectives and/or structure of one component are consistent with the need, demands, goals, objectives and/or structure of another component."[7] Essentially, the need to achieve fit means that HR practices, as one component must be congruent with strategy as another component, to facilitate the achievement of organizational goals. For example, in the context of a nonprofit organization, the structure and processes of the organization are affected by contingencies in the external environment such as funding, societal needs, social values, competition, public policy, the legal and regulatory environment.[8]

Following from this background knowledge, the task for nonprofit managers is first to understand the important interactions in the environment. Second, nonprofit managers must also understand how each interaction impacts the formulation and implementation of the strategy developed to facilitate the goals of the organization. The third imperative for nonprofit managers is to understand the three-way relationship between the external environment, corporate strategy and an internally consistent bundle of HR practices and the human resource pool. We will return to this discussion in detail in Chapter 4.

Theoretical Perspectives

In the meantime, understanding the various theoretical foundations of SHRM will help you to better grasp the relationship. In this brief overview, we highlight the core theoretical perspectives and introduce social exchange theory as a particularly relevant perspective in the context of nonprofits.

General Systems Theory

The notion that the understanding of the environment is important in the effectiveness of an organization is central to *Systems Theory* (Box 2.3). Organizations are in continuous interaction with the environment. Resources such as raw material, human, financial and energy are imported as inputs from the environment.[9] These resources are transformed through the production process into products or services and exchanged in the environment. In effect, the environment is critical to the survival of the organization. The inability of the environment to provide resources the organization requires for production or the lack of market for the products or services of the organization mean the organization will be unable to survive. Organizations must therefore continuously monitor, scan and adapt to the feedback from the environment. Organizations are seen as complex and open systems. As such, they are dynamic and made up of interdependent parts.[10] As a result, an intervention and/or change in one part may result in unexpected impacts on other parts of the organization.[11]

BOX 2.3 EXCERPT FROM AN ARTICLE THAT DRAWS ON SYSTEMS THEORY IN NONPROFIT RESEARCH

The research note utilizes von Bertalanffy's general systems theory to argue that nonprofit organizations are open systems maintaining themselves in an environment in which the supply of critical resources is insecure. Accordingly, commercial activities must be seen as the self-regulatory mechanism that enables, rather than hinders, nonprofit organizations to deliver their missions in hostile environments, as they often are today.

Source: Moeller, L. & Valentinov, V. (2011) "The Commercialization of the Nonprofit Sector: A General Systems Theory Perspective," *Systemic Practice and Action Research* (August 2012), 25(4): 365–370.

Organizations source, acquire and leverage human capital from the environment. An organization's HRM subsystem is designed to motivate and retain the human resource pool recruited from the environment.[12] Scholars suggest that through acquisition, deployment and optimization of human capital, HRM can bring about sustained competitive advantage or competitive vulnerability. In many ways, systems theory underlies HRM functions in organizations. For example, Swanson[13] suggested that systems theory is one of the three dominant schools of thought that are integrated in the discipline of human resource development which he noted has the core purpose of sustaining and advancing its host system. The challenge of fostering system-thinking continues to drive emerging perspectives in HRM such as human capital and talent management. Systems theory underlies many of theoretical perspectives on organizations.

Agency Theory

Agency theory focuses on the problems that arise in the relationship between parties in which one party (the principal) engages another party (the agent) to perform work or provide a service.[14] The relationship could become inherently problematic for a number of reasons. One, the principal and the agent may have conflicting goals. Two, it is expensive or difficult for the principal to monitor and validate the performance of the agent.[15] The conflict is often caused by human nature characteristics such as self-interest and risk aversion, conflicting goals among organizational members and information asymmetry.[16] With information asymmetry, one party may have undue advantage because they have more or superior information than the other.

The key contribution of agency theory is in terms of how best to align the interests of the principal and the agent through control mechanisms that foster cooperative behaviors at minimal cost to the principal.[17] In other words, what type of system or process can we deploy to ensure that the interests of Manager A and Shareholder B who the manager is representing, are aligned? The goal here is not to eliminate the diverse interests of the parties, especially the agent, but to find a control mechanism through contract that will ensure that the agent is more likely to exercise behavior that supports the interest of the principal (Box 2.4).[18]

BOX 2.4 EXCERPT FROM AN ARTICLE THAT DRAWS ON AGENCY THEORY IN NONPROFIT RESEARCH

Yet findings in this study indicate that nonprofit board members do not expect conflict between the executive director and the purpose for which the organization was created. The board believes that the executive management will not act opportunistically and that what management actually does is ensure goal alignment and convergence in its relationship with principals.

Source: Miller, J. L. (2002) "The board as a monitor of organizational activity: The applicability of agency theory to nonprofit boards," *Nonprofit Management & Leadership*, 12(4): 429–450.

To achieve this goal, the employer (the principal) has the option of deploying HR practices such as pay for performance or control mechanisms, or a combination of the two to influence performance of the employee (agent).[19] The principal must also deploy effective socialization and practices that will help to gain the commitment of the individual (agent) which contributes to the reduction of the goal conflict between the parties.[20] However, studies have suggested that the control mechanisms which are the basis of commitment behaviors are dependent on contingency variables in the internal and external environments of the organization.[21] In other words, HR practices that are based on the control mechanism of the principal in one environment at one point in time will vary with the internal and external environments.[22] This is the basis of contingency theory, the perspective we will review next.

Contingency Theory

Contingency theory is premised on the thesis that achievement of organizational goals is relative to the extent of fit or alignment between contingency variables that constitute the environment and structural characteristics, processes and practices of organizations (Box 2.5).[23] Effectiveness is dependent on the impact of the contingencies on the organization and its capacity to adapt to change in the operating environment.[24] The notion that organizations are shaped by their environment is explicit in contingency theory,[25] especially by the need to fit the internal organizational characteristics such as task uncertainty and size with external environmental uncertainty.[26]

BOX 2.5 EXCERPT FROM AN ARTICLE THAT DRAWS ON CONTINGENCY THEORY IN NONPROFIT RESEARCH

Indeed, in responding to the changes in the external environment, organizations in this study were more likely to report choosing revenue-generating and image-enhancing activities than cost-cutting options.

Source: Foster, M. K., & Meinhard, A. (2002) "A contingency view of the responses of voluntary social service organizations in Ontario to government cutbacks," *Canadian Journal of Administrative Sciences*, 19(1): 27–41.

A subsequent perspective on contingency theory known as strategic choices noted that while contingencies affect organizational structure, managerial choices including values and power intervene to determine the impact of the relationship.[27] Strategic choices contend that managers ultimately determine the strategy of organizations and shape the impact of the environment on organizational structure, practices and process.[28]

Contingency theory has been a particularly relevant frame of reference in HRM research. As discussed above, SHRM draws on contingency and fit to examine the relationship between HR practices and organizational strategy.[29] The underlying position of the contingency approach to SHRM is that organizational outcomes depend on the alignment of strategy, HRM practices and the environment. Hence, the central question in much of the research is what specific strategic approach best align HR practices, employee skills and behaviors, and the external environment and organizational factors.[30] The contingency perspective is slowly emerging in studies about HRM in nonprofit organizations.

Institutional Theory

Institutional theory focuses on how the institutionalized environment creates, shapes, adapts, renews and invalidates organizational structures and processes (Box 2.6).[31] Meyer and Rowan note that "institutionalism involves the processes by which social processes, obligations, or actualities come to take on a rule like status in social thought and actions" (p. 341): in other words, organizations conform to normative rules in order to gain approval for their structure and performance—and ultimately to survive.[32] Since the external environment is constituted by multiple stakeholders who make access to the resources organizations require to operate possible, organizations conform to normative rules to gain legitimacy and acceptance.[33] The outcome of the pressures of the institutionalized environment is that organizations predictably become similar.[34]

BOX 2.6 EXCERPT FROM AN ARTICLE THAT DRAWS ON INSTITUTIONAL THEORY IN NONPROFIT LITERATURE

This argument arguably captures the key message of Mukerjee's institutional theory for the modern economics of the nonprofit sector. States and markets suffer from their respective endemic problems of excessive centralization and militant individualism. States are inherently coercive; markets preclude the formation of a meaningful social community. Hence, neither markets nor states, by themselves, are able to ensure the all-round development of personality in harmony with the broader societal values. By virtue of being non-coercive and inclusive, the nonprofit sector overcomes these limitations of states and markets and provides people with the opportunity of experiencing a genuine communion of shared values and meanings.

Source: Valentinov, V. (2011) "The institutional theory of Radhamakal Mukerjee: Lessons for modern nonprofit economics," *Journal of Economic Issues*, 45(3): 605.

Institutional theory suggests that HRM is embedded in the social and industry contexts of the organization and could be the result of social construction.[35] Thus to understand HR practices, it is important to understand the historical and social context of the organization.[36] In essence, organizations may adopt HR practices and policies in order to conform and gain legitimacy. The institutionalization process manifests in HR practices in a number of ways. Examples of how institutional theory plays out in HR include wage and safety legislations, accreditation or best employer competition and the copying of HR practices that have been implemented by other organizations.[37]

Resource Dependence Theory

The focus of resource dependence theory is the resource exchange in the relationship between an organization and its constituencies (Box 2.7).[38] This theory suggests that since no organization is self-sufficient or self-sustaining, an organization will depend on other actors to source and provide the critical resources it requires to function and survive.[39] As a result, power is an inherent component of the relationship between the organization and other actors. Actors gain power by their ability to define, create and shape the perception of others in terms of the interpretation of uncertainty and importance of resources.[40] More importantly, they also gain power through their control of valued resources an organization requires to operate and achieve its objectives.[41]

BOX 2.7 EXCERPT FROM AN ARTICLE THAT DRAWS ON RESOURCE DEPENDENCY THEORY IN NONPROFIT RESEARCH

The findings suggest that an organization is more likely to increase the degree of formality of its collaborative activities when it is older, has a larger budget size, receives government funding but relies on fewer government funding streams, has more board linkages with other nonprofits, and is not operating in the education and research or social services industry.

Source: Guo, C. & Acar, M. (2005) "Understanding collaboration among nonprofit organizations: combining resource dependency, institutional, and network perspectives," *Nonprofit and Voluntary Sector Quarterly*, 34 (3): 340–361.

Taylor, Beechler and Napier[42] proposed that resource dependence is determined by three factors. First, the extent to which the resource is critical to the functioning and survival of the organization.[43] This suggests that any resource that could make or break an organization could very likely create a dependence situation. Second, the degree of discretion that actors have on how the resource is allocated and used.[44] In other words, if an actor has a significant say on how a resource required by an organization is allocated and used, there is a good chance that there will be a resource dependence relationship between the actor and the organization. The example of nonprofits discussed in Chapter 3 fits this scenario. Finally, whether there are alternatives to the resource[45]. The thinking here is that the more the alternative to a resource, the better the ability of the organization to avoid a resource dependence relationship with the actor who provides the resource. These three determining factors underlie the varying degree of dependence between an organization and its constituencies.

HR practices are influenced by factors that reside within the control of other organizational players. For example, research suggests that a parent company's HR practices would influence HRM in its subsidiaries.[46] Similarly, since the SHRM function plays a critical role in the recruitment, retention and reward of human resources, HR practices are dependent on the power of other departments and actors in the organization.[47] Conversely, the ability of these departments and actors to attract, motivate and retain employees is dependent on the HR function for the same reasons.

Resource-Based View

From the perspective of the resource-based view (RBV), organizations are "heterogeneous bundles of idiosyncratic, hard-to-imitate resources and capabilities."[48] Organizations are made up of diverse resources and capabilities that they require to function and achieve a competitive advantage. Hence, the focus of RBV is the characteristics of the resources and capabilities of organizations.[49] The core idea of RBV is that sustained competitive advantage can be derived from the resources of the organization.[50] The ability to acquire, develop, combine and effectively deploy human, physical and organizational resources in ways that are difficult for competitors to imitate sets the organization apart from the competitors.[51] Elsewhere, Oliver proposes that the acquisition and use of resources and capabilities are mediated not only by strategic factor market but also by the social context within which the decisions are made.[52] Oliver argues that the institutional context significantly impacts the resource, how it is selected and the competitive advantage outcome of the process.

In short, RBV emphasizes the importance of intangible socially embedded resources as a strategic source of competitive advantage.[53] The knowledge, skills and capabilities of employees and managers, their social network and those of stakeholders of the organization give it the edge in competition. Both the human and social capital perspectives, which are discussed below, underscore the importance of the RBV in SHRM research (Box 2.8).

BOX 2.8 EXCERPT FROM AN ARTICLE THAT DRAWS ON A RESOURCE-BASED VIEW IN NONPROFIT RESEARCH

This study extends the RBV to a network of not-for-profit organizations by investigating the roles of organizational characteristics, partner attributes, and network structures on organizational ability to acquire monetary and nonmonetary resources through collaborations. . . . As predicted, not-for-profit organizations that provide a broad range of services enhance their effectiveness from collaboration in terms of resource gains.

Source: Arya, B. & Lin, Z. (2007) "Understanding collaboration outcomes from an extended resource-based view perspective: the roles of organizational characteristics, partner attributes, and network structures," *Journal of Management*, 33(5): 697–723.

As explained in subsequent chapters, socially complex resources and capabilities tend to be important paradigms in the activities of nonprofit organizations. Moreover, the question of how resources create sustained competitive advantage is central to strategic management and SHRM in the sector. The RBV has been applied to examine factors that shape HRM in nonprofit organizations.

Social Exchange Theory

Social exchange theory explains the obligations that evolve from the relationship between an organization and employees (Box 2.9).[54] Social exchange has been defined as "favors that create diffuse future obligations, not precisely specified ones, and the nature of the return cannot be bargained about but must be left to the discretion of the one who makes it."[55] At the core of social exchange theory is the norm of reciprocity of action between parties that are not set in any contractual framework to define the form, time and degree of payback obligation. It is a voluntary reciprocal obligation behavior mediated by trust and gratitude that propels the individual making the gratuitous repayment.[56] To put social exchange theory plainly, if the organization treats employees with respect, dignity and trust, the employees will develop a feeling that they owe the organization big time. As a result, the employees will decide on their own how to pay back the good deed of the organization.

BOX 2.9 EXCERPT FROM AN ARTICLE THAT DRAWS ON SOCIAL EXCHANGE THEORY IN NONPROFIT RESEARCH

Statistical data confirmed that perceptions of peer support, social interaction, and audience response were significant predictors of satisfaction and commitment to the particular show and community theater in general. Group members also indicated that disorganized leadership, lack of coordination, and time issues were the most negative aspects of participating.

Source: Kramer, M. W. (2005) "Communication and social exchange processes in community theater groups," *Journal of Applied Communication Research*, 33(2): 159–182.

The social exchange perspective has been used to explain the relationship between HR practices, trust-in-management, employee commitment and employee engagement.[57] This body of research suggests that employee commitment and engagement flow from their perception of organizational support and commitment. In other words, employees interpret HR practices as part of organizational actions, which they draw upon to explain the level of commitment of the organization to them. If they perceive that the HR practices convey that the organization is committed to investing in them and appreciates and recognizes their contribution, employees will develop social exchange as opposed to a purely business relationship with the organization.[58]

If the perception of the employees is that the organization cares about their well-being and values them, not only will they perform better, they will create positive reciprocal exchange relationships in which they will pay back the organization with positive work attitude and behaviors.[59] What employees perceive in the HR policies and practices of the organization form part of the basis of the obligation to pay back the organization in terms of commitment, discretionary effort and organizational citizenship behavior.

Human Capital

The concept of human capital refers to the knowledge, skills and abilities embodied in people.[60] It is essentially the competencies that people—employees, volunteers, community partners—in nonprofit organizations possess. The knowledge, skills and abilities that constitute human capital can be both explicit and tacit.[61] *Explicit* knowledge is exemplified by learning that can be codified and is more likely to be focused on transferrable know-how.[62] It is the type of knowledge "that can be expressed formally using a system of symbols."[63] Explicit knowledge is often acquired through education. *Tacit* knowledge is characterized by learning gained through experience or insight from situations and interactions. This type of knowledge is more likely to be embedded in codified routines and the relationships between individuals.[64] Tacit knowledge therefore tends to be personal and more difficult to transfer from one individual to the other.[65] In short, human capital includes knowledge, skills and abilities that are acquired through different forms of learning.

In essence, people develop human capital through formal learning, non-formal learning, and informal interactions and processes. *Formal* learning generally refers to the institutional ladder that goes from preschool to graduate studies, while *non-formal* learning refers to all organized educational programs that take place outside the formal school system, and are usually short-term and voluntary.[66] These include many of the training and learning opportunities offered by organizations. *Informal* learning is the learning that happens in spaces and places that are not necessarily governed by curricula, experts and timelines; it is learning that can be intentional, unintentional, or through socialization.[67] However, regardless of the source of the learning that creates the human capital, it is first an individual process. It has been suggested that the source and the application of knowledge occur in the minds of knowers.[68] Hence, it is safe to say that a potential primary beneficiary of human capital is the employee who possesses the knowledge, skills and abilities. Employees can leverage their human capital in their current organization, the open labor market and for social outcomes that are in the best interest of the community. In other words, human capital has significant economic and social importance to the employee. For example, employees can leverage the human capital they possess to negotiate higher wages or seek employment with a different organization.[69] Employees can also leverage human capital to build social capital through interactions with direct and indirect stakeholders in the organization.

At the level of the organization, the extensive body of research on human capital has focused on the critical importance of the knowledge, skills and abilities of employees for the organization. It is through the use of human capital that organizations create value and gain competitive advantage.[70] In the resource-based view discussed above, it is posited that the capability of an organization to acquire, develop, combine and effectively deploy its physical, human and organizational resources creates critical value and competitive advantage (Box 2.10). More importantly, it is suggested that since the skills and abilities that are the core of the human capital, such as organization-specific experience, are socially complex, they are difficult to imitate.[71]

BOX 2.10 EXCERPT FROM AN ARTICLE ON NONPROFIT CAPITAL MARKET AND HUMAN CAPITAL IMPACT

The ultimate prize is a social capital market that delivers real impact for the dollars donors contribute. The discipline of such a marketplace would motivate nonprofit leaders to adopt clear models for creating social impact, provide a solid framework for measuring and reporting performance, and help nonprofits develop the leadership and management capabilities they need to achieve their missions. Capital and talent would flow away from the inefficient and migrate toward the most effective, enabling the best to grow in scale and impact to create a stronger and more dynamic social sector.

Source: Kaplan, R. S. & Grossman, A. S. (2010) "The emerging capital market for nonprofits," *Harvard Business Review*, 88(10).

The human capital contribution is a major stream in SHRM research and practice. The point here is that human capital gives the organization a true edge in terms of performance. In the everyday life of an organization, human capital is front and center of the interactions and processes between employees and their customers. As Davenport and Prusak noted, "in organizations, knowledge often becomes embedded not only in documents or repositories but also in organizational routines, process, practices, and norms."[72] It is through these routines, processes and norms that individual employees acquire and develop general human capital, that is, knowledge, skills and abilities that can be used in other organizations as well as the larger society.[73] Basically, employees acquire and develop knowledge, skills and experience which not only add value to their current organization, but are also saleable in the general labor market to the benefit of the individual. These knowledge and skills are also valuable to the wider community. Following from the mission and activities of nonprofits discussed in Chapter 1, it is the intersection of the benefits of human capital for the individual, the organization and the society at large that highlights a potential manifestation of the concept in nonprofit organizations. This point will be reflected in the cases that are discussed in subsequent chapters.

Social Capital

Social capital is about the quality of the interaction and connection among people in a society. The origin of the concept of social capital has been traced to the work of Lyda Hanifan, who described it as "those tangible assets [that] count for most in the daily lives of people: namely goodwill, fellowship, sympathy, and social intercourse among the individuals and families who make up a social unit."[74]

This definition implies the significant impact of the relationships and interactions among people.

While there is no consensus on the definition of social capital, in recent years the importance of relationships and social capital has been rekindled mostly as the result of the work of Robert Putnam. He notes that social capital is the "connections among individuals—social networks and the norms of reciprocity and trustworthiness that arise from them."[75] Putman further suggested two types of social capital: bonding social capital and bridging social capital.[76] *Bonding social capital* develops among people in the same community, age, ethnicity, social background, etc. It is the connection among people who have a social or demographic characteristic in common. *Bridging social capital* develops as a result of connection with people from different and diverse backgrounds. What is clear in social capital is that the relationships and interactions in society have tangible value.

Both the employee and the organization can take advantage of social capital by establishing an extensive social network with their clients and the community.[77] The social networks are an important resource for both the personal and professional goals of the employee as well as the performance of the organization (Box 2.11). Moreover, social capital is unlike human capital in the sense that it is a resource that is available to all. It is not a property that can be traded.[78] Therefore, the ability to build relationships and navigate interactions could have a profound impact for the employees, organizations and the society.

BOX 2.11 EXCERPT FROM AN ARTICLE THAT DRAWS ON SOCIAL CAPITAL IN SOCIAL ECONOMY RESEARCH

The question of competency is evidenced in how members draw upon their social capital to access and leverage resources the organization does not ordinarily have access to due to its unincorporated status. The evidence that some of the organizations access funding and institutional support through formal social economy and public sector organizations illustrates how they mitigate their inability to access resources and overcome the limitation of their unincorporated status by leveraging social networks.

Source: Akingbola, K. (2013) "Resource-Based View (RBV) of unincorporated social economy organizations," *Canadian Journal of Nonprofit and Social Economy Research*, 4(1).

However, similar to social capital which is a source of value not only to those who participate in its creation, but also the larger community,[79] human capital benefits not only the organization that facilitates its acquisition or the individual who possesses the knowledge, skills and experience, but also the larger society.

The discussion about human capital above points out something relevant for social capital: human capital could and does foster the development of social capital. In addition to the economic and social mobility benefits of human capital, the knowledge and skills acquired in organizations could contribute to the creation and sustainability of social capital. In effect, human capital could inextricably lead to social capital for the employee and the organization.

Summary

Together with the introduction to nonprofits discussed in Chapter 1, the brief overview of the relevant theories and perspectives offers an important foundation for the understanding of HRM in nonprofit organizations. While research and new thinking on the theories and perspectives continue to emerge, many of the theories are yet to be used to explain HRM in nonprofits. However, as illustrated in the research abstracts highlighted as examples in this chapter, some of the theoretical perspectives have been used to explain the context and activities of nonprofit organizations. Indeed, knowledge of the theories above can help us to better understand what nonprofits are about, the factors in the environment that underlie their strategy, and how they adapt to change in order to achieve the mission of the organization.

An important takeaway from the relevant research following from the theories is that the context of nonprofits is not only critical, but also unique, as we will discuss in Chapter 3. The factors that contribute to the uniqueness of the context are therefore important for managers to consider in determining how they manage people and link the employee performance to organizational performance.

The development of strategy, the deployment of HR practices and policies that are aligned with strategy and the continuing effort to achieve the mission of the organization depend in large part on the ability of managers to effectively plan for the opportunities and threats in the environment that affect the nonprofit. This is the focus of Chapter 4. In that chapter, the knowledge of the theories and perspectives discussed in this chapter is applied to illustrate the critical players, the factors and processes in a strategic nonprofit human resource management system. In short, the theories and perspective discussed here are used implicitly and explicitly throughout the book to explain how nonprofits can develop a strategic human resource pool and deploy their knowledge and skills to facilitate the achievement of their organizational goals.

Discussion Questions

1. Based on your understanding of systems theory, explain the environment and activities of a nonprofit organization.
2. What are the external contingencies that could impact the HR practices of a nonprofit organization?

3. How is social exchange theory relevant to what you have experienced or read about working in a nonprofit organization?
4. How can social capital benefits nonprofit organizations?

Notes

1 Tamara Baluja, *The Globe and Mail*, Dec 5, 2011.
2 Wright, P. M., & McMahan, G. C. (1992) "Theoretical perspectives for strategic human resource management," *Journal of Management*, 18: 295–320.
3 Lengnick-Hall, M. L., Lengnick-Hall, C. A., Andrade, L. A., & Drake, B. (2009). "Strategic human resource management: The evolution of the field," *Human Resource Management Review*, 19(2): 64–85.
4 Burns, S., & Stalker, G. M. (1961) *The Management of Innovation*. London: Tavistock; Lawrence, P. R., & Lorsch, J. W. (1967) "Differentiation and integration in complex organizations," *Administrative Science Quarterly*, 12: 1–47.
5 Donaldson, L. (2001) *The Contingency Theory of Organizations*. Thousand Oaks, CA: Sage.
6 Ibid.
7 Nadler, D., & Tushman, M. L. (1980) "A congruence model for diagnosing organizational behavior," in R. Miles (Ed.), *Resource Book in Macro Organizational Behaviour* (pp. 30–49). Santa Clara, CA: Goodyear.
8 Bradshaw, P. (2009) "A contingency approach to nonprofit governance," *Nonprofit Management and Leadership*, 20(1): 61–82.
9 Jackson, S. E., & Schuler, R. S. (1995) "Understanding human resource management in the context of organizations and their environments," *Annual Review of Psychology*, 46: 237–264.
10 Katz, D., & Kahn, R. (1978) *The Social Psychology of Organizations*, 2nd Edition. New York: John Wiley.
11 Broedling, L. (1999) "Applying a systems approach to human resource management," *Human Resource Management*, 38(3): 269–278.
12 Lado, A., & Wilson, M. (1994) "Human resource systems and sustained competitive advantage: A comptency-based pective," *Academy of Management Review*, 19(4): 699–727.
13 Swanson, R. A. (2008). "Economic foundation of human resource development: Advancing the theory and practice of the discipline," *Advances in Developing Human Resources*, 10(6): 763–769.
14 Jensen, M., & Meckling, W. (1976) "Theory of the firm: Managerial behavior, agency costs and ownership structure," *Journal of Financial Economics*, 3: 305–360.
15 Eisenhardt, K. M. (1989) "Agency theory: An assessment and review," *Academy of Management*, 14(1): 57–74.
16 Lubatkin, M. H., Lane, J., & Schultze, W. S. (2001) "A strategic management model of agency relationships in firm governance," in M. A. Hitt, R. E. Edwards & J. S. Harrison (Eds.), *The Blackwell Handbook of Strategic Management* (pp. 229–258). Oxford: Blackwell Business.
17 Eisenhardt, "Agency theory."
18 Ibid.
19 Jensen & Meckling, "Theory of the firm."
20 Roth, K., & O'Donnell, S. (1996) "Foreign subsidiary compensation strategy: An agency theory perspective," *Academy of Management Journal*, 39: 678–703.
21 Ibid.

22 Jones, G. R., & Wright, P. M. (1992) "An economic approach to conceptualizing the utility of human resource management practices," in K. Rowland & G. Ferris (Eds.), *Research in Personnel and Human Resources Management*, 10: 271–299.

23 Burns & Stalker, *The Management of Innovation.*

24 Child, J. (1975) "Managerial and organizational factors associated with company performance part II: A contingency analysis," *The Journal of Management Studies*, 12: 12–27.

25 Miles, R. E., & Snow, C. C. (1978). *Organizational Strategy, Structure, and Process.* San Francisco: McGraw-Hill.

26 Donaldson, L. (2001) *The Contingency Theory of Organizations.* Thousand Oaks, CA: Sage

27 Ibid.

28 Child, J. (1972) "Organizational structure, environment, and performance: The role of strategic choice," *Sociology*, 6: 1–22.

29 Delery, J. E., & Doty, D. H. (1996) "Modes of theorizing human resource management: Tests of universalistic, contingency, and configurational performance predictions," *Academy of Management Journal*, 39(4): 802–835; Lengnick-Hall, C. A., & Lengnick-Hall, M. A. (1988) "Strategic human resources management: A review of the literature and a proposed typology," *Academy of Management Review*, 13(3): 454–470.

30 Lepak, D. P., Marrone, J. M., & Takeuchi, R. (2004) "The relativity of HR systems: Conceptualizing the impact of desired employee contributions and HR philosophy," *International Journal of Technology Management*, 27: 639–655.

31 Scott, W. R. (2005) "Institutional theory: Contributing to a theoretical research program," in K. G. Smith & M. A. Hitt (Eds.), *Great Minds in Management: The Process of Theory Development.* Oxford: Oxford University Press.

32 Meyer, J., & Rowan, B. (1977). "Institutionalized organizations: Formal structure as myth and ceremony," *The American Journal of Sociology*, 83(2): 340–363.

33 Ibid.

34 Scott, "Institutional theory."

35 Martin, G., & Beaumont, P. (2001). "Transforming multinational enterprises: Towards a process model of strategic human resource management change," *The International Journal of Human Resource Management*, 12(8): 1234–1250.

36 Jackson & Schuler, "Understanding human resource management in the context of organizations and their environments."

37 Wright, P. M., & McMahan, G. C. (1992) "Theoretical perspectives for strategic human resource management," *Journal of Management*, 18: 295–320.

38 Pfeffer, J., & Cohen, Y. (1984) "Determinant of internal labour markets in organization," *Administrative Science Quarterly*, 29: 550–572.

39 Pfeffer, J., & Salancik, G. R. (1978). *The External Control of Organizations: A Resource Dependence Perspective.* New York: Harper & Row.

40 Pfeffer, J. (1981) *Power in Organizations.* Marshfield, MA: Pitman.

41 Green, S., & Welsh, M. (1988) "Cybernetics and dependence: Reframing the control concept," *Academy of Management Review*, 13: 287–301.

42 Taylor, S., Beechler, S., & Napier, N. (1996) "Toward an integrative model of strategic international human resource management," *Academy of Management Review*, 21(4): 959–985.

43 Blau, P. (1964). *Exchange and Power in Social Life.* New York: Wiley.

44 Pfeffer & Salancik, *The External Control of Organizations.*

45 Pfeffer & Salancik, *The External Control of Organizations*; Blau, *Exchange and Power in Social Life.*

46 Kim, Y. (2003) "Different subsidiary roles and international human resource management: An exploratory study of Australian subsidiaries in Asia," *Journal of Asia-Pacific Business*, 4: 39–60.

47 Pfeffer & Cohen, "Determinant of internal labour markets in organization."

48 Thornhill, S., & Amit, R. (2003) "Learning from failure: Organizational mortality and the resource-based view," Ottawa: Micro-Economic Analysis Division, Statistics Canada, p. 2.

49 Barney, J. B. (1986) "Strategic factor markets: Expectations, luck, and business strategy," *Management Science*, 32(10): 1231–1241; Barney, J. (1991) "Firm resources and sustained competitive advantage," *Journal of Management*, 17: 99–120.

50 Wernerfelt, B. (1984) "A resource-based view of the firm," *Strategic Management Journal*, 5: 171–180.

51 Barney, "Strategic factor markets"; Barney, "Firm resources and sustained competitive advantage."

52 Oliver, C. (1997) "Sustainable competitive advantage: Combining institutional and resource-based views," *Strategic Management Journal*, 18(9): 697–713.

53 Barney, "Strategic factor markets"; Barney, "Firm resources and sustained competitive advantage."

54 Gould-Williams, J., & Davies, F. (2005) "Using social exchange theory to predict the effects of HRM practice on employee outcomes," *Public Management Review*, 7(1): 1–24.

55 Blau, *Exchange and Power in Social Life*, p. 93.

56 Gould-Williams & Davies, "Using social exchange theory to predict the effects of HRM practice on employee outcomes."

57 Saks, A. M. (2006) "Antecedents and consequences of employee engagement," *Journal of Managerial Psychology*, 21(7): 600–619.

58 Shore, L. M., & Shore, T. H. (1995) "Perceived organizational support and organizational justice," in R. S. Cropanzano & K. M. Kacmar (Eds.), *Organizational Politics, Justice, and Support: Managing the Social Climate of the Workplace* (pp. 149–164). Westport, CT: Quorum Books.

59 Aryee, S., Budhwar, P. S., & Chen, Z. X. (2002) "Trust as a mediator of the relationship between organizational justice and work outcomes: Test of a social exchange model," *Journal of Organizational Behavior*, 23(3): 267–285.

60 Coff, R. W. (2002) "Human capital, shared expertise, and the likelihood of impasse on corporate acquisitions," *Journal of Management*, 28: 107–128.

61 Polanyi, M. (1966) *Personal Knowledge: Toward a Post-Critical Philosophy*. Chicago, IL: University of Chicago Press.

62 Liebeskind, J. P. (1996) "Knowledge, strategy and the theory of the firm," *Strategic Management Journal*, 17(Special Issue): 93–107.

63 Davenport, T. H., & Prusak, L. (1998) *Working Knowledge*. Cambridge, MA: Harvard Business School Press, p. 112.

64 Liebeskind, "Knowledge, strategy and the theory of the firm."

65 Nonaka, I., & Takeuchi, H. (1995) *The Knowledge-Creating Company: How Japanese Companies Create the Dynamics of Innovation*. New York: Oxford University Press.

66 Livingstone, D. W. (2002) "Working and learning in the information age: A profile of Canadians," *CPRN Discussion Paper*. Ottawa, Ontario: Canadian Policy Research Network.

67 Ibid.

68 Davenport & Prusak, *Working Knowledge*.

69 Polanyi, *Personal Knowledge*.

70 Barney, J. B. (1991) "Firm resources and sustained competitive advantage," *Journal of Management*, 17(99): 120.

71 Carpenter, M. A., Sanders, W. G., & Gregersen, H. B. (2001) "Bundling human capital with organizational context: The impact of international assignment experience on multination firm performance and CEO pay," *The Academy of Management Journal*, 44(3): 493–512.

72 Davenport & Prusak, *Working Knowledge*, p. 5.

73 Coff, "Human capital, shared expertise, and the likelihood of impasse on corporate acquisitions."

74 Hanifan, L. J. (1916) "The rural school community center." *Annals of the American Academy of Political and Social Science*, 67: 130–138.

75 Putnam, R. (2000) *Bowling Alone: The Collapse and Revival of American Community*. New York: Simon & Schuster, p. 79.

76 Putnam, R. (2001) "Measurement and consequences," *Isuma*, 2(1): 41–51.

77 Hitt, M. A., Biermant, L., Shimizu, K., & Kochhar, R. (2001) "Direct and moderating effects of human capital on strategy and performance in professional service firms: A resource-based perspective," *Academy of Management Journal*, 44(1): 13–28.

78 Herreros, F. (2004). *The Problem of Forming Social Capital: Why Trust?* New York: Palgrave Macmillan.

79 Ibid.

3

CONTEXT AND NONPROFIT HUMAN RESOURCE MANAGEMENT

Learning Objectives

After studying this chapter, you should understand:

1. The unique characteristics of the external environment of nonprofit organizations.
2. The major drivers in the internal environment of nonprofits.
3. How the external environment interacts with the activities of nonprofits.
4. The challenges that result from the external environment that nonprofit practitioners must manage for the organization to be effective.
5. What the context of nonprofits means for strategy in the sector.

The Economy and Susan G. Komen[1]

Susan G. Komen for the Cure is a Dallas, Texas-based nonprofit organization that supports breast cancer research, facilitates community outreach programs and advocacy in collaboration with local nonprofit organizations in more than 50 countries. In the 2010–2011 fiscal year, the organization awarded over $63 million for research projects and distributed $103 million to more than 1,900 nonprofit organizations for community health programs. With an army of over 100,000 volunteers and more than 300,000 advocates, Susan G. Komen's total revenue in fiscal 2011 was $471 million.[1] The fact that most of the revenue was generated from contributions and the Komen Race for the Cure and 3-Day illustrates the grassroots fundraising, network and collaborative strategy of the organization. It also emphasizes the influence of the external environment on the operations and performance of Susan G. Komen.

The influence of the external environment played a major role in the announcement in June 2013 that, starting in 2014 Susan G. Komen for the Cure will no longer hold the 3-Day, 60-mile race in seven cities across the US. The report in the NonProfit Times *noted that the organization identified declining participation and the "economic uncertainty over the last four years" as the rationale for the decision. According to the spokesperson of the organization, "we looked at the markets that weren't generating the kind of return that allows us to invest the most in our mission and we decided to withdraw from those markets."[2]*

Introduction

The next stage in our journey to unearthing the foundation of HRM in non-profits is the understanding of the nature and characteristics of the context of nonprofits. Following from the knowledge of what nonprofit organizations are, their services/products and the size and scope of their undertakings discussed in Chapter 1, it is understandable if one has questions about how they go about their activities. Since nonprofits are not an island unto themselves, they interact with the external environment at different levels and for the different reasons. This suggests that the understanding of the nature and characteristics of the external environment is pivotal to knowing how nonprofits go about their quest for the mission of the organization. The external environment is the source of the opportunities nonprofits must maximize and threats nonprofits must overcome. As explained in many of the theoretical perspectives we examined in Chapter 2, the knowledge of the external environment and its relationship with internal environment is critical to the effectiveness of the organization. Hence, the focus of this chapter is the characteristics and challenges of the environment that underlie HRM in nonprofits. First, we will start by explaining what we mean by the environment and context of an organization.

The Environment

The environment includes all the external elements and influences that affect the operations and performance of an organization.[3] All organizations irrespective of size, scope and sector of the economy, operate within an environment. From the theoretical perspectives discussed in Chapter 2, organizations interact with institutions, stakeholders, government and other organizations in the external environment. Specifically, *General Systems Theory, Contingency Theory* and *Resource Dependence Theory* all emphasize the importance and role of the environment in shaping the operations and influencing the performance of an organization. The reality of the environment is that organizations cannot survive if they are not aligned with the conditions in the environment. The environment is the source of the inputs such as raw materials, human resources and financial resources, which the organization requires to create products or services.[4] It is also the destination and consumer of the products or services of the organization. Hence, it is in the best interests of the organization for managers to continuously analyze the trends, opportunities and threats that are likely to affect the organization in the environment.

At the macro-environment, managers must understand how change in economic activities, such as the 2008 recession, and in how people spend their money could affect the organization. The opening case of Susan G. Komen for the Cure illustrates how the economic conditions can impact revenue and bring about a need to revisit the strategy of a nonprofit organization. The organization noted that there was a decline in revenue and this was due to the uncertain economic condition that resulted from the 2008 recession. Similarly, managers must carefully follow political events to see whether it offers an opportunity or threat to their organization. For example, the election of a new government might suggest a new policy direction that could mean the re-evaluation of the strategy of an organization.

More importantly, managers must understand the opportunities and threats the organization will face by continuously analyzing the environment to gain new knowledge about the needs of clients, activities of their competitors and how to best interact with direct and indirect stakeholders.[5] For example, by knowing the products or services that will meet the demand of clients, managers are better able to position the organization and guide the formulation and implementation of the strategy with respect to products and services. The point about participation highlighted in the Susan G. Komen case is a good illustration of analyzing the environment. However, since the external environment includes numerous factors, it may be impractical and expensive to continuously analyze all the influencers.[6] Thus, it is important to understand the key components of the environment that are particularly relevant to the organization. As we will explain in the discussion of the environment and the challenges of nonprofits, this is even more so for organizations that interact with influencers and influences that often require more than the capabilities and resources of the organization.

Components of the Environment

Broadly, the environment can be divided into two main parts: (1) the general environment; and (2) the competitive environment (Figure 3.1).

The *general environment* includes factors and dimensions in a particular society that influence all organizations within the society. It is sometimes referred to as the macro-environment. The main factors under the general environment are: political/legal, economic, sociocultural, technological, demographic, and global factors.[7] Since the general environment factors are common to all organizations, no organization is immune from their impact. However, the extent of their impact could vary from one organization to the other. For example, the impact of the economy on the revenue from the Komen 3-Day to the Susan G. Komen for the Cure could be similar to the experience of other nonprofit organizations, but the extent of the impact may vary. While these general environment factors are important, similar to organizations in other sectors,[8] nonprofits cannot directly

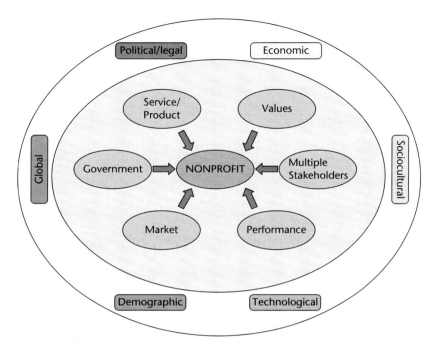

FIGURE 3.1   The General and Competitive Environment of Nonprofits

control these factors. They are beyond the powers of nonprofits. This is why it is critical for nonprofit managers to continuously scan, monitor and understand these factors as well as the unique factors in their competitive environment. We will return to how to scan the environment for the formulation of HR strategy in Chapter 4.

Due to the characteristics of nonprofits, some of the factors in the general environment are more or less part of the competitive factors that influence the operations and performance of these organizations. Before we discuss the unique characteristics and challenges of the competitive environment of nonprofits, it is relevant to provide an overview of the factors in the general environment.

General Environment Factors

- *Political/legal* environment factors include influences that stem from the political system, government policy and relevant legislations that directly or indirectly affect an organization. The political environment also includes public expectations. It is through public expectations that the activities of certain organizations are deemed to be more important to society. As a result, these organizations may be subjected to more regulations than others.[9] Some specific examples of political/legal environment factors that could impact a nonprofit are the requirement to register or incorporate an organization, government policies, taxes and employment legislations. The news report titled "Congressman Calls for Hearing on Charitable Deduction" in Chapter 2 is a good example of the impact of the political environment.

- *Economic* environment factors are determined by the fundamentals and condition of the national and local economy. Inflation, interest rates, exchange rates, monetary and fiscal policies and trade agreements with other countries are examples of factors in the economic environment. Any change in the economy factors could influence the resources available to nonprofits. As evidenced in the example of Susan G. Komen for the Cure, individual and corporate spending, saving and donations could impact nonprofits.

- *Sociocultural* environment factors are influences that result from the norms, values, beliefs and attitudes of the people in society. These factors are the core attributes of the culture. The social institutions of a society such as the family and religious groups generally symbolize its culture. As discussed below, the sociocultural environment is particularly critical to nonprofits due to the social nature of the goods/services they provide and the characteristics of the organization. For example, beliefs about volunteering in the community are directly linked to a vibrant nonprofit and voluntary sector in Canada, the USA and the UK.[10]

- *Technological* environment factors relate to the adoption of technology in everyday life, work processes and production. The opportunity for and the extent of adoption of technology could influence the strategy of a nonprofit to explore a new service/product segment, enhance efficiency or simply better position the organization to respond to emerging needs of the community. For many nonprofits, the question about technology is how to finance the cost of the technology they need for their operations. This need highlights the role of organizations such as TechSoup Global, a nonprofit that partners with leading technology companies to provide technology and knowledge resources to the nonprofit sector to enable social change.

- *Demographic* environment factors or trends are equivalent to the push and pull factors in the population that affect organizations. Factors such as age, level of education, geographic distribution, income level and the family status of the population, are important pointers for nonprofits. Demographic factors impact nonprofits not only in terms of their operations, but also by shaping the demand for social goods and services that are offered by nonprofits. One such influencer is the impact of the aging population for nonprofits. It has been suggested nonprofits that align with the needs of the aging population are positioned for future success.[11]

- *Global* environment factors are those influencers that transcend national boundaries. The concept of globalization which describes the integration and diffusion of the world from an economic, technological, cultural and, to some extent, political standpoint,[12] means that trends and events in one country or part of the world can have domino effects in other countries. People are connected through advanced communication infrastructure, financial system and the push for human rights. Many organizations are able to operate seamlessly across borders. But similar to other environment factors, globalization can be a source of threats and opportunities for nonprofits. As illustrated in the excerpt on Save the Children in Box 3.1, the opportunities and threats are the key drivers in the formulation of the strategy of nonprofits. Recently, one of the aftermaths of the Arab Spring of 2011 is the increased demand for the services of NGOs that provide support to refugees. With the announcement that Canada will work with the United Nations to resettle some high-need refugees from Syria,[13] nonprofits that provide settlement services will likely participate in the initiative and may need to align their strategy to meet the needs of the people.

BOX 3.1 GLOBALIZATION AND NGOs

Globalization is both an opportunity and a threat to people, to societies, and to NGOs. Organizations like Save the Children benefit from global information (e.g., the Internet), global competition between airlines (cheap travel), and corporate fund-raising with global players. At the same time, national fund-raising can become difficult because global firms are looking for global opportunities, competition among NGOs extends beyond national borders, and globalization produces many new tasks that NGOs have to tackle.

Source: Gnaerig, Burkhard & MacCormack, Charles, F. (1999) "The challenges of globalization: save the children," *Nonprofit and Voluntary Sector Quarterly,* 28(4) (Supplement): 140–146.

The general or macro-environment factors represent the broader intersection of nonprofits with the external environment. Even so, these external influences could have considerable impact on the operations and performance of nonprofits. Some of macro-environment factors are the key drivers of change in nonprofits. For example, demographic changes could necessitate the development of new services and the reassessment of strategy of the organization. Table 3.1 provides examples of factors in the general environment.

The point to note is how relevant is the impact of a specific general environment factor for an organization at any particular time. Moreover, as highlighted in the examples above, many of the general environment factors are often inseparable from the competitive environment factors that directly impact the goals and strategy of a nonprofit organization.

TABLE 3.1 General Environment of Nonprofits

Environment	Example
Political/legal	Government policies, Regulations
Economic	Competition, Inflation
Sociocultural	Cultural values, Societal Attitudes
Technological	Knowledge Creation, Information Flow
Demographic	Age, Diversity
Global	Globalization, International Events

Competitive Environment of Nonprofits

The competitive environment factors are the influences in the external environment that could directly impact the mission, the strategic goals and the operations of a nonprofit organization. These influences are the primary drivers that necessitate nonprofit organizations to recognize the need to adapt to change by re-evaluating their strategies, structure and processes. A major differentiating factor between nonprofit, public and for-profit organizations is the characteristics of the competitive environment and how some of the factors overlap with the general environment. Nonprofit managers must plan, coordinate and integrate value-adding activities that are products of the context of the organization. Hence, for the purpose of this chapter, we see the competitive environment as the *context* of nonprofit organizations. These influences are manifested in the strategy and the HR practices of the nonprofit organization and are particularly relevant in shaping its performance. As shown in Figure 3.1, the competitive environment and context factors are: nature of the services, values, performance, market dynamics, multiple stakeholders and government.

Nature of Products/Services

The goods or services that nonprofits produce are essentially personal in nature. This means that nonprofits engage in significant interpersonal transactions. The operational requirement, planning and control needed for performance is a source of daily challenge to any nonprofit organization. In this environment, emotions and how to manage them are part and parcel of the business process. The emotions that are built into the interpersonal transactions of a nonprofit organization's products or services transcend direct service delivery. They are evidenced in strategic transactions such as advocacy, funding of services/products and the relationship with the political environment factors. These interpersonal transactions are also part of the boundary spanning demands that the stakeholders make to nonprofits in terms of the additional services they should provide to meet the needs of clients. The ability of a nonprofit to effectively and efficiently manage interpersonal transactions is important to achieve the performance goals of the organization. To illustrate this point, Box 3.2 highlights the services the American Red Cross provided during the oil spill in the Gulf of Mexico.[14]

BOX 3.2 AMERICAN RED CROSS DURING OIL SPILL

In addition to providing disaster relief during the oil spill in the Gulf of Mexico, the American Red Cross was called upon to provide disaster mental health support to people affected by the spill. Noting the significant emotional issue in the disaster, Rob Yin, Manager for Disaster Mental Health Services at American Red Cross noted that there are mixed emotions such as anger *and* frustration about the disaster.

Source: Mental health issues spill into recovery—July 1, 2010. *The NonProfit Times*.

The personal nature of the products/services further heightens the interpersonal transaction and performance expectation from stakeholders. In terms of managing people, the interpersonal transactions that characterize the products/ services of a nonprofit suggest that HR practices that are developed must fit this important nature of the product or service of the organization. How to attract, engage and retain employees must include consideration for whether the need for quality interpersonal transaction can be met by the human resource management practices adopted. Training must provide employees with the skills to effectively deliver services that are embedded with emotional transactions.

Values

Nonprofits are organizations established primarily to achieve social objectives.[15] Therefore, another way of understanding the context of nonprofits is through the main goals of the organization. The social objectives that are at the core of nonprofits are embedded in the complexities and values of society. The incorporation of nonprofits as organizations has been described as the translation of shared values and common concerns in the community to problem solving activities.[16] In others words, people establish nonprofits in order to solve problems that are common to members or a segment of the society which they have deemed important enough and share similar values on how to address. In the same vein, scholars have found that nonprofits are the product of broader social, political and economic relationships and a complex set of historical forces.[17] These complex forces and factors that underlie nonprofits point to the importance of values that are commonly shared. As a result, the values enshrined in the complex environment are central to what nonprofits are all about.[18] In essence, values are not only important in terms of the core principle and overarching philosophy of the nonprofit, they are also key drivers in the external environment of the organization.

The influence of values points to two critical influences on nonprofits. First, where values are more favourable, nonprofits will grow and flourish. This aspect of the influence of values emphasizes the role of specific institutions in society that are more favourable to the growth of nonprofits.[19] These institutions shape the character of nonprofits. second, values are integral to the social objective that nonprofits set out to achieve and the performance of the organization. At a minimum, the vision, mission and strategic goals of nonprofits must demonstrate these values.[20] Accordingly, the characteristics, operations and performance of nonprofits are shaped by the shared values.

It is therefore imperative for nonprofits to align their strategy, structure and HR practices to the influence of values, a key product of their competitive environment. In one comparative study on high performance HR practices, researchers found that nonprofits adopt those practices that are commonly accepted in order to gain legitimacy.[21] The findings suggest that HR practices in nonprofit organizations result in part from shared values in the competitive environment and society at large. Many nonprofits showcase the importance of values in their HR practices. Also in the behavior of employees illustrated on their website, mission statement and annual report. The excerpt in Box 3.3 below from the career page of Easter Seals Ontario, Canada, illustrates the point about values.

BOX 3.3 EASTER SEALS ONTARIO CORE VALUES

Easter Seals Ontario is dedicated to helping kids with physical disabilities. The people who work for Easter Seals share this dedication. At Easter Seals, we offer our employees a team-oriented environment, with a commitment to continuous learning and development.

Our employees exemplify the core values of our organization. These core values are:

- Commitment
- Respect, honesty and integrity
- Progressive leadership
- Teamwork and communications
- Innovation and creativity.

Source: Career site. http://www.easterseals.org/ Retrieved February 5, 2013.

Values are also essential in the interactions of nonprofit organizations with stakeholders and the political/government environment. This suggests that the organizational values that are supposed to be inherent in the behavior of employees and the leaders of nonprofits could significantly influence the outcomes of these interactions. How nonprofits navigate the contours of ethics and slip into major scandals depend on how well the employees and leaders "live" the values of the organization. The decision of Nike to end its partnership with Livestrong from the fallout over Lance Armstrong's doping scandal discussed in Box 3.4 is a good example.[22] In a nutshell, values are critical factors in the context of nonprofits that could have either a positive or negative impact on the organization.

BOX 3.4 LIVESTRONG AND NIKE SPLIT

Nike, Livestrong Split in Latest Fallout from Lance Armstrong Doping Scandal

By Jim Vertuno

With Nike's help, Lance Armstrong's Livestrong cancer charity turned a little yellow wristband into a global symbol for cancer survivors.

But that partnership, which started in 2004, will soon end. Livestrong announced Tuesday that Nike is cutting ties with the charity in the latest fallout from the former cyclist's doping scandal.

Source: Vertuno, Jim (2013) "Nike, Livestrong split in latest fallout from Lance Armstrong doping scandal," Huffingtonpost.com. Retrieved May 28, 2013.

Performance

For nonprofits, organizational performance is often relative to the unique services/products of the organization, qualitative and not easy to measure. Unlike business organizations that have universally accepted and readily available quantitative performance indicators that are generated through the market, such as quarterly earnings, return on equity, and customer satisfaction scores, nonprofits rely only on their mission. As a result, nonprofit scholars have reminded us that while the bottom line is important, the financial result is not the primary emphasis of the nonprofit enterprise and cannot be an indicator of the performance of the organization.[23] Instead, they noted that the most important indicator of performance is the extent to which nonprofits achieve their mission.[24] The mission communicates the public good the nonprofit intends to achieve and the people the organization intends to serve.

It helps to attract critical resources including funders, donors, volunteers and employees.[25]

One thing scholars agree upon is that organizational performance in non-profits is multidimensional and social in nature.[26] This point explains two viewpoints about performance in nonprofits. First, it reinforces the importance of the context of the organization, particularly the relative perception of what is performance in a nonprofit. In other words, whether a nonprofit is determined to be achieving its mission is based on the perception of those stakeholders who are assessing the performance. It also depends on whether the outcome of the services or products could be assessed without difficulty. Second, the point also highlights the influence of stakeholders in defining what performance the organization should emphasize. What one stakeholder considers a good performance is often different from the performance expectation of another stakeholder.

The bottom line (pun intended) on the unique and multidimensional measure of organizational performance in nonprofits is that it is a major factor in the environment that could influence the strategy and HR practices of the organization. As nonprofits continue to find new ways to highlight their performance and meet the demands of stakeholders who ask for different performance indicators, HRM will have to reflect the different measures of organizational effectiveness. The monitoring and measurement of performance in nonprofits involve different levels of adaptive behavior, skills and knowledge to meet the accountability requirement of funders, donors and clients.

The introduction and excerpts from a 2012 live online discussion on how to measure the performance of a nonprofit in the *Chronicle of Philanthropy* in Box 3.5, illustrate the link between performance measures and employee skills in nonprofits.[27]

BOX 3.5 HOW TO MEASURE YOUR NONPROFIT'S PERFORMANCE

Excerpts from introduction and online discussion

Collecting data is a great way to show donors what your organization has accomplished, but it can also help the staff get better results in their work and make wise decisions.

M: —yes—our research found that, ironically, it was the "soft skills" that differentiated the best measurement directors from the ones that didn't work

(continued)

(continued)

out. These soft skills are: a) interpersonal skills—is this someone who knows how to communicate with, and build rapport with, not just senior leaders but also front-line staff; b) change management skills—is this someone who has led a change process before—that knows how to get people who are reluctant to move in a certain direction to be excited about doing so. Most staff do not immediately believe in measurement—so this is really important.

It isn't that the "hard skills" are unimportant, just that they are not enough to be successful in these roles.

A: The structure actually helped many staff feel less overwhelmed because there was finally a way to organize their work and their efforts with participants that we never had before.

Source: "How to measure your nonprofit's performance," *Chronicle of Philanthropy*, Tuesday, June 19, 2012. Retrieved February 5, 2013. Republished with permission of *The Chronicle of Philanthropy*, http://philanthropy.com

Market Dynamics

One area that is often omitted from the discussion of the competitive environment factors that could influence nonprofits is how the for-profit business market environment affects the activities of nonprofit organizations. While the discussion of the broader market environment is outside the scope of this book, the dynamics of the labor market created by for-profit business organizations is an important competitive environment factor for nonprofits. This is not to suggest that nonprofits do not influence the labor market. The point here is that nonprofit organizations have to manage the constraints of the labor market including those created by the competitive environment of business organizations.

From the perspective of HRM, the business environment could shape the context of nonprofits at three levels. First, the recruitment and compensation practices of business firms could become a relevant factor in the context of nonprofits. How and who business organizations recruit, how much they pay, and the type of benefits businesses offer employees are external environment factors for nonprofits. In essence, the extent to which the business environment interacts and shapes the nonprofit context creates a unique competitive environment for HR practices in nonprofits.

Second, the introduction and adoption of a business culture in nonprofits could factor into the employee issues an organization must address and the HR practices that are developed to manage the issues. Employee relations issues are often related to the culture and conflict in organizations. This was the situation when Roy Soards took over as the CEO of St. Vincent de Paul Rehabilitation Service, Inc. The Portland, Oregon, organization provides employment opportunities for people with disabilities. The nonprofit operated previously as a sheltered work-shop that relied mainly on social service fees and charitable giving. After the previous CEO, Charley Graham, transformed the organization into an affirmative business focused on producing and selling quality goods and services, a culture war emerged between production staff in the factory and the rehabilitation staff who provided social services.[28] This culture war resulted from the tension between the need to meet the business goals in production and the need to provide social support to the adults the organization trained for employment. The orientation and values of the two groups highlighted the tenuous relationship between business and social outcomes in nonprofits.

Third, the activities of business organizations in terms of whether they encourage and support their employees to volunteer could impact the context and influ-ence the HR practices nonprofit organizations develop. For-profit organizations sponsor or encourage their employees to volunteer primarily to enhance the cor-porate social responsibility brand of the organization, boost employee morale and enhance their relations with their local community.[29] The IBM's Corporate Service Corps program is a good example. In addition to the community service goal of the program, it also doubles as a leadership academy for the organization.[30] Each year, thousands of employees compete for the 500 spots in the program. Participants have reported that the program contributed to the job performance, skills and desire to build careers at IBM. In all, 430,000 IBM employees spent 3.2 million hours volunteering in 2011.[31] This and other employer-sponsored volunteering in turn become part of the context that influences HR practices, co-production between employees and volunteers, employee relations, and vol-unteer recruitment and retention. We will return to this topic in Chapter 10. What is important to note here is that employer-sponsored volunteering has implications for the competitive context of nonprofits not only in terms of the HR practices, but also employee knowledge, skills and behavior.

Multiple Stakeholders

The social objectives and the public goods/services that characterize non-profits mean that they have multiple primary stakeholders.[32] Stakeholders are the individuals and groups who can affect, and/or are affected, by the mission, strategic goals and the performance of a nonprofit organization.[33] Stakeholders are very important to nonprofits to the point that they cannot afford to alien-ate anyone.[34] More than in other organizations, the effectiveness of nonprofits depend significantly on multiple stakeholders who are connected to the orga-nization and influence management decisions.[35] Also to a larger extent than in other organizations, nonprofit stakeholders are not limited to individuals who directly impact or are directly impacted by these organizations. Stake-holders include those who have some level of influence on the outcomes of the organization.[36]

For nonprofits, stakeholders include clients, employees, volunteers, funders, advocacy groups, government, media, umbrella organizations such as the United Way, and the community. Although, not all of these stakeholders are directly connected to the operations and activities of nonprofits and therefore may not impact the performance of the organization, nonprofit scholars note that there is an inherently higher level of expectation for nonprofit organizations to satisfy multiple stakeholders and interests. Essentially, the multiple stakeholders' context of nonprofits fosters a continuous state of balancing of interests for the organizations. This environment factor impacts the strategy and HR practices of nonprofits in different ways which will be discussed in subsequent chapters. For the purpose of this chapter, we highlight the broader impacts.

First, since nonprofits depend on the resources and relationships with stakeholders in order to gain legitimacy and to survive,[37] when a nonprofit meets the performance expectations of a stakeholder, one should expect that the funding and non-financial support from that particular resource provider to the organization would likely continue. However, as noted above, because there are multiple stakeholders with different expectations for the organization, there is no guarantee that other stakeholders will accept the same performance. This suggests that the nonprofit must align its strategy and HRM with the diverse performance expectations of the stakeholders. The implications of such diverse performance expectations could mean a drain on the resources of the organization due to the incongruent expectations of certain stakeholders. It would also impose additional barriers to achieving a vertical fit between strategy and HRM and a horizontal fit across HR practices. The reality of managing multiple stakeholders with diverse expectations compels nonprofits to go the extra mile by consulting and engaging with stakeholders to ensure they have the buy-in of these influencers when they are planning and/or implementing a major change. The example of Place2Be, the UK charity that provides counselling to children in schools, is illustrative of this approach.[38] Box 3.6 details how the nonprofit consulted extensively with stakeholders to build its new website.

BOX 3.6 PLACE2BE

Organization: Place2Be
Agency: Sift Digital
Spend: £46,000

The national charity that provides counselling for children in schools decided to put the children it works with at the heart of its new website.

Development

Place2Be brought in the creative agency Sift Digital to meet children, volunteer counsellors and staff at a Place2Be school in Cardiff to find out more about the charity and what the website should include. The charity conducted workshops with stakeholders and a survey of existing staff, volunteers and supporters to decide on the content of the new site.

Source: Quainton, Gemma (2012) "Place2Be," *Third Sector*, 17 December.

Second, the fact that nonprofits have to deal with multiple performance expectations from different stakeholders also means that they may have to contend with conflicting values among their stakeholders.[39] The conflicting interests, values and dependency on multiple stakeholders are unique challenges to nonprofits. Not only do they have to manage the dependency relationships, they have to consider the influence of and impact of stakeholders in decision-making and operations of the organization. Research suggests that employees must grapple with the often conflicting expectations of the mission, the bottom line and the accountability of nonprofits.[40] Nonprofit managers must continuously understand and balance the different expectations of stakeholders as they play out in their HR practices.

Government

For nonprofits, the government is more than just an enactor of public policies and legislation that govern their activities. Different types of nonprofits have varying levels of interaction with the government. The interaction could range from explicit contracts to provide a public service, partnership in community economic development, and civic engagements to the regulation of activities of incorporated nonprofit organizations. Government is a major stakeholder and core source of revenue for many nonprofits.[41] A comparative study of nonprofits in many countries found that 48 percent of the revenue of nonprofits in developed countries and 35 percent of the revenue internationally come from government.[42]

This resource dependence has prompted researchers to single out government funding as the most drastic and difficult challenge in the environment of nonprofits.[43] Government is not simply a component of the political factor in the general environment of nonprofits. Government is by and large an integral part of the competitive environment and context of nonprofits. Hence, research has also found that government funding is a major factor why nonprofits change their strategy.[44] It is therefore no surprise that many nonprofits focus more on fundraising strategy to mitigate the loss of government funding rather than to implement cost containment strategy.[45] Not knowing whether funding will be renewed for the next year or if the service will be discontinued without warning creates an environment of extreme uncertainty and limits the ability of nonprofits to engage in real strategic planning.

The challenge of government as a major factor in the context of nonprofits is not limited to competition, type of funding or government policy. It could become particularly intractable for the management and effectiveness of non-profits when government uses direct political interference to control nonprofits. While this could generate a major controversy, the end result is that the services of *nonprofits* are affected.

In summary, the unique context that includes the *competitive environment* factors defines nonprofit organizations. The competitive environment directly impacts the activities, decision-making and performance of nonprofits. It is the source of the major challenges nonprofits must overcome in order to achieve their strategic goals. Nonprofit managers must pay careful attention to the dynamics of the com-petitive environment as it plays out in different ways. Managers must engage in systematic and continuous analysis of these key factors including how their com-petitors are addressing similar challenges. It is critical for managers to understand the emerging threats and opportunities a nonprofit will confront. This chapter ends with an overview of the current challenges in the competitive environment of nonprofits and a review of the main sources of the core resources and capabili-ties of a typical nonprofit. Both the challenges and resources are important to the formulation and implementation of an effective HRM system and strategy.

Current Issues in the Environment of Nonprofits

The context and competitive environment factors of nonprofits are manifested in many of the challenges of organizations in the sector. In the scanning, monitoring and forecasting of the trends in the environment that could affect the organization which we will discuss in Chapter 4, it is important for managers to pay particular attention to the following current challenges of nonprofit organizations at a high level.

- *Government funding* is perhaps one of the toughest challenges in the competi-tive environment of nonprofits. As evidenced in the overview in Chapter 1, not only has the services/products provided by nonprofits increased due to the outsourcing of services previously provided by the government, the gov-ernment is the primary source of revenue for many nonprofit organizations.[46] As a result, scholars have suggested that the relationship between government funding and HRM functions in nonprofits is one of the significant challenges of the sector.
- *Contract-based funding* has become the de facto model for the funding of nonprofits by government and other funding bodies. Funders, especially the

government, often use contracts which are based on an annual term to support specific services or products that are offered by nonprofits.[47] The challenges of contract-based funding are extensive and are played out in HR practices such as recruitment, training and compensation.[48] We will discuss this further in subsequent chapters.

- *Competition* for funding, human resources and social legitimacy have increased in the environment of nonprofits.[49] Not only do nonprofit organizations compete with other nonprofits for funding, the challenge of competition for nonprofits includes market competition with for-profit business. This has necessitated nonprofit organizations to constantly reassess their strategy to ensure that they are operationally efficient and positioned to achieve their performance goals.

- *Accountability* is a challenge in the competitive environment of nonprofits from different perspectives. First, it must be noted that accountability is linked to the challenges we have discussed above, especially contract-based funding. Hence, the chief area in which the challenge of accountability is prominent is in terms of what to measure, how to measure and how to report the performance of nonprofits. It has been noted that the accountability requirements of the funding environment of nonprofits is a source of stress and job dissatisfaction among child welfare employees.[50]

- *Efficiency* is not a challenge that is unique to the environment of nonprofits. However, the risk of efficiency overshadowing the social objectives of nonprofits has been highlighted as a challenge. For nonprofits, efficiency has to do with minimizing the cost of providing services (input) while maintaining quality and reaching those who need the services (output). Basically, nonprofits must learn to do more with less. The efficiency challenge is related to questions about what is performance in nonprofits and has also contributed to competition.

- *The changing needs of the community* have necessitated the emergence of nonprofits as a major player in the social, economic and political spheres of society. The real challenge in relation to the emerging needs of the community is whether nonprofits are able to effectively respond to the pace of change. From demographic, social and economic changes to the dizzying pace of change in technology, how nonprofits create services/products to meet the dynamics of the new types of demand for public goods require each organization to embrace permanent change readiness. For nonprofits that deploy a growth strategy, it also involves the balancing of strategic priorities based on their resources.

These challenges are some of the major threats to the operations, performance and survival of nonprofit organizations across many countries. The challenges are broad categorizations with many subcategories. For example, technology, which is noted under changing needs of the community, is a distinct threat that affects what services are needed from nonprofits as well as the operational efficiency of the organization. Depending on one's perspective, it could be argued that the challenges of nonprofits include many other threats some of which could fall under the threats above.

Resources and Capabilities

The resources and capabilities of a nonprofit organization represent the core ingredient in the formulation of strategy to maximize the opportunities in the external environment. A typical analysis of the competitive advantage of a nonprofit must also identify how well the organization is positioned to deploy its resources and capabilities to mitigate the threats from the external environment. Such analysis would highlight the weaknesses of the organization especially vis-à-vis its competitors.

Considering the complex unpredictable nature of the external environment, the unique competitive environment and how volatile factors impact nonprofits, the resources and capabilities of a nonprofit could be a reliable tool for its competitive advantage. Although the environment and context are different, the importance of resources and capabilities in nonprofits is similar to those noted by scholars for business firms.[51] The perspective that emphasizes the role of resources and capabilities reflects the resource-based view discussed in Chapter 2. We will now review the main sources of the resources and capabilities of nonprofits.

In a 2013 paper,[52] I suggested that there are three major types of resources and capabilities that originate from the complex interactions and processes in the general and competitive environment of nonprofits.

- First, nonprofits generate resources and capabilities from their structural characteristics, that is, their characteristic as nonprofit organizations. Since nonprofits do not distribute or return profits they generate to owners or directors, they are able to channel surplus revenue to enhance the resource base of the organization. Similarly, volunteer participation creates a cost advantage in the labor market and increases the quality and diversity of the human resource pool.[53] The ability to deploy this human capital for coproduction of outcomes will create a competitive advantage for the organization. Conversely, how a nonprofit uses any surplus revenue could mediate the quality of employee and volunteer skills, behaviors and interactions in the organization.
- Second, institutional resources and capabilities are another source of competitive advantage for nonprofits. These resources and capabilities are a by-product of the union of social, political and economic relationships and the complex set of historical forces that give rise to nonprofits.[54] Institutional resources and capabilities are at the core of the unique context and competitive environment

of nonprofits. Nonprofits are dependent on different individuals, groups and organizations in the external environment. This impacts strategic processes and management practices. Through social interactions, nonprofits acquire, develop and deploy competencies, social networks and tangible assets to gain a competitive advantage.

- Third, nonprofits may also use the values that differentiate the organization from the competition to gain and sustain a competitive advantage. Scholars have suggested that the ability of nonprofits to emphasize the values-driven side of strategy over operational efficiency will result in sustainable competitive advantage.[55] The meeting of minds in terms of similar values between employees, volunteers, other stakeholders and the nonprofit could enhance the performance of the organization. For example, since employee engagement is one of the antecedents of job performance and organizational citizenship behavior, and contributes to organizational performance,[56] the values that constitute the core characteristic of nonprofits are a critical resource and source of capabilities that can be deployed to achieve a competitive advantage.

The role and importance of these resources and capabilities are evidenced in the two examples presented in this chapter—see Susan G. Komen and St. Vincent de Paul Rehabilitation Service, Inc.—and throughout the book. The valuable resources and capabilities, including the intangible assets that are derived from the reputation of the nonprofit, are important drivers for the formulation of strategy and development of HRM systems.

Summary

This chapter provides an overview of the external environment and the characteristics of the context of nonprofits. The topics covered in this chapter are important to understand the factors that could impact the operations, the performance and, ultimately, the survival of a nonprofit. The external environment and the unique context of nonprofits are not only the gates to the opportunities and the origins of the threats managers must consider in formulating strategy and HR practices, they give root to the mission of each organization.

The differences in the context of strategy and HRM mean that managers must pay particular attention to the relevant factors in scanning, monitoring and assessing the impact of the external environment. How well managers position the organization to ensure that each nonprofit can acquire, develop and leverage its core resources and capabilities depends on the understanding of the external environment and the context of nonprofits. As we will explain in Chapter 4, one principal resource and capability that managers must focus on is the knowledge, skills and behavior of employees and the HR practices developed to effectively deploy this human resource. The need to adapt to change and the pressure to do more are also intricately linked to HRM.

Discussion Questions

1. Select a nonprofit organization and outline the general environment factors that affect the organization. What are the implications of the environment for the organization?
2. Search online for the annual report of a nonprofit. In the report, determine the percentage of the funding of the organization that is from government sources. Outline how government funding could impact the organization.
3. Outline how the aging population is relevant to nonprofit organization.
4. Stakeholders have different expectations for nonprofit organizations, what are some of the ways nonprofits can balance the conflicting interests of stakeholders?

Notes

1 Susan G. Komen for the Cure. 2010–2011 Annual Report. http://ww5.komen.org/uploadedFiles/Content/AboutUs/Financial/FY11%20report%20FINAL%20100812.pdf
2 Sullivan, Patrick (2013) "Embattled Komen canceling many 3-day races," *The Nonprofit Times*. June 5, 2013. http://www.thenonprofittimes.com/news-articles/embattled-komen-canceling-many-3-day-races/. Retrieved June 14, 2013.
3 Hitt, M. A., Ireland, R. D., Hoskisson, R. E., Sheppard, J. P., & Rowe, W. G. (2009) *Strategic Management: Competitiveness and Globalization-Concepts*. 3rd Canadian Edition. Toronto, ON: Nelson.
4 Jackson, S. E., & Schuler, R. S. (1995) "Understanding human resource management in the context of organizations and their environments," *Annual Review of Psychology*, 46: 237–264.
5 Hitt, Ireland, Hoskisson, Sheppard, & Rowe, *Strategic Management*.
6 Grant, R. M. (2012) *Contemporary Strategy Analysis*. 7th Edition. Chichester, West Sussex, UK: Wiley.
7 Hitt, Ireland, Hoskisson, Sheppard, & Rowe, *Strategic Management*.
8 Hitt, Ireland, Hoskisson, Sheppard, & Rowe, *Strategic Management*.
9 Fottler, M. D. (1981) "Is management really generic?" *Academy of Management Review*, 6(1): 1–12.
10 Hall, M. H. (2006) "The Canadian nonprofit and voluntary sector in perspective," in V. Murray (Ed.) *Management of Nonprofit and Charitable Organizations in Canada* (pp. 25–50). Markham, ON: LexisNexis.
11 Espy, Siri N. (1992) "The aging of America: Implications for nonprofit planning," *Nonprofit World*, 10(2): 31.
12 Hirst, P., & Thomson, G. (1995) *Globalization in Question: The International Economy and Possibilities of Governance*. London: Polity Press.
13 "Canada to help resettle some Syrian refugees." Canadian Broadcasting Corporation News. Posted: Jun 20, 2013, 7:53 PM ET.
14 "Mental health issues spill into recovery" *The Nonprofit Times*. 07/01/2010, http://www.thenonprofittimes.com/article/detail/mental-health-issues-spill-into-recovery-2840. Retrieved October 14, 2011.
15 Quarter, J. (1992) *Canada's Social Economy: Cooperatives, Nonprofits, and Other Community Enterprises*. Toronto, ON: James Lorimer.
16 Smith, R., & Lipsky, M. (1993) *Nonprofits for Hire: The Welfare State in the Age of Contracting*. Cambridge, MA: Harvard University Press.

17 Salamon, L., & Anheier, H. (1998) "Social origins of civil society: Explaining the non-profit sector cross nationally," *Voluntas: International Journal of Voluntary and Nonprofit Organizations*, 3: 213–248.

18 Jeavons, T. H. (1992) "When management is the message: Relating values to management practice in nonprofit organizations," *Nonprofit Management and Leadership*, 2(4): 403–417.

19 Salamon & Anheier, "Social origins of civil society."

20 Moore, M. (2000) "Managing for value: Organizational strategy in for-profit, nonprofit, and governmental organizations," *Nonprofit and Voluntary Sector Quarterly*, 29: 183–208.

21 Kalleberg, A. L., Marden, P., Reynolds, J., & Knoke, D. (2006) "Beyond profit! Sectoral difference in high-performance work practices," *Work and Occupations*, 33(3): 271–302.

22 Vertuno, Jim (2013) "Nike, Livestrong split in latest fallout from Lance Armstrong doping scandal," Huffingtonpost.com, May 28, 2013.

23 Brown, W. A., & Yoshioka, C. (2003) "Mission attachment and satisfaction as factors in. employee retention," *Nonprofit Leadership and Management*, 14(1): 5–18.

24 Moore, "Managing for value."

25 Bradach, Jeffrey L., Tierney, Thomas J., & Stone, Nan (2008) "Delivering on the promise of nonprofits," *Harvard Business Review*, December 2008.

26 Herman, R. D., & Renz, D. O. (1997) "Multiple constituencies and the social construction of nonprofit organization effectiveness," *Nonprofit and Voluntary Sector Quarterly*, 26(2): 185–206.

27 "How to measure your nonprofit's performance," *Chronicle of Philanthropy*, June 19, 2012. http://philanthropy.com/article/How-to-Measure-Your/132139/. Retrieved February 5, 2013.

28 The story of St. Vincent dePaul Staffing Services. http://www.socialent.org/pdfs/St_Vincent.pdf. Retrieved October 21, 2011.

29 Basil, D., Runte, M., Barr, C., & Easwaramoorthy, M. (2006) "Employee volunteerism: Benefits and challenges for businesses," University of Lethbridge and Imagine Canada. http://sectorsource.ca/sites/default/files/resources/files/ULeth_Benefits_FS.pdf. Retrieved March 15, 2010.

30 Brady, Diane (2012) "Volunteerism as a core competency," *Bloomberg Businessweek*, November 8, 2012. http://www.businessweek.com/articles/2012-11-08/volunteerism-as-a-core-competency. Retrieved April 1, 2013.

31 Ibid.

32 Herman, R. D. (2004) "The future of nonprofit management," in R. D. Herman (Ed.), *The Jossey-Bass Handbook of Nonprofit Leadership and Management, 2nd Edition* (pp. 731–735). San Francisco: Jossey-Bass: Quarter, J., Mook. L., & Armstrong, A. (2009) *Understanding the Social Economy: A Canadian Perspective*. Toronto: University of Toronto Press.

33 Jones, T. M., & Wicks, A. C. (1999) "Convergent stakeholder theory," *Academy of Management Review*, 24: 206–221.

34 Courtney, R. (2002) *Strategic Management for Voluntary Nonprofit Organizations*. London: Routledge.

35 Stone, M. M., Bigelow, B., & Crittenden, W. (1999) "Research on strategic management in nonprofit organizations," *Administration & Society*, 31: 378–423.

36 Ibid.

37 Moore, M. (2000) "Managing for value: Organizational strategy in for-profit, nonprofit, and governmental organizations," *Nonprofit and Voluntary Sector Quarterly*, 29: 183–208.

38 Quainton, Gemma (2012) "Place2Be," *Third Sector*, 17 December 2012. Retrieved February 6, 2013.

39 Handy, C. (1988) *Understanding Voluntary Organizations*. Harmondsworth, UK: Penguin.

40 Kim, S. (2005) "Three big management challenges in nonprofit human services agencies," *International Review of Public Administration*, 10(1): 85–93; Sowa, J., Selden, S. C., & Sandfort, J. (2004) "No longer unmeasurable? A multidimensional integrated model of nonprofit organizational effectiveness," *Nonprofit and Voluntary Sector Quarterly*, 33(4): 711–728.

41 Quarter, J., Mook. L., & Armstrong, A. (2009) *Understanding the Social Economy: A Canadian Perspective*. Toronto: University of Toronto Press; Scott, K. (2003) *Funding Matters: The Impact of Canada's New Funding Regime on Nonprofit and Voluntary Organizations*. Ottawa: Canadian Council on Social Development.

42 Hall, M. H., de Wit, M. L., Lasby, D., McIver, D., Evers, T., Johnson, C., et al. (2005) *Cornerstones of Community: Highlights of the National Survey of Nonprofit and Voluntary Organizations*. Ottawa: Imagine Canada.

43 Hall, M., & Banting, K. (2000) "The nonprofit sector in Canada: An introduction," in K. Banting (Ed.), *The Nonprofit Sector in Canada: Roles and Relationships* (pp. 1–28). Kingston, ON: Queen's University School of Policy Studies: Smith, R., & Lipsky, M. (1993) *Nonprofits for Hire: The Welfare State in the Age of Contracting*. Cambridge, MA: Harvard University Press.

44 Alexander, J. (2000) "Adaptive strategies of nonprofit human service organizations in the era of devolution and new public management," *Nonprofit Management & Leadership*, 10(3): 287–303; Smith & Lipsky, *Nonprofits for Hire*.

45 Foster, M. K., & Meinhard, A. (2002) "A contingency view of the responses of voluntary social service organizations in Ontario to government cutbacks," *Canadian Journal of Administrative Sciences*, 19(1): 27–41.

46 Scott, K. (2003) "Funding matters: the impact of Canada's funding regime on nonprofit and voluntary organizations," Ottawa: Canadian Council on Social Development.

47 Smith & Lipsky, *Nonprofits for Hire*.

48 Akingbola, K. (2004) "Staffing, retention and government funding," *Nonprofit Management & Leadership*, 14(4): 453–465.

49 Dees, J. G. (1999) "Enterprising nonprofits," *Harvard Business Review*, 76: 135–166.

50 Howe, P., & McDonald, C. (2001) *Traumatic Stress, Turnover and Peer Support in Child Welfare*. Washington, DC: Child Welfare League of America. http://www.cwla.org/programs/trieschman/2001fbwPhilHowe.htm. Retrieved October 1, 2005.

51 Grant, R. M. (2012) *Contemporary Strategy Analysis*. 7th Edition. Chichester, West Sussex, UK: Wiley.

52 Akingbola, K. (2013) "A model of strategic nonprofit human resource management," *Voluntas: International Journal of Voluntary and Nonprofit Organizations*, 24(1): 214–240.

53 Liao-Troth, M. A. (2001) "Attitude differences between paid workers and volunteers," *Nonprofit Management and Leadership*, 11(4): 423–442.

54 Salamon & Anheier, "Social origins of civil society."

55 Frumkin, P., & Andre-Clark, A. (2000) "When mission, markets, and politics collide: Values and strategy in the nonprofit human services," *Nonprofit and Voluntary Sector Quarterly*, 29(1): 141–164.

56 Saks, A. M. (2006) "Antecedents and consequences of employee engagement," *Journal of Managerial Psychology*, 21(7): 600–619.

4

STRATEGIC HUMAN RESOURCE MANAGEMENT

Learning Objectives

After studying this chapter, you should be able to:

1. Explain the concept of strategy, and types of strategy.
2. Discuss human resource management and strategic human resource management.
3. Describe the challenges of managing human resources in nonprofit and non-governmental organizations.
4. Discuss the importance of human resource management to nonprofit and non-governmental organizations.
5. Explain the role of human resource management in the strategy of nonprofit and non-governmental organizations.
6. Understand the process of implementing strategic management in nonprofit and non-governmental organizations.

Human Resources and Performance of Save the Children USA

Save the Children USA is a non-governmental organization (NGO) that is committed to inspiring breakthroughs in the way the world treats children. The organization provides nutrition, medical care and education services to children across five continents. In a 2010 independent survey of 2,733 southern partners of 25 northern NGOs, Save the Children USA was rated higher than most NGOs in the cohort for most aspects of its interactions with respondents.[1] The feedback from partners emphasizes that they highly value the inter-action they had with employees and volunteers of Save the Children USA. In effect, one of the most important performance outcomes for Save the Children USA is made possible by employees and volunteers.

Introduction

This chapter describes the process of strategic human resource management (SHRM) in the nonprofit sector. It examines the *drivers* that necessitate SHRM, *functions* that must be performed, and *challenges* that will need to be managed to deploy SHRM in a nonprofit organization. The chapter also presents a *process* model that outlines the steps for the formulation and implementation of SHRM. Each of these components illustrates the methods adopted in the remaining chapters of this book. The chapter lays a foundation for subsequent chapters of the book.

Why Human Resource Management in Nonprofits?

Similar to other sectors, nonprofits understand the importance of strategic management to organizational performance. They are aware of the need to provide quality service to clients/customers (many of whom are vulnerable), to engage employees, volunteers, funders, communities, and to manage cost simultaneously. As a result, the activities of nonprofits such as American Red Cross, Habitat for Humanity and Oxfam are designed to help the organization to satisfy the performance expectations of stakeholders who are affected by their actions. Since the work of nonprofits is very labor-intensive, the importance of strategic management is particularly pronounced in how they deploy people to achieve the performance goals of the organization.

One reason why nonprofits work is labor-intensive is that the "service" is exchanged directly between the provider and the consumer. The employees and volunteers who deliver the service often interact directly with the consumer/client. Although most of the services are social and personal in nature, many economic services that nonprofits provide such as community economic development and micro credit do have a social side to them. Due to this direct interaction, it has been observed that employees and volunteers who make up the human resources of nonprofits are the main asset of the organization.[2] Service delivery and ultimately achieving the performance goals of nonprofits simply cannot happen without competent and committed employees and volunteers.

Given the importance of the skills, competencies and commitment of employees and volunteers, nonprofits managers must pay particular attention to activities related to attracting, recruiting, retaining and developing human resources. Managing the performance of human resources and understanding the factors in the external and internal environment that influence them are critical in order to help the organization to achieve its goals. The type of work that employees and volunteers perform in nonprofits suggests that managers must recognize that the organization cannot survive without its people.

The brief introduction on Save the Children USA shows that how a nonprofit organization meets its challenges and the performance expectations of stakeholders such as partners depend significantly on how effectively it manages the skills, competencies, and commitment of employees and volunteers. In essence, the knowledge, skills, and behavior of human resources in nonprofits are directly linked to the core competencies that will give the organization a competitive advantage and enable it to achieve its mission and strategic goals.

Human resource management must relate to and be aligned with the mission and strategy of the organization. It is impractical to expect employees to deliver on performance, without having the behavior and skills that are related to the mission and strategic goals of the nonprofit. Although we will highlight the importance of strategy in the process model later in the chapter, it is imperative to briefly introduce strategy before we discuss HRM, in order to lay the foundation for our understanding of the relationship between HR and strategy.

What Is Strategy?

Strategy is essentially about achievement. As Robert Grant puts it, strategy is about winning.[3] He goes on to explain that "common to the definitions of business strategy is the notion that strategy is focused on achieving certain goals; that the critical actions that make up a strategy involve allocation of resources; and that strategy implies some consistency, integration, or cohesiveness of decisions and actions."[4] The essence of strategy is to provide a roadmap of the choice of the organization on how it would stand out from competition. This explains why strategy has been described as the process of taking an organization from its present position to its desired position, that is, from point A to B in terms of its objectives.[5]

For nonprofits, strategy is defined as an integrated set of actions and processes that are developed and implemented to enable the nonprofit to use its resources to deliver value to stakeholders, adapt to change, and gain competitive advantage.[6] Essentially, strategy indicates that the nonprofit is working to achieve the goals that are important to stakeholders. When Ottawa-Carleton Association for Persons with Developmental Disabilities, a Canadian nonprofit with a mission to support people with developmental disabilities through a holistic approach, stated that its strategy is to leverage existing competencies and services to diversify into new areas in order to achieve the mission of the organization, the leadership has outlined the roadmap that will guide how the organization will deliver value to stakeholders.

Levels of Strategy

Following from the understanding that strategy guides the actions and processes the organization adopts to achieve its goals, scholars have explained that there are two main levels of strategy: corporate strategy and business strategy.[7]

Corporate strategy is focused on the overall commitments, actions, and alternatives that an organization adopts to create value for stakeholders. It includes the diverse services and markets of the organization. For nonprofits, the corporate strategy will focus on the services/products or subsector within which the organization operates. It tends to focus on long-term growth and includes strategies such as restructuring, growth and diversification. The term organizational strategy is used instead of corporate strategy.

Business strategy is a set of plans, actions, and commitments that are deployed to build competitive edge in one particular line of service, industry, or market. The key focus of business strategy for a nonprofit organization is how the organization will compete in a particular service/product segment or industry. For example, a nonprofit that offers youth services and a housing service would have a business strategy for the two areas. We will use the term *service strategy* in place of business strategy.

Generic Strategies in Nonprofits

To explain what strategy is in the context of nonprofits, especially the choices the organizations have made to be competitive and adapt, scholars have proposed general types of strategy in nonprofits. Drawing from this body of work, I have suggested that there are three generic strategies in nonprofits:[8]

- *Growth strategy* is one in which the organization focuses on innovation, expansion or diversification as the main game plan of the nonprofit. The range of choices that are part of a growth strategy are extensive. Examples include new product/service innovation; merger or joint venture partnership with other nonprofits; a new subsidiary; and a for-profit business venture to support the nonprofit enterprise. A nonprofit with a growth strategy would continuously leverage its resources to explore emerging community needs, funding and revenue opportunities. However, the organization might run the risk of mission creep. Mission creep or drift is a situation in which a nonprofit organization unknowingly deviates from its mission due to pressures from the resource base.[9]
- *Preservation strategy* is a competitive game plan that maximizes the opportunities in a particular service, product or mission focus. Preservation strategy is about creating a unique niche. Nonprofits with a preservation strategy adapt to change in the environment primarily by extending current service to new geographic areas or creating additional resources to support the same service.[10] Some also cut costs to maximize resources. The challenge with this strategy occurs when there is a change in the resource base or funding that supports the service(s)/products. How does the organization preserve the mission?
- *Root strategy* means a nonprofit purposefully uses only volunteer human resources for service delivery and management.[11] In other words, a totally volunteer organization. This strategy tends to focus on the implementation

of community development enterprise, social impact, or mutual interest goals of stakeholders. Nonprofits that adopt a root strategy generally steer clear of activities and initiatives that would require significant professional human resources. While such an organization may have a few employees to coordinate administrative tasks, the service delivery is provided by volunteers. Nonprofits that use root strategy such as *Habitat for Humanity* vary in size, scope and level of development. The strategy is common in mutual associations that serve a membership or service clubs that support organizations that provide the services.

Each of the three generic nonprofit strategies has an inherent impact for HR. As the nonprofit navigates the opportunities and threats in the environment to formulate and implement an effective strategy, the human resource pool and the HR system required to achieve the goals of the organization are front and center of the strategic management process.

What Is Human Resource Management?

All managers play a direct or indirect role in how human resources can make a difference in the performance of a nonprofit organization. How managers play this role is the domain of human resources management. Human resource management includes those functions, activities, programs and processes that are developed and implemented in order to attract, acquire, engage, maintain and retain employees and volunteers of a nonprofit organization. The traditional human resource management functions include recruitment and selection, training and development, performance management, compensation, employee and labor relations. These functions are discussed in detail in subsequent chapters. However, to set the stage for the discussion of strategic human resource management, it is important to discuss the challenges in the environment of nonprofits, the organizational characteristics, and the implications of these for nonprofits and how they manage human resources.

Challenges of Human Resources Management

As we discussed in Chapter 3, similar to business and public sector organizations, nonprofits are affected by factors in the external environment of the organization. Many of these influences are unique to the *environment* of nonprofits. You will recall that the current issues in the environment of nonprofits that we highlighted in Chapter 3 are:

- government funding
- contract-based funding
- competition

- accountability
- efficiency
- the changing needs of the community.

These same challenges and other related influences in the competitive environment are the sources of the opportunities and threats that could underlie the HR practices of nonprofits. You will recall that in Chapter 2, we explained that contingency theory emphasized the *fit* between the external environment, strategy and the HR practices of the organization as the basis of SHRM. The starting point of the process of achieving the alignment with the external environment is scanning, monitoring and assessing these challenges. You will also recall that in Chapter 3, we noted that scholars have researched the relationship between government funding and HR functions in nonprofit organizations, and found it to be one of the significant challenges for the sector. Our understanding of the theories we examined in Chapter 2 and the unique context of nonprofits emphasize why we must look at HRM in organizations with social objectives using the tools of SHRM. Simply looking at HRM as a function that is not aligned to the strategy of a nonprofit would not help to meet the need to develop HR systems and the human resources pool required to achieve the goals of the organization. To get us thinking about the impact of these challenges, Figure 4.1 shows examples of HR practices that are likely to be impacted by the dependence on government funding.

What Is Strategic Human Resource Management?

The definition of human resource management noted above outlines the traditional view which focuses on functions of the field. Over the years, this view

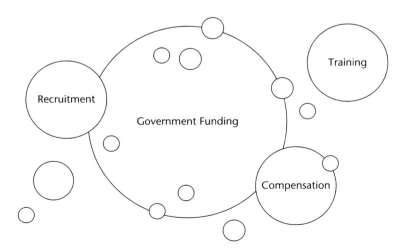

FIGURE 4.1 Government Funding and Nonprofit HR Practices

has been refined to capture other important subfields within human resource management. According to Boxall, Purcell and Wright (2007), there are three major subfields of human resource management: micro human resource management, strategic human resource management and international human resource management.[12]

1. Micro human resource management focuses on the sub-functions of human resources policy and practice. It is more or less the traditional area of human resource management that includes two main categories: how to manage individuals and small groups through functions such as recruitment, selection, orientation, training and development, performance management, and compensation; and how to manage work organization and systems such as labor relations.
2. Strategic human resource management takes the role a step further. Its focus is on the overall human resources strategies organizations adopt and the impact on their performance. Strategic human resource management aims to explain "the pattern of planned human resource deployments and activities intended to enable the organization to achieve its goals."[13] Planning, implementation and measuring performance are very important in strategic human resources management.
3. International human resource management is focused on what organizations in different countries do. This subfield includes how human resource management reflects the different international context. However, if the discussion relates to how human resource management impacts the performance of the organization, regardless of the country, it is part of strategic human resource management.

In essence, scholars have emphasized that SHRM is the core of HR. It connects HR practices to strategy and the performance of the organization. One important takeaway from SHRM is that for an organization to be effective, HR practices must *fit* the strategy of the organization.[14] SHRM continuously scans, analyzes and considers the environment through the eyes of strategy, in order to develop and deploy appropriate HR practices. According to Nadler and Tushman,[15] congruence or fit is "the degree to which the needs, demands, goals, objectives and/or structure of one component are consistent with the need, demands, goals, objectives and/or structure of another component." Essentially, HR practice, as one component, must be congruent with business strategy, as another component, to facilitate the achievement of organizational goals. It has been suggested that the determinants of fit in SHRM are based on three factors:

1. HR functions,
2. personal factors, and
3. firm level factors.

TABLE 4.1 Implications of Strategic Direction for HR

Strategy	HR Implications
Focus on differentiating our service based on quality	Emphasize training, internal career path, recruitment at entry level, and performance management.
Focus on innovation in our services	Emphasize recruitment of top talents at all levels, cross training, teams, incentive compensation.
Focus on partnership to grow our services	Emphasize teamwork, recruitment based on industry knowledge, employee involvement.
Focus on extending our services to new regions/states	Emphasize performance management, internal career path, project-based teams.
Focus on client needs where services are weak	Emphasize training, project-based teams, incentive compensation
Focus on costing and deliver more value to clients	Emphasize training, performance management, HR analytics
Focus on entrepreneurial activities to support our nonprofit services	Emphasize recruitment, teams, incentive compensation.
Focus on technology to change how we provide services	Emphasize HR analytics, training.

HR function factors include HR policy, options of HR practices, and the investment or budget of HRM. The personal factors of fit are the capability of HR managers, ability and support of senior managers, and employee knowledge and skill. At the firm level, the determinants of fit are the nature of strategy, and values and culture.[16]

Table 4.1 shows some examples of how strategic decisions have implications for HR practices. How these examples could play out in nonprofit organizations is discussed in more detail in subsequent chapters.

SHRM in the Nonprofit Sector

The idea of SHRM has not been paramount in nonprofit organizations. As noted above, the type of work performed by nonprofits is labor-intensive. It has a social dimension which includes emotional transaction. Hence, the ability of nonprofits to perform and generate social value for stakeholders depends significantly on the knowledge, skills and behavior of employees and volunteers. Moreover, nonprofits cannot simply substitute the work of frontline employees and volunteers by investing more in physical capital and technology.[17] As a result, the need for SHRM is heightened in nonprofits. Each nonprofit organization must carefully deploy its human capital to achieve the mission of the organization. This can only happen by aligning HR practices with the strategy of the nonprofit organization. The managers need to understand better:

- What SHRM means in nonprofits.
- What role SHRM plays in the performance of nonprofits.
- What SHRM looks like for nonprofits.
- How to implement SHRM in nonprofits.

These questions are answered in the next section and throughout the book with examples. Before presenting a process model of SHRM in a nonprofit organization, which will illustrate how to develop and implement SHRM in a nonprofit organization, it is important to point out that research in SHRM nonprofit organizations is limited. However, it has gained momentum in recent years. One recent study found that larger nonprofits, those affiliated with national organizations, younger nonprofits, as well as educational nonprofits are more likely to implement SHRM.[18]

A Process Model of Nonprofit SHRM

Figure 4.2 illustrates a process model of SHRM for nonprofits. It shows how a nonprofit organization must start SHRM from the mission and values of the organization. By starting with an emphasis on the mission, the foundation of the link between HR and strategy is set. Strategy formulation and implementation process determine how the organization intends to deploy its internal resources and adapt

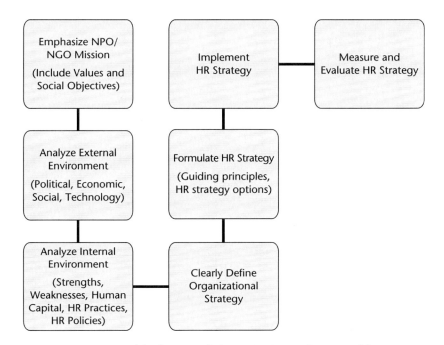

FIGURE 4.2 Process Model of Nonprofit Strategic Human Resource Management

to opportunities and threats from the external environment. The process brings together the competitive environment factors that shape the mission, strategic goals, and the organizational performance of a nonprofit organization. The non-profit SHRM process consists of seven main steps which are summarized below.

Step 1: Emphasize Organizational Mission

The mission of a nonprofit organization is the most unique characteristic of the organization. This is because it is generally tied to a social goal. The mission is what the organization is all about. As explained previously, the mission is the public good that the nonprofit organization intends to serve. The mission is the starting point of the SHRM process in nonprofits. For example, the mission of Easter Seals Arkansas, USA, is "to provide exceptional services to ensure that all people with disabilities or special needs have equal opportunities to live, learn, work and play in their communities."[19] This mission statement is encoded with important principle that will facilitate the formulation of HR policies and prac-tices. It suggests that learning and equal opportunity should be emphasized in HR. Coupled with organizational values, the mission will inform and guide managers on what to emphasize in terms of HR practices. For example when VTCT, a UK professional qualification charity, wanted to introduce a new approach to staff training, the nonprofit emphasized one of its core values that stipulates that it should endeavour to "include everyone and treat everyone equally and fairly."[20] The HR manager communicated the new approach to senior management with emphasis on the core values of the organization. She also tasked them to "feed the changes down to other managers." Research has shown that nonprofits do adopt HR practices that are commonly accepted, in other words consistent with their values, in order to gain legitimacy.[21]

Step 2: Analyze External Environment

As indicated in the discussion of the competitive environment, nonprofit organi-zation managers must carefully assess both the general and competitive environ-ment of the organization. This is critical in SHRM. The pace and dimension of change in terms of how nonprofits deliver services, how they generate revenue, how they compete with other nonprofit and for-profit organizations, and their accountability for funding mean that each organization must assess the opportu-nities and threats in its environment.

The need to keep pace with the *external environment* requires managers of a nonprofit organization to position the organization for constant change that is beyond a one-in-three-year assessment. Opportunities and threats for a nonprofit organization now come fast and often furious. The *economic environment* is one such area of constant threat that nonprofit organization managers must continuously track.

Economic conditions can impact nonprofits in both positive and negative ways. An economic boom can boost donations and options to seek funding from more sources. Inversely, economic downturn can seriously reduce funding opportunities and decrease donations to nonprofits. It also generally increases the demand for the services of nonprofits. A recent example in the United Kingdom of how local councils responded to the aftermath of the recession illustrates the threat of the economic environment to nonprofits (Box 4.1).[22] Economic threats and opportunities often go hand in hand with political undertows in the form of changes in public policy. The impact of a change in public policy could bring about a change in the strategy of nonprofits.

Political environment could mean that a nonprofit organization has to focus on a new service or product which public policy has made a priority.[23] Through funding and public policy, the economic and political environments directly impact the competitive environment of nonprofits. Managers must scan the environment to know the change that will affect their organizations. With strategy, they can prepare to maximize the opportunities and manage the threats. Moreover, government and other funding organizations impose stringent accountability requirements that may make an opportunity less attractive to a nonprofit organization. By scanning the environment, nonprofit managers can plan and implement actions to meet the requirements of the government and funding organizations when they formulate their strategy.

BOX 4.1 FUNDING CUT

A United Kingdom survey of local councils in 2012 found that budget allocation for voluntary sector funding was cut by an average of 19 percent. In fact, NPOs in some cities were hit particularly hard. In addition to placing restrictions on street fundraisers, the City of Liverpool cut funding for the sector by 48 percent over the previous year.

Source: Plummer, J. (2011) "Analysis: Sector budgets feel the squeeze," *Third Sector*, March, 21 2011.

The *social environment* is a similarly important source of opportunities and threats for nonprofits. One trend in the social environment affecting nonprofits is the aging population. On the one hand, this will increase the demand for services of nonprofits that serve this demographic group. Services such as Meals on Wheels, congregate dining, and adult day services will see an upsurge in demand. From an HR point of view, the aging population and the resulting extension of the working careers of baby boomers is an opportunity for nonprofits to leverage the talent of these vastly experienced workers. A survey by MetLife/Civic Ventures found that more than half of the 427 nonprofits cited the benefits of hiring matured workers.[24] On the other hand, nonprofits must develop HR practices that cater to the needs of the matured workforce. Although more details about benefits and compensation will be provided in subsequent chapters, it is important to note that targeted HR strategies must be developed to deploy the talent of the matured workforce. A matured workforce strategy allows a nonprofit organization to maximize the energy and experience of older workers.

Technology offers an excellent opportunity for nonprofits to be more efficient in reporting and accountability. As noted above, due to the interpersonal characteristic of the services of nonprofits, they cannot replace employees and volunteers with technology. However, technology can be an important tool in administration and human resources management. Telecommuting can provide flexibility in work schedule. Employees can also use technology to coordinate the work of volunteers who provide support to the organization online.

Scanning the competitive environment will elicit opportunities and threats which can directly impact the operations of nonprofits. Specific competitive factors such as government policy and the priority of funding organizations relating to the services of a nonprofit organization will point to service segments that are more attractive to the organization. Even in a downturn economy, managers can position a nonprofit organization to maximize opportunity to grow services and expand the operation of the organization. The nonprofit organization can seek opportunities to increase earned income in service areas relevant to the mission. One strategy nonprofits have adopted is to market the organization to gain increased mindshare of funders during a downturn in the economy in order to position itself ahead of the competition. Box 4.2 illustrates this strategy.[25]

BOX 4.2 JEREMIAH PROGRAM GOES NATIONAL

Jeremiah Program is a charity in Minneapolis, United States. Jeremiah provides safe, affordable housing for low-income single mothers with young children. In the midst of the recession in 2009, the human services nonprofit organization's board voted to expand to new cities. The goal is to open at least one new program by 2012.

Comment: The strategy emphasized the commitment of the organization to the mission. Moreover it brought publicity that placed the organization in the radar of donors.

Source: Russell, S. (2009) "Twin Cities-based Jeremiah Program goes national," *MinnPost*, March 16, 2009.

Step 3: Analyze Internal Environment

In addition to scanning the external environment for opportunities and threats, nonprofit managers must also assess their *internal environment*. Human capital and human resources practices must be assessed because of the critical importance of employees and volunteers. For nonprofits, the human capital consists of the knowledge, skills and capabilities of employees and volunteers that have both social and financial value to the organization. This human capital is simply the most valuable asset of a nonprofit organization. In fact, due to the characteristics of the products/services nonprofits provide, scholars have suggested that non-profits cannot replace their human capital with investment in physical capital such as machines. Managers must assess whether the organization has the required knowledge, skills and capabilities to benefit from the opportunities in the external environment. This becomes a key part of how the nonprofit organization attracts, recruits, develops, motivates and retains employees and volunteers. Essentially, human resources practices and policies must be developed to support the strategy of the nonprofit organization. Recruitment and selection are focused on finding and hiring employees who have the knowledge and skills the nonprofit organization needs. Training is designed to build knowledge and skills that the nonprofit organization needs but employees do not possess. HR policies must reinforce the values of the nonprofit organization. Also, it must foster the type of workplace environment that will motivate employee performance.

In assessing the internal environment, managers must identify the impact of external opportunities and threats on the internal strengths and weaknesses of the nonprofit organization. How the organization adapts its internal resources and capabilities to meet the change in the opportunities and threats in the external environment must be a paramount question for managers. The characteristics of the environment of nonprofits discussed above mean that there is a continuous need to position the internal environment to be able to develop adaptive strategy when factors change in the external environment. Thus, managers must focus on the immediate effects of the opportunities and threats on the strengths and weaknesses of the organization. Nonprofit managers must also build in flexibility to meet the need of the organization to continue to adapt in order to maintain a link between these factors in the external environment and the internal environment.

Either formally declared or not, matching external opportunities and threats to internal strengths and weaknesses is the basis of the strategy of a nonprofit organization. To achieve their mission, nonprofits must formulate and implement organizational strategy that aligns the challenges and opportunities in the environment with the capabilities of the organization by leveraging the human capital and human resources practices of the organization. SHRM in nonprofits helps managers to achieve the goals they have outlined in their strategy and link the mission, values and objectives with the environment of the organization.

Step 4: Clearly Define Strategy

For a nonprofit organization to achieve its mission, the organization must first carefully define a clear strategy. Simply stated, the purpose of strategy is to take the organization from its present position to a defined performance outcome(s) by drawing on its internal resources, maximizing external opportunities and mitigating threats. It guides the behavior—commitments and actions—the organization deploys to gain a competitive advantage. Given this understanding that strategy guides the behavior of organizations and it is made up mainly of the *substantive vision of the value the organization intends to produce*,[26] strategy is fundamental to the mission of a nonprofit organization. Strategy is the tool for actualizing the mission. Strategy is a process, the starting point of which is to clearly articulate the performance outcomes organizational actors would like to see.

As noted previously in the chapter, there are two main levels of strategy: organizational strategy and service strategy. *Organizational strategy* is focused on the overall commitments, actions and alternatives that an organization adopts to manage its diverse interests, services and markets. It tends to focus on long-term growth and includes strategies such as restructuring, growth and maintenance. The Arizona Children's Association (AzCa) provides a good example of corporate strategy that is focused on growth. Between 1999 and 2008, the organization completed six mergers that increased the services to the youth and families.[27] *Service strategy* is a set of plans, actions and commitments that are deployed to build a competitive edge in one particular line of service, industry or market. The key focus of business strategy for a nonprofit organization is how the organization will compete in a particular service/product segment or industry.

With the mission that specifies the services/products and the clients the organization intends to serve as the reference point, nonprofit organization managers must clearly state the strategy of the organization. They must state what the content or makeup of the nonprofit organization strategy is. The strategy must by necessity enable the organization to satisfy the needs of their clients and expectations of other stakeholders. What managers are saying to stakeholders is that these are:

a) the specific strategic goals we will achieve for you;
b) the actions we will deploy to maximize internal strengths, take advantage of the opportunities in the environment and mitigate the threats in the competitive environment; and
c) the commitments we will make to position the organization in the event that the environment should change.

We can illustrate the importance of clearly defining the strategy of a nonprofit organization with the example of Big Brothers Big Sisters (BBBS), Ottawa, Canada. The mission of the BBBS, Ottawa is to provide mentors to all children who need caring adult role models, mentors who can help expand their horizons, realize their potential and enrich their futures—in effect, changing their lives.[28] First, the organization outlined six key planning assumptions that were based on consensus among stakeholders. The assumptions are principles used to guide the goals that clearly map out what BBBS, Ottawa, will deliver for the 2011–2014 strategic plan. Second, BBBS, Ottawa, identified five priority areas for action from the considerable feedback generated through consultation with stakeholders. Finally, the organization clearly defined specific strategies based on the priority areas. Boxes 4.3 and 4.4 show the priority areas and one of the strategies in each area.

BOX 4.3 PRIORITY AREAS FOR BIG BROTHERS BIG SISTERS, OTTAWA, CANADA

- Excellence in Programming
- Optimal Workplace
- Diversification of Revenue
- Strengthening Our Brand-Marketing and Communications
- Leadership in Mentoring

The end result of a clearly defined strategy for a nonprofit organization will ensure that employees and stakeholders know the strategic goals. They will have a clear idea of the unique path the organization will tread in order to achieve its strategic goals. More importantly, clearly defined strategic goals will communicate the kind of actions expected from employees. Together, the mission and clearly defined strategic goals will facilitate insights that will help to guide how to formulate and implement an HR strategy.

Step 5: Formulate and Implement HR Strategy

Once a clearly defined strategy has been outlined from the mission of the non-profit organization, the next step in the process is to formulate and implement an HR strategy for the organization. It is important to remember that strategy is an indication of the context of an organization and that it is through strategy that managers understand the context of events at multiple levels of an organization.[29] Hence, the manager must thoroughly review and fully understand the results of the environmental scanning, steps 2 and 3, as well as the strategic goals defined in step 4. These two make up the foundation required to formulate the HR strategy. There are three sub-steps in the formulation and implementation of HR strategy.

BOX 4.4 STRATEGY IN PRIORITY AREAS

Excellence in Programming	Optimal Workplace	Diversification of Revenue	Marketing and Communications	Leadership in Mentoring
Improve quality assurance measures through evaluation	Create a balanced enrollment process resulting in successful matches	Create an environment that prioritizes and supports innovation and employee commitment	Implement a progressive donor retention/ conversion and upgrade program	Market BBBSO as the "go-to" organization for mentoring excellence and community investment	Attract, engage and retain community leaders as key stakeholders

Source: Big Brothers Big Sisters (BBBS), Ottawa, Canada.

Sub-step 1. With the preliminary step completed, the manager is now ready to frame what HR can do to support the strategy of the organization. For non-profits, the choices in terms of HR strategy may include consultation with or a role for the board of directors. This is because many nonprofits have working boards. Working boards are intimately involved in the day-to-day operations of the organization. As part of the process of formulating an HR strategy, the manager will also consider whether there is internal HR expertise within the organization. If necessary, the organization may need external expertise to guide or facilitate some part of the HR strategy formulation process. What the manager has to outline in the formulation phase is the content of the HR strategy. In other words, the manager is asking these questions:

- What HR guiding principles and policies do we need to be the bedrock of our HR strategy? For example, a nonprofit organization that has to foster a *democratic workplace* as a core HR principle will reflect this in its HR practices. The principle will influence the type of HR practices the organization adopts, as illustrated in the example of VTCT above. The UK nonprofit translated a core value into an HR guiding principle and reflected this in the new approach to staff training.
- What HR practices do we adopt that will enable the organization to deploy employee skills and behaviors required to achieve its strategic goals? Following from the core HR principle example above, the HR practice must include some form of employee participation to be consistent with the principle of a democratic workplace. Employees may participate in the decision-making process about training.
- What do we need to change in our current HR practices? Still using the same example, the nonprofit organization may introduce employee survey follow-up to ensure that feedback leads to improvement, action and communication.

The answers to these questions and how well HR practices align with the principles and the need for change will set the stage for how a nonprofit orga-nization will use the human resources it has to deliver the strategic goals of the organization. The answers and action items that follow from addressing these questions will also help to ensure that the nonprofit organization's HR functions are aligned with how the organization manages the effects of the interactions and processes between mission, multiple stakeholder relationships, and dependence on funders. However, to get these results, the manager must take ownership of the process to make things happen.

Sub-step 2. Next, the manager must outline the HR strategies that will best support the strategic goals of the nonprofit organization. These are HR strategy options that will address the question about HR practices and change noted above. Of course, the HR strategies must also be consistent with the principles. They should explicitly or implicitly incorporate the values spelled out in the HR principles. Each HR strategy option should be examined with a critical lens to determine whether it is relevant, viable and congruent with the HR principle of the nonprofit organization. In brainstorming the HR strategies, the manager must examine the upsides and downsides of each HR strategy. It is critical to know what value each HR strategy will contribute to the strategic goals of the nonprofit. The manager must consider this as well as the questions below, where applicable:

- What specific strategic priorities does the HR strategy support?
- What specific desired outcomes will the HR strategy deliver?
- Does the culture of our organization support this strategy or does it support our culture?
- How does this HR strategy fit with our other HR practices?
- What are the potential roadblocks or risks of proceeding with this strategy?
- Do we have the skills to follow through with the HR strategy?
- What worked well in our previous HR strategy? (if applicable)
- What learning can we carry forward from our current HR strategy? (if applicable)

The result of this process is a clear map of what HR will contribute to bring about the achievement of the strategic goals of the nonprofit organization. It is the unambiguous connection between HR and the strategic goals of the organi-zation. To make this connection possible, the manager must certainly consider whether the organization has the resources. If the resources are not available, can the organization afford to acquire them? Since the HR strategies must be designed to facilitate the required skills and behavior from the pool of human resources in order to support the performance of the nonprofit organization, the manager must focus on strategies that will foster high performance behavior, skills development and intrinsic rewards. As discussed above, the latter is especially important in nonprofits because employees are committed to the social mission of the organization. Over the years, research has shown that specific HR strategies are a good fit for different types of strategy.

Figure 4.3 illustrates one example of the link between type of strategy and HR practices proposed by Miles and Snow.[30] They demonstrated the relationship between HRM and strategy by illustrating HR practices that align with each of the types of strategy they proposed. For example, they explained that organizations that adopt a *Defender* strategy will embrace a "building human resource" strategy with emphasis on internal career paths, promotion, recruitment at entry level, training, and a compensation system that is based on organizational hierarchy. Organizations that use a *Prospector* strategy will emphasize "acquisition human resource" and continuously acquire and redeploy human resources at all levels to different management and technical assignments to enable development of competencies. And finally, organizations that embrace an *Analyzer* strategy will combine the acquisition and building of human resource strategies of both the *Defender* and *Prospector*. This is because *Analyzer* is a dual strategy that includes features of both the *Defender* and *Prospector*. Regardless of the strategic choice of a nonprofit organization, there are broad categories of strategies or plans that are commonly included in an HR strategy.

1. *Human resources planning.* Activities under the umbrella of *human resources planning* can help to set the stage for the formulation and implementation of HR strategies of an organization. For example, job analysis provides information about jobs, the behavior and breakdown of tasks required in each job. The information obtained through job analysis is very valuable for the HR strategies

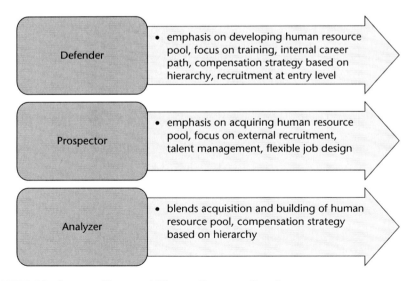

FIGURE 4.3   Strategy Types and Human Resource Practices

of a nonprofit organization. In fact, all major HR functions including recruitment, performance appraisal and compensation use the information to develop and implement practices. First, human resources planning activities must provide the baseline number of people and their skill level for the purpose of formulation of strategy. Nonprofits can anticipate and provide for movement of employees such as turnover, promotion and lateral position change by using human resources planning.

2. *Recruitment strategy.* This is developed to provide a roadmap and set of actions the organization will use to attract, recruit and select qualified candidates to meet its human resource needs. In addition to attracting and recruiting qualified candidates, the recruitment strategy is important in order to identify candidates who have a passion to help others and achieve the strategy goals of a nonprofit organization. A number of HR activities feed into and are included in the recruitment strategy. Job analysis is a systematic process of collecting information about jobs to determine the duties, tasks and required behaviors. Recruitment activities include how the organization will source qualified candidates and how it will attract them.

3. *Performance management.* Basically, performance management is an ongoing dialogue process through which managers foster a supportive work environment for employees. The emphasis in performance management is how to provide feedback that will enable employees to perform, grow and contribute their best to the organization. It is an important source of determining training needs and impacts other HR functions such as compensation. For nonprofits, performance standards include the "hard to measure" outcomes that are connected to the mission of the organization. This could make implementing a performance-management system complicated in nonprofits.

4. *Employee engagement.* Employee behaviors such as commitment and organizational citizenship behavior are very important to a nonprofit organization. These desirable behaviors are the goals of employee engagement. The focused energy and discretionary effort that result from engagement drive how employees motivate themselves to perform their jobs and identify and connect with the mission of a nonprofit organization. Engagement engenders the type of employee desire and behavior that is focused on helping the organization succeed largely by providing discretionary effort or going the extra mile. Empirical research has shed more light on the true meaning of, condition for, and dimension of employee engagement such as job, behavioral and organization engagement.[31] Rich, Lepine and Crawford (2010) found that employee engagement is one of the antecedents of job performance. It is because of this importance that *employee engagement strategy* is either explicitly or inexplicitly included in HR strategy.

5. *Compensation strategy.* Consistent with SHRM, compensation must be aligned with the business strategy and other HR strategies of the organization. Compensation entails the policy and practices of a nonprofit organization in terms of what salary or wage rates employees are paid and how these are paid. Based on the personal characteristics of the service/product of nonprofits and the significant interpersonal transactions involved in service delivery, employee compensation is a major cost to nonprofits. For many nonprofits, it is the single largest budget item. Generally, nonprofit research often emphasizes the importance of intrinsic factors such as employee buy-in to the mission to explain compensation practices, particularly wage levels in nonprofits.[32] While this addresses the question of how to motivate employees, the question of strategic compensation and how managers can align compensation to the strategic goals of nonprofits needs more work. The thought exercise in Box 4.5 illustrates the dilemma of compensation strategy in nonprofits.[33]

BOX 4.5 NONPROFIT COMPENSATION SCENARIO

Imagine that you've built a business that generates $10 million in revenue per year. What would be a fair level of compensation to expect? Now, imagine that this enterprise is a program that helps low-wage workers receive Earned Income Tax Credit funds, and that the $10 million is the net amount of value the program brings to low-income neighborhoods. How did this change your estimate of fair compensation?

Source: Pete Manzo (2009) "Rethinking compensation for nonprofits," *Stanford Social Innovation Review.* Copyright © *Stanford Social Innovation Review.* Reproduced in *Managing Human Resources for Nonprofits.*

The question of compensation strategy will be discussed in detail in Chapter 5. What is important to note here is that the characteristics of nonprofits create a unique context for how managers can effectively manage compensation.

Step 6: Implement HR Strategy

Once an HR strategy that will best help to facilitate the goals of the nonprofit organization has been defined using the questions outlined above as a guide, the manager must now address how the strategy will be implemented. One option for rolling out an HR strategy is to translate each strategy to specific HR deliverables. Each HR deliverable is then set to a performance milestone and timeline. For example, a community care nonprofit that has an HR strategic goal to *build exceptional teams* could translate the goal into an HR deliverable that is stated as *attract and increase retention of Registered Nurses*. The implementation of the HR strategies could also involve translating the deliverables into tactical actions that are included in the annual operating plan of the nonprofit organization. This will ensure that the HR deliverables are properly integrated into and reported as part of the key performance metrics of the organization. In addition to linking HR strategies to the goals of a nonprofit organization, the goal of including HR deliverables in the operating plan is to clearly communicate the expectations to members of the management team who are not directly involved in the HR function. Not only will this establish a supportive working environment for the rollout of HR strategies, it will also provide opportunity to elicit feedback from members of the management team. Whether HR strategies are implemented using a separate HR document or integrated into the operating plan as part of a scorecard, it is important to develop a workplan to guide the implementation process.

Step 7: Measure and Evaluate HR Strategies

If human capital is truly the most important asset of nonprofits, the need to measure the contribution and performance outcomes of HR strategies is paramount. How the HR strategies contribute to the strategic goals of a nonprofit organization and how well each HR function is doing can be determined by using HR metrics. HR metrics are measures or indicators of the performance of HR strategies, practices and functions. Generally, the need for HR metrics has been emphasized as one of the ways for HR professionals to clearly communicate their role as strategic partners to top management. It is through HR metrics that HR professionals can showcase systems thinking by measuring deliverables that are important to the organization.[34] Not only do the HR metrics measure the effectiveness of HR strategies and functions, they provide an effective tool for strategic planning. In short, HR professionals can improve their ability as internal consultants when they use HR metrics.

Before proceeding further with the discussion of what metrics are measured in HR performance and outcomes, one would be remiss not to mention the challenges of measuring performance in nonprofits. A major defining characteristic of nonprofits is the lack of a universally accepted measure of organizational performance, particularly one that is similar to the bottom line indicator of performance of for-profit business organizations.[35] As a result, research on nonprofits has reminded us that while the bottom line is important, the financial result is not the primary emphasis of the nonprofit enterprise and cannot be an indicator of the effectiveness of the organization.[36] Instead, it is argued that the essential indicator of performance is the extent to which nonprofits achieve their mission.[37] As explained previously, since there are multiple stakeholders, who are directly or indirectly affected by the activities of the nonprofit organization, what is performance in relation to the mission is open to the perception of the stakeholder. However, one consensus in the literature is that nonprofit organization effectiveness is multidimensional and social in nature.[38] For example, one group of stakeholders of the American Red Cross may emphasize disaster relief work done locally as a key measure of the performance of the nonprofit while another group of stakeholders may define performance in terms of the contribution of the organization to international relief efforts. The multidimensional indicators of effectiveness in nonprofits mean that what is accepted as performance depends on the context and who is involved.

Perhaps HR metrics can help to clarify those metrics that cut across different performance standards in nonprofits. In a recent report by *HR Focus*, in which the second largest participant group included government, education or nonprofit organizations, 92.3 percent of the organizations in the group indicated that they use HR metrics to indicate department achievements and progress.[39] Generally, some of the common types of metrics used to measure HR performance and outcomes include turnover rate, cost per hire, absenteeism, demographic metrics, training costs and vacancy rate. The HR Metrics Service, a joint service of three Canadian provincial Human Resources Professional Associations (British Colombia, Manitoba and Ontario), uses 23 key metrics, which are outlined in Table 4.2.[40] As can be seen, each measure is divided into metric categories such as compensation, productivity and HR efficiency.

TABLE 4.2 Key HR Metrics*

Metric Name	Metric Category
Labour Cost per FTE	Compensation
Labour Cost Revenue Percent	Compensation
Labour Cost Expense Percent	Compensation
HR FTE Ratio	HR Efficiency
HR Costs per Employee	HR Efficiency
HR Costs per FTE	HR Efficiency
Absenteeism Rate	Productivity
Human Capital Return on Investment	Productivity
Revenue Per FTE	Productivity
Profit Per FTE	Productivity
Vacancy Rate	Recruitment
1st Year Resignation Rate	Recruitment
Turnover	Retention
Voluntary Turnover Rate	Retention
Involuntary Turnover Rate	Retention
Resignation Rate	Retention
Cost of Voluntary Turnover	Retention
Retirement Rate	Retention
Average Retirement Rate	Retention
Average length of Service	Workforce Demographics
Average Age	Workforce Demographics
Union Percentage	Workforce Demographics
Promotion Rate	Workforce Demographics

*HR Metrics Service. A joint service of BC HRMA, HRMAM & HRPA.

These metrics provide opportunities for organizations, including nonprofits, to link HR strategies and practices with organizational goals. They can also be useful benchmarks to compare performance among organizations in similar and different sectors.

So, what HR metrics should the nonprofit manager measure? This question will be discussed in detail in Chapter 13. The point is that the HR metrics must be aligned with the strategic goals of the nonprofit organization. This is critical to ensure that HR is evidently a strategic partner. As explained further in Chapter 13, developing and using metrics will ensure that HR professionals in nonprofits support frontline managers to be effective. According to a recent survey in the UK, 36 percent of nonproft employees think their managers are ineffective.[41] With limited financial resources, the strategic role of HR is important to help nonprofit managers to grow and develop.

Summary

This chapter introduces the process of SHRM in nonprofits. It offers important definitions of HRM, SHRM and key HR functions to build an in-depth understanding of HRM in the sector. By examining the major factors in the environment that constitute the key challenges of HRM and the relationship between these contextual factors, organizational characteristics and dimension of HR practices in nonprofits, the chapter lays the foundation for the process of formulating and implementing SHRM in these organizations. The chapter draws on HRM literature to develop a process model of SHRM for nonprofits. The examples in the chapter illustrate the application of the concepts and the importance of HRM to nonprofits. It emphasizes that detailed attention to the requirement of the social, strategic and contingent factors is vital to our understanding of SHRM in nonprofits. While it is important to note that research on SHRM structure, strategy and practices is still at an early stage, the process model provides a broader and in-depth step-by-step process for rolling out HR in nonprofits. The case examples and emphasis on the environment illustrate the methods adopted in the remaining chapters of this book

Discussion Questions

1. What are some of the unique characteristics of HR in nonprofits?
2. Why does a nonprofit need to link its strategy to its mission? What are some of the implications if the mission is not reflected in the strategy of a nonprofit?
3. As the HR manager of a nonprofit, you have been asked to develop an HR strategy for the organization. Who are the stakeholders you will engage in the process and why?
4. Search online for a nonprofit that has posted its HR strategy. Review the strategy and identify three top HR priorities of the organization.

Notes

1 NGO Partner Survey. Partner Feedback Report: Save the Children US. http://www.savethechildren.org/atf/cf/%7B9DEF2EBE-10AE-432C-9BD0-DF91D2EBA74A%7D/save-the-children-us-partner-survey-report-2011.pdf. Retrieved October 1, 2011.

2 Light, P. C. (2003) *The Health of the Human Services Workforce.* Washington, DC: Brookings.

3 Grant, R. M. (2012) *Contemporary Strategy Analysis,* 7th Edition. Chichester: Wiley.

4 Ibid, p. 3.

5 Burack, E. H., & Mathys, N. J. (1996) *Human Resource Planning: A Pragmatic Approach to Manpower, Staffing and Development.* Northbrook, IL: Brace-Park Press.

6 Akingbola, K. (2013) "A model of strategic nonprofit human resource management," *VOLUNTAS: International Journal of Voluntary and Nonprofit Organizations,* 24(1): 214–240.

7 Light, *The Health of the Human Services Workforce.*

8 Akingbola, "A model of strategic nonprofit human resource management."

9 Scott, K. (2003) *Funding Matters: The Impact of Canada's New Funding Regime on Nonprofit and Voluntary Organizations.* Ottawa: Canadian Council on Social Development.

10 Foster, M. K., & Meinhard, A. (2002) "A contingency view of the responses of voluntary social service organizations in Ontario to government cutbacks," *Canadian Journal of Administrative Sciences,* 19(1): 27–41.

11 Quarter, J., Mook, L., & Richmond, B. J. (2003) *What Counts: Social Accounting for Nonprofits and Cooperatives.* Upper Saddle River, NJ: Prentice-Hall.

12 Boxall, P., Purcell, J., & Wright, P. (2007) "Human resource management: Scope, analysis and significance," in *The Handbook of Human Resource Management* (p. 23) Oxford: Oxford University Press.

13 Wright, P. M., & McMahan, G. C. (1992) "Theoretical perspectives for strategic human resource management," *Journal of Management,* 18: 295–320.

14 Miles, R. E., & Snow, C. C. (1984) "Designing strategic human resource systems," *Organizational Dynamics,* 13(1): 36–52; Schuler, R. S., & Jackson, S. (1987). "Linking competitive strategies with human resource management practices," *Academy of Management Executive,* 1: 207–219; Wright, P. M., Dunford, B. B., & Snell, S. A. (2001). "Human resources and the resource based view of the firm," *Journal of Management,* 27: 701–721.

15 Nadler, D., & Tushman, M. L. (1980) "A congruence model for diagnosing organizational behavior," in R. Miles (Ed.), *Resource Book in Macro Organizational Behaviour* (pp. 30-49). Santa Clara, CA: Goodyear.

16 Wei, L. (2006) "Strategic human resource management: Determinants of fit," *Research and Practice in Human Resource Management,* 14(2): 49–60.

17 Akingbola, K. (2006) "Strategy and human resource management in nonprofit organizations: Evidence from Canada," *International Journal of Human Resource Management,* 17(10): 1707.

18 Guo, C., Brown, W. A., Ashcraft, R. F., Yoshioka, C. F., & Dong, H.-K. D. (2011) "Strategic human resources management in nonprofit organizations," *Review of Public Personnel Administration,* 31(3): 248–269.

19 Easter Seals Arkansas. http://ar.easterseals.com/content/mission-statement. Retrieved November 20, 2011.

20 Interview: Gemma Beardsmore of VTCT. *Third Sector,* November 22, 2010. http://www.thirdsector.co.uk/news/1041944/Interview-Gemma-Beardsmore-VTCT/. Retrieved November 24, 2011.

21 Kalleberg, A. L., Marden, P., Reynolds, J., & Knoke, D. (2006) "Beyond profit! Sectoral difference in high-performance work practices," *Work and Occupations*, 33(3): 271–302.

22 "Analysis: Sector budgets feel the squeeze by John Plummer," *Third Sector*, March 21, 2011. http://www.thirdsector.co.uk/Finance/article/1060843/analysis-sector-budgets-feel-squeeze/. Retrieved November 24, 2011.

23 Reed, P. B., & Howe, V. J. (1999) *Voluntary Organizations in Ontario in the 1990s*. Ottawa: Statistics Canada.

24 "Tapping Encore Talent: A MetLife Foundation/Civic Ventures Survey of Employers, MetLife Foundation/Civic Ventures, October 2008, pp. 8–9.

25 Russell, S. (2009) "Twin Cities-based Jeremiah Program goes national." MinnPost March 16, 2009. http://www.minnpost.com/business/2009/03/twin-cities-based-jeremiah-program-goes-national.

26 Moore, M. (2000) "Managing for value: Organizational strategy in for-profit, non-profit, and governmental organizations." *Nonprofit and Voluntary Sector Quarterly*, 29: 183–208.

27 Butzen, J. (December 12, 2009) "An example of strategic mergers in the nonprofit sector: Arizona Children's Association." *Stanford Social Innovation Review*. http://www.ssireview.org/blog/entry/an_example_of_strategic_mergers_in_the_nonprofit_sector_arizona_childrens_a

28 http://www.bbbso.ca/site-bbbs/media/ottawa/BBBSO%20Strategic%20Plan%20 2011.pdf. Retrieved February 14, 2012.

29 Taggar, S., Sulsky, L., & MacDonald, H. (2008) "Subsystem configuration: A model of strategy, context, and human resources management alignment," in Michael D. Mumford, Samuel T. Hunter, & Katrina E. Bedell-Avers (Eds.), *Multi-level Issues in Creativity and Innovation* (Research in Multi Level Issues, Volume 7), pp. 317–376.

30 Miles, R. E., & Snow, C. C. (1984) "Designing strategic human resource systems," *Organizational Dynamics*, 13(1): 36–52.

31 Rich, B. L., Lepine, J. A., & Crawford, E. R. (2010) "Job engagement: Antecedents and effects on job performance," *Academy of Management Journal*, 53: 617–635.

32 Barbeito, C. L., & Bowman, J. P. (1998) *Nonprofit Compensation and Benefits Practices*. New York: John Wiley.

33 Pete Manzo (2009) "Rethinking compensation for nonprofits," *Stanford Social Innovation Review*. http://www.ssireview.org/blog/entry/rethinking_compensation_for_nonprofits. Retrieved March 11, 2012.

34 Jamrog, Jay, & Overholt, Miles (2004) "Building a strategic HR function: Continuing the evolution," *Human Resource Planning* 27(1): 51–62.

35 Herman, R. D., & Renz, D. O. (2004) *Investigating the Relation Between Good Management, Financial Outcomes and Stakeholder Judgement of Effectiveness in Donative and Commercial Nonprofit Organizations*. Los Angeles: Association for Research on Nonprofit Organizations and Voluntary Action.

36 Brown, W. A., & Yoshioka, C. (2003) "Mission attachment and satisfaction as factors in. employee retention," *Nonprofit Leadership and Management*, 14(1): 5–18; McFarlan, W. (1999). "Don't assume the shoe fits," *Harvard Business Review*, Nov/Dec.

37 Moore, M. (2000) "Managing for value: Organizational strategy in for-profit, nonprofit, and governmental organizations," *Nonprofit and Voluntary Sector Quarterly*, 29: 183–208.

38 Crittenden, W. (2000) "Spinning straw into gold: The tenuous strategy, funding, and financial performance linkage," *Nonprofit and Voluntary Sector Quarterly*, 29: 164–182; Herman, R. D., & Renz, D. O. (1997) "Multiple constituencies and

the social construction of nonprofit organization effectiveness," *Nonprofit and Voluntary Sector Quarterly*, 26(2): 185–206; Herman, R. D., & Renz, D. O. (1999) "Theses on nonprofit organizational effectiveness," *Nonprofit and Voluntary Sector Quarterly*, 23(2): 107–126.

39 *HR Focus*. Special Report on HR Metrics. July 2010.
40 HR Metrics Service. A joint service of BC HRMA, HRMAM & HRPA http://www.hrpa.ca/Pages/HRMetricsService.aspx.
41 Stothart, Chloe (2012) "Forty-two per cent of sector staff think their line managers are ineffective," *Third Sector Online*, February 29, 2012. http://www.thirdsector.co.uk/news/1119634/Forty-two-per-cent-sector-staff-think-line-managers-ineffective/?DCMP=ILC-SEARCH.

5
HUMAN RESOURCE PLANNING IN NONPROFITS

Learning Objectives

After studying this chapter, you should be able to:

1. Explain the concept of human resource planning.
2. Discuss the objectives of human resource planning.
3. Illustrate the types of human resource planning.
4. Describe the relationship between human resource planning and the strategy of the organization.
5. Discuss the issues and importance of human resource planning for nonprofit organizations.

Human Resource Planning at JEVS Human Services[1]

To bridge the shortage of leaders in some of its units and help the organization to grow, JEVS Human Services sets out to attract talented mature workers from the for-profit sector and the construction trades. The Philadelphia-based nonprofit organization has a mission to benefit members of the community by enhancing their employability and self-sufficiency through a broad range of support programs. The corporate strategy of JEVS Human Services is focused on fostering understanding of customer needs to identify social enterprises opportunity. Flowing from this strategy, an HR planning initiative was formulated and implemented. The plan centered on a Pilot Boomer Task Force to look at: positions and functions JEVS should target for recruitment, where to look for potential sector switchers, and which for-profit skills are most transferable to a nonprofit setting. The outcome was that HR planning enabled JEVS Human Services not only to align HR to its strategy, but also to develop and enhance its recruitment strategy, selection practices, onboarding and ultimately employees' connection to the mission of the organization.

Introduction

The process model of nonprofit strategic human resource management discussed in Chapter 4 encapsulates two main processes: the formulation of the organization's strategy and the development of the human resource strategy. First, the corporate and business strategies are developed to provide a roadmap for the organization and its core businesses or services. Second, strategy is followed by or is simultaneously developed with the human resource strategy that would outline the talent pool, HR practices and policies the organization would deploy to facilitate the implementation of its strategy. The human resource strategy involves the core HR functions to which we will devote our attention in this book. One of the functions and perhaps the linchpin function is the focus of this chapter.

This chapter addresses HR planning. It discusses important planning questions that are critical to all HR functions, practices and policies. Following from Chapter 4, you will see that the organization must consider these questions to formulate and implement an effective HR strategy. Moreover, the chapter also shows how the information and impact of the external environment of nonprofits we examined in Chapter 3 play out in the HR practices and policies of an organization. To achieve this end result, the chapter will describe the issues, methods and tools for HR planning in nonprofits. It reiterates the link between a nonprofit organization's strategy and its HR plan. Hence, we start the chapter with an overview of strategic planning.

Strategic Planning

Planning is inevitable to an organization. Both operational planning and strategic planning are critical to the performance of the organization. The determination of the organization's mission is the beginning of the planning process. The goals, actions, policies and the coordination must be integrated to support the mission of the nonprofit organization through planning. Put differently, strategy is formulated through planning.[2] Specifically, we are talking about strategic planning (Box 5.1).

The purpose of a strategic plan is to outline an organization's future direction, performance targets and approaches to achieve the targets.[3] Therefore, strategic planning generally incorporates the analysis of the environment, market, the existing competencies, opportunities, threats and the options the organization could implement.

BOX 5.1 FUNCTIONS OF STRATEGIC PLANNING

1. Facilitate forward scanning for nonprofits.
2. Guide longer time frame analysis by management of nonprofits.
3. Communicate strategic goals and resource allocation to stakeholders.

4. Provide framework for short-term plan and integration.
5. Tool for decision-making and performance analytics.
6. Facilitate change management.
7. Support the analysis of external environment.
8. Help managers to connect priorities and trends.
9. Market nonprofit to funders, community, and stakeholders.

Source: Greer, C. R. (2001) *Strategic Human Management: A General Managerial Approach,* 2nd Edition. Upper Saddle River, NJ: Prentice-Hall.

Strategic planning must also include the flexibility for strategy to be refined in order for the organization to be able to adapt to any change that is not evident at the time of planning. Likewise, it should allow the discontinuation of an ineffective strategy. The point here is that while analysis is important in strategic planning, it is essential to allow change, modification or enhancement of the original strategy.[4] This explains why many management scholars and managers contend that the formulation of an effective strategy combines planning and experimentation.

Strategic planning could be *formal* or *informal*. Many small and large nonprofit organizations engage in formal strategic planning in which one or more days are designated for planning sessions. Participation of the senior leadership, middle managers, and some form of insight from the employees of the organization are common in strategic planning sessions. Facilitators are often engaged to guide the analysis and brainstorming process. The sessions could be held on or off-site of the organization. An example of a formal strategic planning process used at Ottawa–Carleton Association for Persons with Developmental Disabilities, a Canadian nonprofit organization (OCAPDD) is presented in Box 5.2.

BOX 5.2 FORMAL STRATEGIC PLANNING AT OTTAWA-CARLETON ASSOCIATION FOR PERSONS WITH DEVELOPMENTAL DISABILITIES (OCAPDD)

A two-day work session to develop a three-year strategic plan and to explore team-building strategies and tools.

Activities for developing the strategic plan consisted of

- reviewing the current Vision and Mission statements to reach a common understanding of the statements;
- conducting an environmental scan of each program;
- analyzing external linkages in the community;

(continued)

(continued)

- identifying internal strengths and weaknesses; and
- identifying external opportunities and threats.

Following these activities, members of the management team identified strategic directions and goals for each direction.

Source: Akingbola, K. (2013) "Contingency, fit and flexibility of HRM in nonprofit organizations," *Employee Relations*, 35(5): 479–494.

For many nonprofit organizations, strategic planning is an informal process. It could involve ongoing discussions that are focused on emerging trends, opportunities and threats in the operating environment as well as the competencies of the organization. Such discussions are necessitated by operational planning, reporting, or a specific requirement that is part of a funding process. Relative to the size of the nonprofit organization, the discussions could include highlights of conversations at staff and managers' meetings which are rolled up to senior management for decision-making. Intrinsically, there is an element of incremental planning involved in informal strategic planning especially in terms of how the short-term focus is used to address the need for change and develop adaptive capability of the organization in the long run.[5] What is important is that the informal process should be recognized as an incremental process for addressing the strategic planning needs of the organization. However, as Greer noted, the use of formal and informal strategic planning is not mutually exclusive. Organizations tend to use or at least combine elements of both approaches.

Strategic Planning Process

Organizations use different approaches for strategic planning. The use of a particular approach compared to the others could depend on the size, the sector, or the structure of the organization. Some of the steps we outlined in the process model of strategic nonprofit human resource management in Chapter 4 are part of the strategic planning process. However, a generic strategic planning process would include all of the steps summarized in Figure 5.1.[6]

Strategic planning ultimately sets the groundwork for an effective HR strategy. It includes important elements that would flow into HR planning. It triggers pertinent questions that will drive SHRM. For example, when the Royal Society for the Protection of Birds (RSPB) identified leadership as an important component of the charity's strategy, it appears to have triggered a number of HR planning questions that resulted in an actual HR strategy.[7] For many organizations, how to determine the number of employees is one such question. Beyond the questions which we will discuss further below, it is important to note that

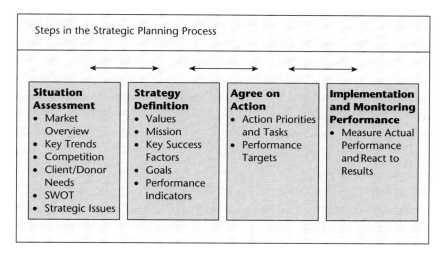

FIGURE 5.1   Steps in the Strategic Planning Process

Source: Adapted from Rogers, G., Finley, D. S., & Galloway, J. R. (2001). *Strategic Planning in Social Service Organizations: A Practical Guide.* Toronto: Canadian Scholars Press, Figure 3.1, p. 25.

HR strategy provides input and flags concerns that feed into the strategic planning. This is common in organizations where both processes are well integrated. For example, HR planning would identify the knowledge and skills that could influence the competitiveness and future direction of the organization.[8]

What Is HR Planning?

HR planning is critical in SHRM. As a result, it is an important tool HR managers must deploy to influence the performance of an organization. HR planning is concerned with the systematic assessment and forecasting of an organization's future need for human resources. The first basic purpose of HR planning is to estimate the number and type of employees, especially the knowledge, skills and behavior that will be required to support the strategic goals of the organization. The emphasis is on matching the future demand of the organization for employees who have the required competencies to the supply of the identified employee group.[9] The second basic purpose of HR planning is to facilitate the formulation of strategies to address the gap between the demand and supply of employees with the required knowledge and skills. This is the problem-solving role of the HR planning process. Generally, the process would involve the review of the knowledge and skills of current employees vis-à-vis the future direction of the organization. As we highlight in the outline of the HR planning process below, a great deal of effort is extended to analyzing the internal and external environment to forecast how the factors we discussed in Chapter 3 could drive the demand for and supply of employees.

Although it is critical, the focus on the forecasting of the demand for and supply of employees is considered to be the traditional perspective of HR planning.[10] Belcourt and McBey explain that the approach fails to consider the connection of HR planning to the practices and policies that are required to support the diverse strategies of the organization. In essence, it limits the contribution of HR to the strategy of the organization. For example, how HR practices support the corporate leadership strategy of the RSPB cannot be limited to the number, skills and knowledge of employees who will help the organization to achieve the goal(s) of this strategy. It must also consider the implications of the strategy for HR functional practices in compensation and training.

Thus, at the level of SHRM, the third basic purpose of HR planning is to facilitate the development of HR practices that will support the strategy of the organization. It involves making proactive assumptions, anticipation of probable change in the environment and industry environment, and facilitating the development and deployment of HR practices to address the changes in a proactive way.[11] From this perspective, HR planning is not only aligned to the strategic planning process: it is equipping the organization with the readiness to adapt to change and maintain fit with the operating environment. The ability of an organization to manage change by deploying a relevant HR strategy could depend to a significant extent on how well the HR planning process has set up the groundwork or framework for analyzing the scenario and the required strategic options. Instead of reacting to the change, HR planning makes it possible for the organization to adapt to the change in the environment and industry factors[12] that we discussed in Chapter 3. Essentially, HR planning supports the strategy of the organization by aligning HR practices with specific strategies and by enabling the organization to adapt to change through the system it has put in place.

Similar to strategic planning, HR planning must have built-in flexibility to allow for midway change, total overhaul, or the deployment of a brand new strategy in the event that the scenarios are not working out quite as anticipated. Organizations must be able to tweak or replace an original plan in the face of unanticipated shift in the environment, industry, and operational factors.[13] As Mello noted, a change to any planning initiatives is an indication that the organization is continuously scanning the environment and adapting to change accordingly. It should not be seen as a weakness. In fact, it is specifically for this reason among others that the need for flexibility has been emphasized by SHRM scholars.[14] They noted that flexibility positions the organization to effectively adapt to change in the environment. This is perhaps more critical in an unstable environment such as the one in which nonprofit organizations operate. The need for flexibility must be engrained in both strategic planning and HR planning in order for the organization to achieve its performance goals or simply to survive. Managers must use HR planning to prepare the organization for sudden shock to the system from contingencies such as funders, government policies, and competition.

Importance of HR Planning

From the foregoing section, HR planning is about HR strategy, forecasts, assumptions and scenario planning. It is more than the accuracy of any projections. This value-adding contribution to HR strategy and corporate strategy provides a number of important benefits for the organization. HR planning:

- *Simplifies* how the organization determines human resource shortages, surpluses and measures to address any gaps. This functional contribution ensures that the organization is always ahead of the curve in terms of workplace planning and the required knowledge and skills of employees.
- *Rationalizes* the need for more attention and/or change of direction in specific HR functional practices. Gaps identified through HR planning could trigger the need for more attention and resource allocation to specific HR practices. It is also possible that the identified gaps could support the need to change the direction of specific HR practices.
- *Facilitates* the link between HR practices and policies and the corporate strategy of the organization. As discussed previously, the HR planning process could be a simultaneous process that feeds into strategic planning in organizations where both processes are integrated. It could also be a consecutive process in which the set strategic goals of the organization are decoded into the priorities in HR practices and become the roadmap for planning. Many organizations blend the two approaches. Regardless of the process that is adopted, HR planning ensures that HR practices and policies are better integrated with strategy.
- *Drives* the integration of and consistency in HR practices and policies in the organization. HR planning ensures that practices and policies work together as a bundle with a unified goal of managing employees to use their knowledge, skills, and behavior to support the strategy of the organization. HR planning is one of the tools that can be used to avoid having siloed, disjointed and incoherent organizational practices.
- *Enhances* the ability of managers to better understand the operational environment of the organization. In making assumptions and analyzing scenarios during the HR planning process, managers not only advance their skills on how to understand the key factors in the external environment, they also learn how to stay in tune with events in the environment.
- *Flags* why change should be considered. Through the scanning of the environment and making assumptions, HR planning leads managers to issues, trends and practices that could be the driver or impetus for change. Basically, HR planning is a proactive change tool. If used effectively, the organization would be better positioned to monitor change.

- *Improves* organizational performance. HR planning is the front end of HR strategy that links employees' contribution directly to the strategic goals of the organization. As noted above HR planning interfaces with all HR functional practices. It shapes how the organization attracts, motivates and retains employees. As emphasized in Chapters 3 and 4, this strategic value of HRM is a prime ingredient for improving organizational outcomes, especially in nonprofits.
- *Boosts* the status of the HR department as a strategic partner. For HR practitioners, HR planning offers a credible tool that can further legitimize their strategic partnership role with operational managers and the senior leadership of the organization.

HR planning is one of the core functions in SHRM. It is not only a planning tool and process, but also a continuous improvement mechanism, the starting point of a change management framework, and the provider of the roadmap for delivering human capital for a nonprofit organization to gain competitive advantage. Nonprofits must deploy HR planning as one of the important tools for managing the difficult challenges and uncertainties which have heightened the need for change over the past decades. It will ensure that there is clarity of focus and the targeting of the scarce resource to strategic priorities.

HR Planning Process

The HR planning process must be interactive with the strategic planning. It must flow from and into strategic planning for the organization. This means that the nonprofit manager must be concerned with how to formulate an effective corporate strategy as well as plan for the human resource pool and competencies at the same time. For example, program development and funding strategy must translate into questions about human resource practices and policies. As such, human resource planning would include the steps illustrated in Figure 5.2.

Strategy and Human Resource Planning

The starting point of the HR planning process is strategic planning. It is essentially the coming together of the two processes. From Chapter 3, the mission that outlines the public good and the people the nonprofit intends to serve underlies strategy. It is the reference point for the strategic analysis, environment scan and the funding strategy of the nonprofit. The strengths, weaknesses, opportunities and threats analysis is used to guide the functional plans and decision-making on priorities, and to provide input for change management. This interface stage ensures that the content and the direction outline in HR plan is aligned with the objectives of the organization.

As noted above, it is also through this phase that HR provides input and flags concerns for strategic planning. Also, important people-related issues that are germane to the execution of strategy must flow back into the planning process.

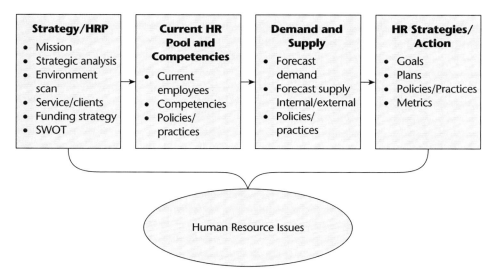

FIGURE 5.2 Human Resource Planning Process

Current HR Pool and Competencies

Following from step 2 in Figure 5.2, the organization must assess its current human resource pool. Here, the goal is to identify whether the number and competencies of the current employees match the strategic requirements of the nonprofit. This internal analysis is a key step in HR planning because it enables the organization to take full account of its people and, more specifically, its current human capital. For a nonprofit, it is imperative to identify employees who have the unique knowledge and skills the organization needs to implement its strategy. Another vital people-related analysis is how well current policies and practices best support the strategy of the nonprofit. This ensures that the link between HR and strategic planning is beyond forecasting numbers.

Forecasting Demand and Supply

The analysis of the current human resource pool, competencies, and gaps in HR policies and practices is followed by forecasting the demand of the nonprofit for people and specific competencies. It involves managers making assumptions about the future human resource pool and their knowledge and skills. To forecast the supply of people with the skills required by the organization, nonprofit managers must complete a comprehensive environment scan and analysis of labor market trends. Many of the general and industry environment factors we discussed in Chapter 3 impact the demand for and supply of labor to nonprofit organizations. In addition, technology and how technological changes shape the jobs must also be considered. Regardless of the factor, the key for managers is to anticipate the people the nonprofit would require and make decisions on whether to hire externally, move people from within the organization, or blend both approaches. The outcome of forecasting often highlights different strategies for employees with different skills. For example, a 2011 report found that US charities plan to hire significantly more employees who provide direct services to expand their service capacity than managers and support employees.[15] Managers must consider new and revised policies and practices that the nonprofit would implement to support the execution of the strategy of the nonprofit.

HR Strategies/Action

The outcome of the HR planning process includes a comprehensive HR plan with clearly outlined goals. Action steps are mapped for implementation. The HR plan could be seen as an antecedent that will permeate most of the functional HR practices. It will also signal how the organization intends to deploy people to adapt to change in the environment. One core outcome of HR planning is how the nonprofit will address the results of forecasting. Bearing in mind that managers of a nonprofit would have made some assumptions and forecasted the demand for specific skills and the supply of those competencies from within and outside of the organization, the HR plan outlines how they intend to effectively deal with the workforce shortages or surpluses that are based on the forecast. It provides a roadmap for linking people, jobs and the organization's strategic goals.

At a minimum, the outcome of the HR plan will provide information for the recruitment strategy. It will highlight the expected turnover and any potential challenges in the recruitment of employees who have the unique competencies the organization requires. In staffing, the HR plan is essential not only when a nonprofit is dealing with increased demand for its services but also when the organization is under pressure to restructure due to changing factors in the environment. This was the situation the Royal Society for the Prevention of Cruelty to Animals (RSPCA) in England and Wales found itself in recently (see Box 5.3). The information from the HR plan also flows into the process for identifying training needs.

BOX 5.3 RSPCA RESTRUCTURING AND STAFFING REVIEW

Facing multifaceted pressures of increased demand for its services, rising costs, pension deficit and flat investment return, the RSPCA needed to make tough decisions. The charity had 1,600 employees, an income of £115.3 million, and an expenditure of £122.6 million in 2010. It was imperative that the RSPCA managed the pressures in order to continue to deliver top notch services to animal welfare clients.

A key element of HR planning, a staffing review, was utilized to facilitate decision-making. The result was a restructuring that included the protection of over 1,000 front-line staff working directly with animals and an increase of inspectors to be employed in the long term. However, over 130 non-frontline positions were restructured.

Source: Ricketts, A. (2012) "Animal welfare charity says it will protect front-line services," *Third Sector Online*, April 2, 2012, http://www.thirdsector.co.uk/news/1124966/RSPCA-expects-lose-130-jobs-staffing-review/. Retrieved June 15, 2013.

Since different organizations have different people needs, the HR planning process could be adapted to address the specific HR practices, policies and programs of each nonprofit. Particularly, it is important to consider the organization culture in order to effectively adapt the process to the unique context of the nonprofit. But most importantly, the key challenge for managers is to ensure that the process is aligned front and center with the organization's mission business and corporate strategies.

HR Planning Methods

One of the goals of HR planning is to enable the organization to streamline the planning process for efficient resource allocation and to ensure better outcomes. The goal of efficiency and effectiveness means that the planning process must be based on systems or approaches that have evidence of success. This section explains the basic approaches of HR planning through a discussion of the three fundamentals of the process: forecasting demand for employees: analysis of supply of labor; and implementation of measures to address the gap between the demand and supply of employees.[16] The use and effectiveness of the approaches depend on how well managers understand the specific context and requirements of their nonprofit organization.

Forecasting Demand for Human Resource

The drivers of demand for employees are varied. The same factors that shape the strategy and operations of nonprofits underlie the demand for employees. From factors in the general and industry environment to change implemented as part of the strategy of a nonprofit or change in the staffing mix of employees and volunteers due to professionalization of service delivery, nonprofits increase or decrease their demand for employees to achieve specific objectives. For example, the RSPCA noted that due to the increased demand for its services, the organization must sustain and extend frontline services. As a result, the management decided to protect over 1,000 front-line employees and also to increase the number of inspectors to be employed in the long term.

Demand for employees is a continuous balancing act for many nonprofits. Consistent with the RSPCA example, the national data that we discussed in

Chapter 1 shows that many nonprofits are reporting increased demand for services. However, the precarious revenue situation means that managers must prioritize the areas where the need for employees is most critical to the mission and strategic goals of their organization. It is therefore not surprising that research and industry reports seem to point to revenue as a major determining factor in the demand for employees by nonprofits in the US, the UK and Canada. The requirements of government funding, competition and accountability also impact the demand for employees.

Basic Methods

The basic method of forecasting demand for employees is mainly quantitative. However, qualitative approaches have also gained some ground. Both approaches recognize the drivers of demand for employees based on number and the characteristics of employees.

One of the approaches used by experts to forecast employment needs is the **Delphi technique**. It involves asking a group of experts by survey to estimate the future demand for employees. The experts could be managers or frontline professionals with significant knowledge of the department, the organization or the industry. The results of the survey are summarized and provided to the experts. The original survey questions could be refined based on the information provided by the experts. Participants communicate through a coordinator or facilitator. The *Delphi technique* requires that face-to-face interaction between the experts is minimized at least initially to facilitate objectivity and eliminate the influence of individuals on the estimates of participants.[17] The process is continued until a consensus is reached with the HR department coordinating the survey.

The following steps, adapted from Burack and Mathys, are typical in the *Delphi technique*. First, define the problem or question the organization wants the experts to answer. Second, review the survey questionnaire for relevance and clarity. It is important that the experts understand and are able to respond to the questions. Third, identify and select individuals who will provide expert opinion. The experts must have an orientation as part of this step. Fourth, circulate a first-round questionnaire to the experts. Fifth, the facilitator will receive, analyze and summarize first-round responses of the experts. Sixth, if necessary, the facilitator will send out a revised questionnaire based on the responses of the experts with the summary of the results of the first-round survey. Finally, the facilitator will receive, analyze and summarize the second-round responses of the experts and determine whether they are close to reaching a consensus. The facilitator may organize a face-to-face meeting to resolve differences in the estimates provided by the experts.

Another approach used by experts to forecast human resource needs is *trend analysis*. It involves using past trends to forecast future human resource needs of the organization. Two examples of *trend analysis* are *indexation* and *extrapolation*.[18]

In *indexation,* future human resource needs are matched to growth projected for an organizational index. For example, a human service nonprofit organization such as the Salvation Army could match the organization's human resource needs to the number of under-housed clients who visit its drop-in center. In this case, the organization may project that for every 20 new under-housed clients, the drop-in center would need an additional frontline employee. In effect, the number of clients who visit the drop-in center is the key predictor of the human resource needs of the organization. Alternatively, the Salvation Army could use the number of employees it has hired in the past to forecast its future staffing needs. This *trend analysis* method is known as *extrapolation.* If the Salvation Army has recruited five employees each year over the past five years for the drop-in center, it could extrapolate that five employees will likely be recruited next year.

With the availability of sophisticated computer software and applications, there are many options for organizations to choose from in terms of forecasting demand for human resource. Staffing tables and scenario planning are included in some workforce planning and Human Resource Information System (HRIS) software. The Nominal Group Technique (NGT) that elicits and ranks the opinion of managers/professionals on an issue in a facilitated meeting is also an option. Except for the meeting, the NGT and the *Delphi technique* are similar.

Forecasting Supply of Human Resources

One essential question for many nonprofit organizations once they have transitioned from depending entirely on volunteer labor is how to meet the need for professional human resources that have the knowledge and skills as well as a desire to buy into the mission of the organization. Basically, they will ask the question, where and how do we get the employees to meet our needs, including connection to our mission? In effect, it may not be good enough for nonprofits to think about the supply of human resources once they have forecasted the demand; they must always think about it in relation to their mission. The nature of the mission of nonprofits makes the question about the supply of human resources a recurring issue.

Basic Methods

Nonprofits have three main sources of supply of professional human resources— paid employees, volunteers, current employees and external supply. Volunteers are an important source of supply of employees for nonprofits. Research has found that there is a high degree of interchange between the roles of volunteers and paid employees in nonprofit organizations.[19] Volunteers are also known to use their role as a stepping stone towards employment with nonprofit organizations. Current employees are a source of supply through reassignment, promotion and lateral transfer into vacant positions. External sources of supply of professional human resource include potential employees from other nonprofit organizations, for-profit businesses, public sector and the open labor market.

Internal Supply

Although not exclusively, forecasting the supply of human resources starts from the internal environment for many nonprofit organizations. Hence, the variety of approaches available to these organizations could be used to tap into volunteer labor and current employees as sources for the supply of human resources.

Volunteer management systems offer a rich database of the knowledge, skills and experience of volunteers. A detailed analysis of the database would provide a nonprofit organization the opportunity to develop **volunteer skills inventories**. The analysis of the inventories would provide information on the potential supply of labor from the volunteer pool by matching volunteer talent to current and future positions. In addition to the knowledge and skills populated in the systems, relevant profile information, type of volunteer work and the training they have completed can be mapped as part of the analysis to determine supply of human resources. Figure 5.3 shows an example of a volunteer skill inventory form for Greater Cleveland Habitat for Humanity.

A simple tool that is important in forecasting the supply of human resources from current employees is the *staffing tables*. It is basically an overview of all positions in the organization and the number of employees in those positions. Information from the staffing tables is used in the forecasting techniques discussed below.

Employee skills inventories are commonly used to provide a comprehensive profile of the educational background, skills, work experience, interests, general abilities and current and previous positions of employees in an organization. With the advancement in software programs, both customized and off-the-shelf HRIS systems come with modules that include data required to build a skills inventory. With detailed data collection and regular updating of a skills inventory, the HR department can use analytics to provide the specific data required by managers to forecast the potential supply of human resources for specific positions from current employees. *Analytics* is simply the collection and use of data to enhance decision-making. Information for a skills inventory should start with the standard employee documentation at the time of hire. HRIS systems with self-serve features can enable employees to update their information. **Management inventories** provide similar information with additional data on management experience, training and specialization.

When an employee leaves a position due to promotion, demotion or turnover, it is likely to trigger movement of additional employees in the organization.[20] To manage the impacts of such movements, nonprofits can develop *replacement analysis* or *movement analysis* for their organization.

Replacement analysis identifies the individual employee who will replace a current job holder if there is a vacancy in the position (Figure 5.4). The analysis

Greater Cleveland

Habitat
for Humanity®

Volunteer Skill Inventory

STOP! Each volunteer must *first* fill out his/her own Volunteer Registration Form. If you have not, please do so now.

Volunteer Name and contact info: _____ Date: _____

Construction

If you are **new to construction**, but interested in learning as a general volunteer, please check here: ☐
You do not need to indicate your level of experience below.

Others use the scale below to indicate your level of experience next to the following skills:

1 I am **highly skilled or a professional** in this area and can lay out activities and supervise others.

2 I am **skilled and experienced** in this area and feel comfortable performing these activities.

If you do not have skills or experience in a particular area, leave the line blank.

Example: _1_ **Architecture** (for professional architect)

___Architecture	___Electrical	___Green Building	___Plumbing
___Carpentry	___Electrical Engineering	___Heating/HVAC	___Roofing
___Carpeting	___Engineering/Surveying	___Insulating	___Siding
___Concrete (flat work)	___Equipment Operation	___Land Acquisition	___Tree Removal
___Demolition	___Finish Carpentry	___Landscaping	___*Other (specify)
___Drafting/CAD	___Flooring	___Masonry	
___Drywall Finishing	___Framing	___Mechanical Engineering	_____
___Drywall Hanging	___General Contracting	___Operating Engineer	
	___General Home Repair	___Painting	

ReStore

If you are **new to retail**, but interested in learning as a general volunteer, please check here: ☐
You do not need to indicate your level of experience below.

Others use the scale below to indicate your level of experience next to the following skills:

1 I am **highly skilled or a professional** in this area and can plan activities and supervise others.

2 I am **skilled and experienced** in this area and feel comfortable performing these activities.

If you do not have skills or experience in a particular area, leave the line blank.

Example: _1_ **Cashier** (for professional level)

___Cashier	___ Pricing
___ Customer Service	___Retail/Sales
___ Donation Solicitation	___ Stocking
___ Lifting (30-50 lbs.)	___ Truck Driving
___Merchandise Display Design	___ *Other (specify)
___Merchandise Cleaning/Prepping	_____

Greater Cleveland Habitat for Humanity, 2110 W. 110th Street, Cleveland, Ohio 44102   9/19/2009
Phone (216) 429-1299 Fax (216) 429-3629 ReStore (216) 429-3631 www.clevelandhabitat.org

FIGURE 5.3 Skills Inventory Form for Greater Cleveland Habitat for Humanity

would include relevant information about the replacement such as performance summary, readiness for the next level position, strengths and weaknesses. With the increased attention to succession planning in nonprofit organizations in recent years, information provided by *replacement analysis* is used as part of the **succession planning** process.[21] Succession planning is a process designed to identify and develop employees with the knowledge, skills and abilities in preparation for advancement to senior management position in the organization.[22]

Movement analysis is a tool for analyzing the ripple effects of an initial job change, promotion or turnover in terms of the resulting movements of other employees in the organization.[23] The goal is to help the organization to identify and summarize vacant positions and the corresponding movements of employees that result from filling the vacant positions. *Movement analysis* helps managers to determine how best to balance a promotion-from-within policy with external supply of human resource.[24]

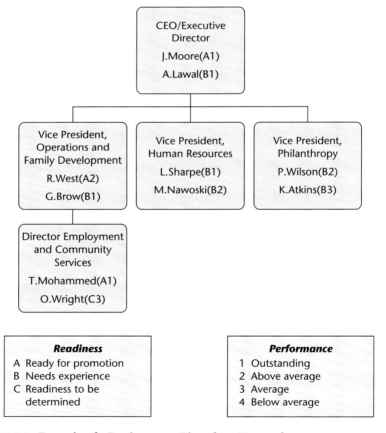

FIGURE 5.4 Example of a Replacement Chart for a Nonprofit

Markov analysis is a commonly used technique for predicting supply of human resource that is based on movement of employees within the organization. It provides detailed patterns of movement such as the number and percentage of employees who move to and from the various jobs as well as those who remain in each job in the organization.[25] One of the goals of the Markov analysis is to forecast the future numbers of employees in the different categories of jobs.[26]

Although there is currently minimal evidence of the use of some of the approaches for forecasting internal supply of human resources in nonprofit HR planning, one would expect that the increased attention and importance of the strategic HR function to the performance of nonprofit organization would expedite the use of the techniques.

External Supply

The external labor market is both a rich and challenging source of supply of human resources for nonprofit organizations. As a result, the general and industry environment factors discussed in Chapter 3 could influence the labor market to present opportunities and problems for forecasting the supply of labor to non-profits. Whatever the case, a nonprofit must consider not only its internal supply of qualified candidates from volunteers and current employees but also external sources to meet its demand for labor. The external supply of labor reflects different aspects of the opportunities and challenges of the HR function in nonprofit organizations.

The primary forecasting method for determining the external supply of human resources is the *labor market analysis*. It is through a labor market analysis that is conducted in conjunction with constant scanning and monitoring of the industry and general environment of a nonprofit that the organization can relatively forecast the available supply of labor to meet its demand for human resources. One key indicator in the labor market analysis is the unemployment rate. Generally, a high unemployment rate suggests that there is a relative supply of skills to meet the demand of employers, and organizations would not find it difficult to attract and recruit new employees. A low unemployment rate would suggest the opposite. However, the reality of the unemployment rate is that it could vary by region and profession. High unemployment rates do not often affect some highly skilled professions in the same way as other professions. Conversely, the implications of the unemployment rate vary for different sectors in society. In a tight labor market with a low unemployment rate, it has been suggested that nonprofits may find it difficult to attract qualified candidates due to relatively lower wages in the sector.[27] We will return to this point in the next chapter on recruitment.

Another key indicator that is central in the labor market analysis is the demographic trend. It could provide information about the potential supply of human resources for the different categories of employees over a period of time. In recent years, demographic trends have highlighted the aging population as an important trend for managers and HR professionals to consider in their analysis of the labor market. For nonprofits, the same demographic trend that has pointed to the aging population has presented a unique opportunity for the recruitment of experienced baby boomers in nonprofit organizations in the US, Canada and the UK. A US Conference Board report explains that baby boomers offer nonprofits critical expertise, experience and passion for the mission of the organization.[28] This trend is similar for nonprofits in Canada.

For many nonprofit organizations, ***community engagement and advocacy activities*** play a part in their external supply of human resources for their organizations. For one, such activities could help the nonprofit to assess the level of interest of potential volunteers in the mission of the organization. The transition of these potential volunteers to actual volunteers builds the talent pool that is available to the nonprofit. As discussed above, the volunteer pool is a source of supply of labor for nonprofit organizations. Similarly, the advocacy activities could also trigger interest of potential employees to explore job opportunities with the organization. As a result, it is not uncommon for a nonprofit to use advocacy activities as a source of recruitment. In essence, the community engagement and advocacy activities connect nonprofits to the external labor market.

Summary

The formulation and implementation of an effective SHRM system depend to a great extent on the information provided by and the linkages created through HR planning. Therefore, HR planning is pivotal to SHRM in nonprofit organizations. In this chapter, we examined the critical link between strategic planning and HR planning. We discussed how the strategic planning process provides a road map for the HR planning and the interconnection between the two processes. The HR planning function and process drive key interactions between the external environment, the organizational goals and the HR practices of a nonprofit organization. Forecasting demand and supply of human resources could also provide tools and insights for managing other organizational initiatives.

The need for a nonprofit to effectively deliver quality services and achieve the goals of the organization in a dynamic and competitive environment requires constant monitoring of demographic, social and economic trends and changes. SHRM and HR planning in particular is key to anticipating and making provisions for uncertainties and helping managers to develop adaptive strategies that are consistent with values of the organization. At the most basic level, HR planning ensures that the movement of employees with the knowledge and skills the organization requires to perform its mission is coordinated, systematic and aligned with the gaps. Whether a nonprofit is dealing with a situation of growth or restructuring, HR planning is essential to forecast the people needs, to identify the potential gaps, and to outline plans that will feed into key HR functions such as recruitment.

Discussion Questions

1. Why is the mission of a nonprofit organization important in HR planning? How would you ensure that the mission is a reference point in HR planning?
2. Organizational strategy impacts HR planning in many ways. How can HR planning impact organizational strategy?
3. What is the role of HR planning in SHRM in a nonprofit where there is no HR professional?
4. You are the only HR professional in a small nonprofit organization and the strategic planning process is in progress. However, you have been told that you should focus on the transactional tasks because those are the immediate needs of the organization. What will you do?

Notes

1   Casner-Lotto, J. (2009) *A Perfect Match? How Nonprofits Are Tapping into the Boomer Talent Pool.* The Conference Board, Research Report R-1447-09-RR.
2   Crossan, M., Fry, J. N., & Killing, J. P. (2005) *Strategic Analysis and Action*, 6th Edition, Toronto: Pearson.
3   Thompson Jr, A., Strickland III, A. J. & Gamble, J. E. (2005) *Crafting and Executing Strategy*, 14th Edition. New York: McGraw-Hill/Irwin.
4   Ibid.
5   Greer, C. R. (2001) *Strategic Human Management: A General Managerial Approach*, 2nd Edition. Upper Saddle River, NJ: Prentice-Hall.
6   Rogers, G., Finley, D. S., & Galloway, J. R. (2001) *Strategic Planning in Social Service Organizations: A Practical Guide.* Toronto: Canadian Scholars Press.
7   "Charities seek smarter a way," *Third Sector*, July 30, 2013. http://www.thirdsector. co.uk/news/1192947/Charities-seek-smarter/?DCMP. Retrieved August 15, 2013.
8   Greer, *Strategic Human Management.*
9   Schwind, H., Das, H., & Wagar, T. (2007) *Canadian Human Resource Management*, 8th Edition. Toronto: McGraw-Hill Ryerson.
10 Belcourt, M., & McBey, K. (2007) *Strategic Human Resources Planning*, 3rd Edition. Toronto: Nelson.
11 Mello, J. A. (2011) *Strategic Human Resource Management*, 3rd Edition. Mason, OH: South-Western Cengage Learning.
12 Ibid.
13 Ibid.
14 Wright, P. M. & Snell, S. A. (1998) "Toward a unifying framework for exploring fit and flexibility in strategic human resource management," *Academy of Management Review*, 23(4): 756–772.
15 Frazier, E. (2011) "Nonprofit hiring shows signs of recovery in 2011, new survey of employers finds," *Chronicle of Philanthropy.* http://philanthropy.com/article/Outlook-for-Nonprofit-Staffing/127134/. Retrieved June 15, 2013.
16 Burack, E., & Mathys, N. (1996) Human Resource Planning a Pragmatic Approach to Manpower Staffing and Development. Northbrook, IL: Brace-Park Press.
17 Ibid.

18 Schwind, Das & Wagar, *Canadian Human Resource Management*.

19 Chum, A., Mook, L., Handy, F., Schugurensky, D., & Quarter, J. (2013) "Degree and direction of paid employee/volunteer interchange in nonprofit organizations," *Nonprofit Management & Leadership*, 23(4): 409–426.

20 Burack & Mathys, *Human Resource Planning*.

21 Carman, J. G., Leland, S. M., & Wilson, A. J. (2010) "Crisis in leadership or failure to plan? Insights from Charlotte, North Carolina," *Nonprofit Management & Leadership*, 21(1): 93–111.

22 Mello, *Strategic Human Resource Management*.

23 Belcourt & McBey, *Strategic Human Resources Planning*.

24 Burack & Mathys, *Human Resource Planning*.

25 Belcourt, M., Bohlander, G., Snell, S., & Sherman, A. (2002) *Managing Human Resources*, 3rd Edition. Toronto: Nelson Education.

26 Belhaj, R., & Tkiouat, M. (2013) "A Markov model for human resources supply forecast dividing the HR system into subgroups," *Journal of Service Science and Management*, 6(3): 211–217.

27 Salamon, L., & Geller, S. L. (2007) *The Nonprofit Workforce Crisis: Real or Imagined?* Communique No. 8, Listening Post Project. Baltimore, MD: Johns Hopkins University Center for Civil Society.

28 Casner-Lotto, *A Perfect Match?*

6

RECRUITMENT AND STAFFING IN NONPROFITS

Learning Objectives

After studying this chapter, you should be able to:

1. Describe why recruitment is important in nonprofit SHRM.
2. Discuss the challenges of recruitment in nonprofits.
3. Develop and implement a recruitment plan.
4. Identify recruitment methods related to the context of nonprofits.
5. Outline how to evaluate recruitment outcomes.

Recruitment Is Core at Teach For America[1]

Teach For America is always recruiting. Established in 1990, the American nonprofit organization has a mission to "eliminate educational inequity by enlisting high-achieving recent college graduates and professionals to teach for at least two years in high-need schools and to become lifelong leaders." As a result, recruitment is central to achieving the goals of the organization. To meet this important need, a key recruitment strategy Teach For America has adopted is to hire recruiters who have participated in the charity's two-year teaching program. About 76 percent of the organization's 140 recruiters have participated in the program. The recruiters understand that they must be able to relate to the experience and questions of their candidates in order to effectively communicate the mission and attract new graduates and professionals. The strategy appears to be working. In 2011, it was reported that more than 48,000 soon-to be college graduates applied for the 5,000 teaching positions. In all, 11,000 corps members currently teach in the Teach For America program across urban and rural areas in the United States.[2]

Introduction

This chapter examines the recruitment function as a critical component of SHRM in nonprofit organizations. The chapter is divided into two broad sections. The first will briefly discus the key concepts in recruitment and staffing. This section will also present an overview of the challenges of recruitment in nonprofits. In the second section, the chapter presents how-to steps, relevant tools and strategies nonprofit managers can use to attract and recruit qualified candidates for current and expected job opportunities. Since mission and values are important characteristics of nonprofit organizations, both are reflected in the decision-making about recruitment and staffing. Moreover, further to the discussions in Chapter 3, the impact of the environment and context of nonprofit organizations is discussed in this chapter.

Recruitment, Selection and Staffing

The term *recruitment* refers to the process of sourcing qualified applicants and attracting them to apply for job opportunities with an organization. Basically, recruitment involves finding potential employees and connecting them with the organization for the purpose of becoming an employee. The process starts when an organization reaches out to the external labor market either directly or indirectly. How a nonprofit organization connects to the labor market depends on many factors such as type of job opportunities, financial resources and the talent pool available inside the organization including volunteers. On paper, the recruitment process is supposed to end once the new employee has formally joined the organization.

In between attracting potential candidates and the commencement of employment, there must be a *selection* process. During this process, successful applicants are evaluated and selected based on their ability to meet the outlined requirements of the vacant position. The process generally entails a thorough review and analysis of the knowledge, skills and abilities as well as the experience of the candidates through screening, interview and reference checks. Since nonprofits also select candidates based on their mission and values, the candidate should fit into the culture of the organization. Selection is perhaps the most difficult decision-making phase of the recruitment process because it involves choosing one candidate over the others. An ineffective selection process could be very costly and damaging to the performance of the entire organization.

Staffing is an umbrella process that encapsulates the recruitment, selection and endpoint of filling a vacant position. The term staffing is also used to mean having the appropriate number of employees to meet the operational need of an organization. For example, hospitals and human services nonprofits with 24-hour operation have staffing formula for different shifts during a 24-hour period. Related to this second meaning is the type of staffing contract. Broadly, there are two main types of staffing: traditional or permanent staffing, and alternative staffing.[3] Traditional staffing is based on the assumption of a permanent employment relationship between the employee and the employer. Alternate staffing involves short-term and non-permanent employment relationship. Common forms of alternative staffing include the use of temporary contracts, part-time contracts, and independent contractors. Although for the purpose of this book, the focus is on staffing as the overall process of recruitment and selection, a brief overview of permanent and alternative staffing is relevant to understanding the staffing process in nonprofits. Staffing is the goal of recruitment and selection. It is not uncommon for managers to use the terms staffing and recruitment interchangeably.

Staffing is critical for nonprofit organizations. As noted, candidates must not only possess the knowledge and skills required in the positions for which they are recruited; they must also buy into the mission of the nonprofit because the mission is the business of the organization. Moreover, the fact that people are truly the primary asset of nonprofits coupled with the social and labor intensive nature of the nonprofit enterprise means recruitment directly impacts the performance and survival of the organization.[4] The opening example of Teach For America illustrates this point. By underscoring that recruiters not only understand the program but also have experience with the two-year teaching program, the nonprofit is making important linkage between the mission, performance and recruitment practices of the organization. For the potential candidate, this recruitment strategy stresses that Teach For America is in the business of building human and social capital.

The critical importance of recruitment suggests that nonprofits must align how they attract and recruit employees with the unique challenges, opportunities and interactions within and outside of the organization. The decision-making about recruitment involves strategic choices that test a manager's understanding and ability to effectively manage these dynamics.

Staffing Choices

The means by which an organization decides to fill a vacant position in terms of the form of staffing is a strategic choice. The broad question is whether the organization should hire employees on a permanent basis or use one of the alternative forms of staffing. As discussed in the next section on the challenges of recruitment, the decision on whether to fill a vacant position with a permanent employee or use an alternative form of staffing is familiar to many managers in nonprofit organizations. Each option has a number of advantages and disadvantages.

Permanent Employees

Permanent employees generally have employment contracts with indeterminate end dates, benefits and vacation pay. The assumption is that "unless the employee resigns or is fired, he or she will remain with the employer until death or retirement."[5] Permanent employment relationship contributes to the effectiveness and efficiency in a nonprofit organization at many levels and in different ways. First, permanent employees would enable the nonprofit to plan for the long-term. With information on the knowledge, skills and abilities available to it, the organization is better able to develop core competencies and strategy that will help to achieve its mission. Second, due to the social nature of nonprofit services, permanent employees are more likely to deliver better value to clients of the organization through consistency of practice, continuous improvement, and knowledge of the needs of clients that they have developed over time. Third, permanent employees could help nonprofits to attract and retain qualified candidates because they would signify a relative sense of job security. Potential employees sometimes use the information they glean from current employees to assess the level of job security in the organization. Fourth, although not absolute, permanent employees mean better retention. At the least, the nonprofit would reduce the number of its employees who are actively seeking other jobs due to their non-permanent employment contract. Fifth, hiring employees on a permanent basis could be more cost effective to the nonprofit in the long term. Considering the direct and indirect costs that are related to the higher turnover that could characterize non-permanent employees, permanent employees could offer a significant advantage for SHRM. The costs will be discussed in the section on recruitment process below. Permanent employees would also figure into the ability of a nonprofit organization to adapt to change, a point we will discuss in detail in Chapter 12.

Non-Permanent Employees

Non-permanent employees hired under alternative staffing arrangement are generally recruited on short-term basis. The common types of non-permanent employees such as temporary employees on limited time contracts or hired through temp agencies are recruited to meet staffing needs that are related to special projects, as backfill for permanent employees, or for contingency requirements of the organization. Non-permanent employees could give nonprofit organizations the flexibility to manage the uncertainty related to forecasting future staffing needs and fluctuation in service or production level. However, they could impact the bottom line and the performance of the nonprofit in the short and long term. In addition to the opposite of the advantages of the permanent employees highlighted above, there are other impacts of reliance on non-permanent employees. First, the rate of pay for a temporary staff from an employment agency is generally higher than the comparable pay for a regular employee. Second, there is a question about the predictable turnover. Since most non-permanent employees are actively seeking permanent jobs, employee turnover and cost of recruitment tend to increase with alternative staffing. Third, reliance on non-permanent employees could affect the ability of the nonprofit to develop and sustain the human capital the organization needs to build its core competencies and drive strategy. Fourth, related to the foregoing, there are questions about the level of motivation of non-permanent employees due to the temporary nature of their employment.[6] It could be difficult to motivate employees who are on temporary contract for goals that are beyond their time with the organization.

The choice between permanent and non-permanent employees is a contentious issue for many nonprofit organizations. Box 6.1 shows excerpts from an article on the use of temporary fundraisers in US nonprofits which highlights some of the issues. The characteristics of nonprofits and the quality and continuity required in the services they provide mean that over-dependence on non-permanent employees could affect the organization. However, the imperative imposed by industry factors, especially contracting and funding, have forced nonprofits to use non-permanent employees to the detriment of their performance. These factors are highlighted in the challenges of recruitment discussed in the next section.

BOX 6.1 TEMPORARY FUNDRAISERS CAN EASE THE STRAIN OF RAMPANT TURNOVER

A Temporary Team

Finding a replacement can take several months, and often longer, so the temporary arrangement "gives the organization some breathing space, rather than having to get someone because the wheels are falling off," says Timothy Higdon, the former chief development officer at Girl Scouts of the USA.

Can Be Costly

"I'm not sure that the interim position helps minimize the ill effects of turnover, because the person is usually not there long enough to be fully integrated into the organization," BT, a Boston fundraising consultant. "It's a way to cope, not a long-term answer."

Interim fundraisers usually command higher pay than other development officers, often charging a day rate that can be as high as $1,500 or more.

"When a charity reaches out to an interim fundraiser, it's a sign they have some weakness in staffing." Sometimes the request comes after new leaders try to shift an organization's culture and face resistance. Or the chief executive's position is vacant and the charity is reluctant to hire a permanent fundraiser until a new leader can select the person to fill that role. BG, an interim fundraiser.

(continued)

(continued)

Coaching Sessions

When temporary fundraising assignments work well, they usually have multiple benefits. For example, interim fundraisers can pave the way for more junior development officers to take over, keeping them from job hopping, says Ms. T.

Source: Excerpt from Hall, H. (2013) "Temporary Fundraisers Can Ease the Strain of Rampant Turnover" *The Chronicle of Philanthropy*, May 9, 2013.

Recruitment Choices

When it comes to recruitment, one key decision nonprofit managers must make is whether to recruit internally from among current employees and volunteers or target qualified candidates from external sources. Although some may argue otherwise, volunteers are part of the internal pool of human resources available to a nonprofit. Moreover, the strategy of the nonprofit will also be a major consideration as discussed in Chapter 4.

Internal Recruiting

Internal recruiting offers a number of benefits to the nonprofit organization. First, the organization and the employee are known to one another. The organization is familiar with the employee's knowledge, skills and abilities. The employee is familiar with the organization's systems, processes and culture. This familiarity by both parties puts the recruitment process at an advanced stage.

Second, internal recruiting within an organization motivates employees to perform and helps to facilitate retention. Internal recruiting through promotion signals to the employees that the nonprofit recognizes their performance and is willing to provide a career path with progressive opportunities. Third, internal recruiting lessens the financial and social costs of recruitment. The financial costs and the time required for job posting, orientation, and training are reduced because of the employee's knowledge of the organization. Similarly, the internal social capital cost is reduced as the employee would at least have working relationships with colleagues. Fourth, since the nonprofit is familiar with the performance of employees from their performance evaluation, concerns about the performance is minimized. Depending on the length of the employee's service, performance evaluation can provide insight into the growth and development of the employee.

Internal recruiting is not without disadvantages. First, it could lead to intense competition among employees for the limited promotion opportunities. This could contribute to internal conflict and building of alliances, and ultimately impact teamwork and collaboration in the nonprofit. Second, internal recruitment can be inimical to change in nonprofit. Because employees have similar experience, they may not see the need for improvement or misunderstand the drivers of change. Hence, they may want to preserve the status quo. Although resistance to change is not exclusive to internal recruiting, the lack of diversity of ideas that could be contributed by new employees with a different experience would likely heighten resistance. Third, internal recruiting can demotivate employees who are not selected for promotion. Such employees might read the unsuccessful promotion effort as an indication of lack of recognition of their performance. This would likely contribute to employee turnover. Fourth, a strict policy of internal recruiting would have a domino effect.[7] One job filled by an internal candidate would lead to subsequent vacancies and recruiting across levels of the nonprofit. The repeated recruiting resulting from the initial vacancy would affect the operations of multiple departments and create inefficiencies especially for small nonprofits with limited resources.

External Recruiting

A nonprofit that has adopted a strategy that is focused on service innovation would emphasize external recruiting in order to continuously renew its human resources pool and better position the organization to adapt to change.[8] Beyond strategy, the advantages of external recruiting counteract the disadvantages of internal recruiting. First, external recruiting would provide, at the very least, the nonprofit access to new knowledge, skills and abilities that may not be available in the organization. The new competencies could also include knowledge of best practices from competitors and experience with diverse service or product market segments.

Second, external recruiting also increases the probability of eliciting different perspectives on issues and fresh ideas from employees. An external recruit will bring exposure to other context(s) that would have shaped their decision-making, problem-solving and work orientation. Third, external recruiting could also extend the social capital of a nonprofit organization. It is not uncommon for new employees to call upon or use the professional network and contacts they established in their previous employment for their new organization. For example, the relationship a new employee has built with suppliers, client groups and officials of funding bodies could be leveraged to get answers to questions and clarify processes.

External recruiting is not without demerits. First, it is more costly to recruit externally. The direct and indirect costs of external recruiting could affect the financial resources of small nonprofit organizations. Second, the learning curve about the nonprofit organization's policies and the socialization process for external recruits often takes a longer period of time. This could impact the ability of the organization to maximize the benefits of a new employee. Third, although the recruitment process should give the organization a good insight into the knowledge, skills and abilities of an external recruit, there is no guarantee about the performance of the new employee. Even with information about past performance of the external candidate through a good reference checking process, the actual performance of the new employee in the new organization is unknown. Fourth, excessive external recruiting especially for senior positions could demotivate current employees who have applied for such positions. This could contribute to the turnover of high-performing employees who will see the emphasis on external recruiting as an indication of a lack of a career path for them in the organization. Finally, excessive external recruiting could jeopardize the culture and values of a nonprofit organization. Since a nonprofit is a values-based organization and it takes time for new employees to adapt to the culture of an organization, excessive external recruiting could affect the consistent adoption of the values of the nonprofit in organizational practices and decision-making.

The decision to recruit internally or externally should consider both the unique external and industry factors of a nonprofit as well as the internal factors in the organization. The characteristics of a nonprofit such as size, age and the type of social cause the organization is involved in are also relevant in shaping the decision to recruit internally or externally. These factors would often necessitate some form of balance that would blend internal and external recruiting (Table 6.1).

TABLE 6.1 Internal or External Recruiting

Positive Aspects	Negative Aspects
Internal Recruiting	
• Familiarity between employees and organization	• Competition among employees for the limited promotion opportunities
• Motivates employees to perform and helps to facilitate retention	• Fosters status quo and resistance to change
• Lessens the financial and social costs of recruitment	• Demotivates employees who are not selected for promotion
• Concerns about the performance are minimized	• Contributes to inefficiency
External Recruiting	
• New knowledge, skills and abilities	• Learning curve and socialization take time
• Different perspectives on issues and fresh ideas	• No guarantee of performance
• Extends the social capital of the organization	• Demotivates current employees who have applied for positions
	• Impacts culture and values of nonprofit
	• Costly

Challenges of Recruitment in Nonprofits

Recruitment effectiveness in nonprofits is dependent on the ability of each organization to understand and manage the specific factors that influence the outcome. Most of these factors are challenges that are unique to the sector. Nonprofit literature has highlighted the following as the important factors to consider in the effort to attract and recruit employees.

Mission of a nonprofit. The mission of a nonprofit could be both a positive and a negative in the recruitment process. As a positive factor, potential employees are attracted and often choose to work for a nonprofit because they identify with the mission of the organization.[9] However, as a negative factor, highly qualified potential candidates who oppose the mission could be dissuaded from applying for a job with the nonprofit. Hence, although it is generally not a condition of employment, the mission of nonprofits plays a significant role in attracting employees.

Skill mix. Many of the competencies nonprofits require to meet the challenges of their operating environment are unique to the sector. The implication of the unique competencies is that the talent pool for some positions in nonprofits is limited to those with experience in the sector. For example, nonprofit managers have to focus not only on basic management functions such as budgeting, planning, decision-making and supervision, but they must also learn to work with a volunteer board, advocacy groups and multiple funding organizations.[10]

Government. The relationship between the government and nonprofit organizations is an important underlying factor in recruitment. Generally, there are two ways the relationship impacts recruitment. One, the dependence on government funding could influence who is recruited and how employees are recruited in nonprofits. Two, the contracting system of government funding means that nonprofits are more likely to recruit non-permanent employees on short-term contracts than recruit permanent employees for services funded by the government.[11] The impact of government is not limited to nonprofits that operate within the US, UK and Canada but also international NGOs from these countries. For example, NGOs such as the Red Cross and Oxfam generate a sizeable percentage of their revenue from government sources.

Small workplace. Most nonprofits are small organizations. For example, the annual expenses of 75 percent of US nonprofits in 2010 was less than $500,000[12] while most UK and Canadian nonprofits have less than 20 employees.[13] It is, therefore, uncommon to find informal and inconsistent recruitment practices. In addition to the impact on the ability of the organization to attract and recruit qualified candidates, the limited organizational capability and resources could make a nonprofit susceptible to the legal risk of violating employment legislation.

Compensation. There is almost a consensus in research that salaries are generally lower for most nonprofit positions compared to similar positions in for-profit and public sector organizations. In fact, research has shown that the difference in salary increases as the position being compared moves to managerial and senior leadership levels of the sectors.[14] This inability to offer competitive salaries is a major challenge for recruitment in nonprofits. It contributes to the difficulty organizations experience in attracting candidates with certain types of skills and experience.

Job advancement. The small size of most nonprofits suggest that there is limited opportunity for advancement in each organization. With limited opportunity for career advancement, employees who are seeking to advance to higher levels may have to change jobs to actualize their career goals.

Coproduction with volunteers. This is another factor that could also be a positive or negative for recruitment in nonprofits. On the one hand, the coproduction between volunteers and employees[15] enhances the pool of human resources of a nonprofit which could be used to attract new employees. The interchangeability of roles could enable the organization to focus on recruiting employees whose roles cannot be substituted with volunteers. On the other hand, interchangeability of roles could be detrimental to recruitment if potential employees are aware that managers may opt to recruit volunteers to do their jobs.

In all, recruitment strategies in nonprofits must underscore the need to address these challenges in order to attract and recruit the employees required to the goals of the organization. How a nonprofit deploys its recruitment strategy could affect how it integrates recruitment with other HR functions. The recruitment strategies and processes used by nonprofits are discussed in the next section.

Recruitment Methods

As evidenced in Chapter 1, nonprofits are facing increasing demand for their services. As a corollary, employment has continued to grow in the sector faster than for-profit and government organizations.[16] This pattern points to a need to find innovative ways to connect with potential candidates. Although a nonprofit employment trends survey by a US consulting firm suggests that nonprofits are increasingly depending on current employees to staff new programs rather than hiring new employees,[17] when they do hire new employees, the recruitment methods they employ are varied. Specifically, research indicates that nonprofits combine traditional and other methods to connect with qualified candidates.

Word of Mouth

It is perhaps unexpected in the age of the internet and social media, but word of mouth remains one of the cost-effective methods of recruiting in nonprofits. Spreading the word through the formal and informal network of stakeholders of the organization could help to promote the vacant job to candidates who are in the immediate and extended community of the nonprofit. In most cases, word of mouth is used to introduce the job to the potential candidates before they view the official job posting and apply for the position. Many nonprofits use word-of-mouth recruiting without formally acknowledging it as a key part of their recruitment method. The reality for many small nonprofits is that recruiting by word of mouth is effective enough for them.

Employee Referral

Closely related to recruiting by word of mouth is employee referral. Current employees formally or informally introduce candidates to the nonprofit. In a formal employee referral program, employees are sometimes recognized or rewarded for referring the successful candidate for a job. There are advantages to using the employee referral method to recruit employees. First, the organization is able to glean some basic information about the knowledge, skills, and experience of the potential candidate even before they apply. Second, if the employee who is referring the potential candidate has worked with him/her, it is very likely that the nonprofit will have an inside track on the past performance of the potential candidate. Third, at least at the initial stage of the employment, the referred candidate is likely to have an obligation not to disappoint the employee who referred him/her. Fourth, the potential candidate has the opportunity to know more about the organization through the employee making the referral before applying for a job. Box 6.2 shows an example from nonprofits that use employee referral as one of the methods of recruitment. However, it is important to note two related disadvantages of employee referral if it is not managed properly. One, it has the potential to facilitate "groupthink," that is, people who think and do things alike. Two, it could also limit recruiting to people who are mainly from the same group. In effect, employee referral could facilitate discrimination.[18]

BOX 6.2 EMPLOYEE REFERRAL AT CATHOLIC RELIEF SERVICES

Catholic Relief Services relies heavily on two key approaches—a fellowship program and referrals—to develop what Mr. Ausmus calls "bench strength."

The charity's International Fellows program is designed to give people interested in careers in international relief and development an opportunity to increase their overseas experience while gaining exposure to how Catholic Relief Services operates.

Participants, like Mr. Steinbeiser, who is working in Jerusalem's West Bank, get hands-on experience for one year in projects involving agriculture, education, health, HIV/AIDS, and peace efforts.

(continued)

(continued)

Each year, 20 candidates are selected and placed in the program. Competition is tough for the fellowships, and those who get selected typically express their desire for a long-term career at the organization. "We tell them when they start out the first year that our goal is to hire [them]," Mr. Ausmus says, and that is typically what happens: Nearly 90 percent of fellows end up as full-time employees of the charity.

The organization also depends on referrals from employees and others who are involved in international relief work. A Catholic Relief Services worker is awarded a $500 bonus when a person he or she recommended is hired. "The referral system is great because it's really such a small community around the world," Mr. Ausmus says. "You can verify someone's skills and ability and experience. When you hire someone it's always something of a crapshoot. It's great when someone you trust can say, 'I know what he or she can do.'"

Both avenues led Mr. Steinbeiser to Catholic Relief Services: A family friend who knew his interests and career goals referred him, and he then applied for the fellowship and received an assignment to the West Bank.

Yet, Mr. Steinbeiser says, to continue attracting people such as himself, international relief charities need to step up efforts to offer competitive salaries—and also publicize the many unexpected benefits the jobs offer. "A lot of NGOs need to market the lifestyle more attractively and more widely, emphasizing the opportunities for personal growth and making the difference in the lives of others," Mr. Steinbeiser says. "There is already a lot of interest in these positions for these reasons, but the persistence of hot spots means the talent pool needs to be continually renewed and enlarged."

Source: Westcott, S. (2008) Excerpt from "Recruiting in dangerous times," *The Chronicle of Philanthropy*, January 24, 2008.

Online Job Posting

For nonprofits that post jobs, the internet offers an array of sources to reach potential candidates. Through its many websites and applications, the internet is an important method for job posting for many nonprofits. According to the nonprofit employment trends survey, online job posting is the most popular method of job posting, second only to informal and formal networks.[19] The survey also found that US nonprofits post their jobs on both online and print editions of newspapers and job posting websites as well as on social media which are discussed below. Online job posting adds value to the recruitment in different ways. First, the global reach of the internet ensures that the jobs posted by a nonprofit can attract qualified candidates from within and outside the local community of the organization. Second, online job posting can be targeted to specific candidate segments to emphasize the knowledge, skills and abilities required in the job. This could save time and resources during the recruitment process by screening out candidates who do not have the relevant competencies. Third, online job posting can increase efficiency in recruitment administration, selection and benchmarking. Basically, it makes it easier to track resumes, download resumes into a database, and search for candidates, all of which enhance the selection process. It also makes it easier to track recruitment metrics such as time to fill and cost of recruitment. This enables the organization to compare the performance of the recruitment function to nonprofit benchmarks in the area.

Beyond the actual recruiting goals and process, online job posting gives the nonprofit an added web presence that could benefit the services and advocacy work of the organization. For small and new nonprofits, online job postings could be another way of building the brand of the organization. Many well-established nonprofits already understand that online job postings enable them to burnish the brand of the organization. It is also a way of constantly maintaining awareness of the nonprofit brand without the significant cost of advertising. Box 6.3 shows highlights from two online job postings that emphasize the brand of the nonprofits.

BOX 6.3 EXAMPLES OF BRANDING IN JOB POSTINGS

Amnesty International

If you are talented and passionate about human rights then Amnesty International wants to hear from you. By working for Amnesty International you will have a chance to make a difference and to help us make more of an impact.

YWCA Toronto

YWCA Toronto is an association of diverse and caring women dedicated to improving the lives of women and girls through dynamic leadership, advocacy and a range of unique and essential services that promote personal growth and economic independence.

Artemis Center, Ohio

Artemis Center—"Guiding victims of Domestic Violence towards hope and healing."

Sources: https://careers.amnesty.org/
https://charityvillage.com/jobs/search-results/job-detail.aspx?id=287688&l=2
http://careercenter.nptimes.com/jobs/#/detail/5968999/3,false

Social Media

Social media is essentially a sub-component of online recruiting with distinctive features. Rather than the general online job postings, social media can target potential candidates based on their interests, affiliation with groups, causes, etc. Hence, it can be inexpensive and more effective. In fact, social media such as LinkedIn, Facebook or Twitter can be used as a word of mouth recruiting method. This happens when employees and stakeholders simply post or send the link for a job to their personal network. Social media is now also used to pre-screen candidates by reviewing their profiles and relevant information. Nonprofits could also search LinkedIn for profiles or use the premium service of the social media site to find candidates. Such premium services and effort to roll out a social media campaign would cost the organization more.

Job Fairs

There are numerous opportunities for nonprofits to participate in job fairs. Although job fairs are often open to organizations from different sectors, there are a few that are focused on nonprofit and public sector organizations. It is also possible for a network of nonprofits in a local area to organize a job fair together. The advantage of job fairs is that the nonprofit will be able to reach a broader applicant base. Job fairs are also a means for nonprofits to create brand awareness for the organization in their local community.

Campus Recruitment

Recruiting on college and university campuses is an effective means of connecting with new graduates. For nonprofits with internship programs, campus recruitment is the major channel for recruiting candidates. It is a particularly important source for building a future talent pool by establishing a recruitment relationship. For example, a recruitment relationship established with second- and third-year students could be leveraged for job opportunities when they are seniors or in the labor market. Campus recruiting is also a way of sourcing candidates for immediate job vacancies that require minimal experience. The number of campus job fairs and how to choose which to attend could pose a decision-making challenge for nonprofits. To overcome this disadvantage, the organization should determine the relevance of the education and skills of the students of the particular college or university to the recruitment needs of the organization. Also, the HR staff may attend some to assess the outcome or yield in resumes from the campus fair.

Recruiting from Volunteers

Nonprofits have a unique advantage based on the access to the diverse talent pool that is available from their volunteers. Recruiting from the volunteer pool has some advantages that are similar to those of current employees such as awareness of the competencies, performance and understanding of the values of the organization. As a recruitment method, nonprofits can interface volunteer management with employee recruitment. First, nonprofits could and do target job postings to volunteers. Job vacancies are posted internally specifically for volunteers either before the external posting or simultaneously with the external posting. Second, the recruiter or hiring manager can review the volunteer skills inventory to determine whether there is a match between the knowledge and skills required in a vacant job and those of current volunteers. Third, the nonprofit could simply encourage volunteers to apply for available job vacancies. Fourth, recruiting from volunteers is less costly and orientation into the organization will likely take less time.

Overdependence on volunteers as a recruitment source has disadvantages. First, it could impact volunteer retention in a nonprofit. Volunteers who have joined a nonprofit with the hope that they will eventually transition to an employee role could be frustrated if such an opportunity does not materialize. Second, if volunteers who are competing with external candidates for vacant jobs are somehow accorded undue consideration due to their role, it could limit the ability of the nonprofit to attract new talent. Volunteers must be considered for vacant jobs based on the knowledge, skills, and the relevant experience they possess in relation to the job. To mitigate the disadvantages of recruiting from volunteers, nonprofits should outline a clear policy and adopt consistent practice on volunteer recruitment. For example, it should be clear whether volunteers should be considered as internal or external candidates.

Additional Methods

Nonprofits also have a number of other methods for recruiting employees. Reports have shown that many nonprofits recruit employees through their *internship* programs. Formal or informal internships are an excellent way of introducing potential employees to the organization, its operation, policies and processes. It is also an opportunity for the interns to check out the nonprofit as a potential organization they would like to work for. It could be considered a form of *realistic job preview* because the candidates will have a firsthand view of the job and the organization.

Advertisement in print *newspapers* is another method for recruiting that nonprofits use. Print advertisement is generally significantly more costly than online job posting. A nonprofit with many vacancies can also organize a recruitment open house. Such an event would include review of resumes and at least pre-screening interviews. If resources are available, more detailed interviews could be organized as part of a recruitment open house.

Recruitment Process for Nonprofits

There is no doubt that the outcome of a recruitment drive is related to a significant extent on the process adopted to achieve the goals of attracting and recruiting qualified candidates to the nonprofit. From a regular recruitment of one or two employees to large-scale recruitment projects, the recruitment process adopted and how it is implemented are critical. As outlined in the discussion on HR planning in Chapter 5, also important is the need to align the recruitment process with SHRM. The recruitment plan and process must facilitate the HR imperative of supporting the organizational goals of the non-profit in terms of recruiting employees with the knowledge, skills and abilities required by the organization. The generic recruitment process presented in Figure 6.1 underscores this goal.

Develop recruitment plan. The recruitment process generally starts with the information provided by the *job analysis* completed as part of HR planning. This information includes clearly defined job requirements which summarize the responsibilities as well as the job specification that describes the knowledge, skills and abilities required for the job. The information is the core of the recruitment plan and must drive the entire recruitment process to ensure that the recruiters and managers involved in the recruitment do not lose sight of the goal. It is important for HR to review the job requirements with the hiring manager to see whether there is need to update the responsibilities and job specification before posting the job. Previous recruitment for the job should also be reviewed to incorporate learning from it into the current plan. The goal of the plan is to provide a roadmap for the recruitment process. As such, it must explore and determine where and how the job will be posted, who will be involved in the

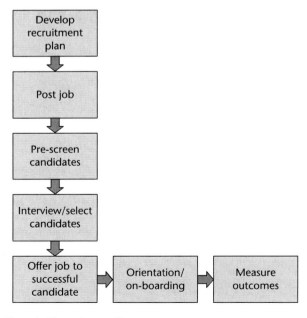

FIGURE 6.1 Generic Recruitment Process

process, and a timeline for the recruitment. The recruitment plan does not have to be elaborate but must include the key components above.

Post job. Generally, there are three aspects in this phase of the process. First, the content of the job posting must communicate the responsibilities, job specification and the brand of the nonprofit. The latter is essential not only to attract potential candidates for the position, but also to build awareness of the brand of the nonprofit. The job posting is another platform nonprofits can use to communicate to the public who they are and what they do. Second, the recruitment method should use sources that are most likely to reach the candidates who have requirements for the job. Many nonprofits combine two or more methods when posting their jobs. It is not uncommon to combine word of mouth with online job posting. Third, the job posting must provide a basis for the pre-screening that will be used to shortlist candidates.

Pre-screening. It used to be that pre-screening was meant to clarify information that was not clear on a candidate's resume and covering letter or provide the opportunity to ask preliminary questions about the candidates in order to create a shortlist when there were many candidates who met the minimum requirements. The purpose of pre-screening has been extended with the use of internet search engines and social networking sites. HR practitioners and hiring managers now routinely use the internet to know as much as possible about a candidate. Information collected surreptitiously is now used to determine whether to invite the candidate for an interview or not. While some of the information gleaned from the internet could be relevant, nonprofit HR professionals and hiring managers should focus on the purpose of pre-screening, which is to clarify information and shortlist candidates for interviews.

Interview and select candidates. This is perhaps the most crucial phase of the recruitment process. An interview is a two-way street. For the organization, it provides an invaluable opportunity for the organization to formally assess the knowledge, skills and abilities of the candidates. The interview is also an opportunity to provide more information about the organization and the job to the candidate: after the application and pre-screening, which generally do not involve face-to-face contact, it is the second level in the pre-employment relationship between the potential candidates and the organization. Hence, it requires special attention. Interview questions should be developed specifically to elicit information that will help the interviewers to determine whether a candidate has the required competencies and experience for the job. The questions should also seek to find out about the possible fit between the candidate and the values of the nonprofit. Potential employees use the interview to learn more about the organization, its people, environment, and operational challenges. Many candidates research organizations they are seeking employment with on the internet and ask questions about the job during the interview.

If interviews are important, interview questions are the centerpiece of the activities and outcome of the recruitment process. The two major types of interview questions are *situational* and *behavioral-based* interview questions. With *situational questions*, candidates are asked how they would respond to a hypothetical situation. The intention is to know what the candidate would do in the particular situation. For example, in a nonprofit that provides settlement services to displaced people, a candidate for a frontline position could be asked this question: what type of information would you ask a client with an identity document to provide? *Behavioral-based interview* questions are designed to find out what a candidate has done in an actual situation. Using the same example of a frontline staff, the candidate could be asked this behavioral-based question: tell us what you did when a client did not provide the information you required to assist him. Interviews could be conducted by one interviewer or by a panel of interviewers. When a panel interview is used, an employee from the department is generally part of the panel.

In addition to the interview questions, different *tests* are available to organizations to aid in the selection process. Currently, the extent to which nonprofits use tests as part of the selection process is not clear. The final piece of information required to facilitate the selection decision is provided through the reference check. A *reference check* is conducted to collect information about the candidate's experience and performance from current or previous organizations. It is generally advisable to conduct a reference check with the direct supervisors of the candidate. Once a final decision has been made, the HR professional and the hiring manager will work out how and when the job will be offered to the successful candidate. Unsuccessful candidates should also be contacted to inform them about the outcome of the selection process.

Orientation. The purpose of orientation is to facilitate the transition of the new employee into the nonprofit. It is intended to educate the new employee about the job, the department, if applicable, and the organization. Orientation helps the new employee to bridge that gap to a new job and adjust to a new role. It also helps the new employee to learn about the performance expectations. In recent years, orientation has been subsumed under a broader socialization process into a new organization known as *onboarding*. Onboarding provides an opportunity for managers to clearly articulate performance expectations, provide coaching and monitor performance against role expectations from the start-up to six months or one year after commencement of employment. More importantly, it enables managers to give new employees ongoing support, education and sense of security. It also gives new employees the opportunity to ask questions, better understand expectations and feel supported as they transition into their new roles (Box 6.4).

BOX 6.4 ONBOARDING AT PRS INC.

At PRS Inc. the strategy on recruitment is exemplified through an emphasis on employee referral and an onboarding program that facilitates the

HR strategy of the organization. The Virginia-based nonprofit provides community programs and services to assist individuals with mental illness, emotional and/or behavioral disorders to achieve personal wellness, recovery and community integration.

PRS nurtured such an atmosphere through its efforts to not only hire the right people, but to ensure those hired fully understand their jobs and how they relate to the PRS's overall goals. A new hire undergoes an entrance interview between three and six months after they start work. The organization wants to gauge how accurately the work was explained during the hiring process, orientation and training; determine initial job satisfaction; and, discover areas that may need improvement.

Virginia Tischner, the director of Human Resources, notes that the organization uses onboarding to ensure that every employee is getting the same information in the same way in a manner that relates to each specific job. Wendy Gradison, president and CEO, adds that all top managers of the organization participate in the orientation so each new hire understands the role of the organization and how it fits into the community, PRS's operations and services, the agency's financial picture and how each individual role affects that picture. "We think it's very important that every employee understand that everything they do helps not only the client, but also helps PRS met its goals."

Source: Excerpt from Morton, Gary (2013) "Employee referrals gets jobs filled, challenges keep them going," *The NonProfit Times Best Nonprofits to Work For*, 2013.

Recruitment metrics. Measuring the outcomes of the recruitment function is important to ensure continuous improvement, effectiveness and efficiency. There are various metrics that are available to provide insight and guide decision-making on recruitment. Generally, recruitment metrics include measures of *cost of recruitment, cost per hire, time to fill, interview to hire ratio, quantity of resumes, offers to acceptance,* and *hire by source*. The metrics will be discussed in detail in Chapter 13. The ability to measure these indicators is dependent on the availability of reliable data. Many recruitment management systems and online job posting sites have features that provide good data. Often the challenge is about combining traditional recruitment methods such as receiving resumes by mail or fax with online systems and limited resources to support the HR analytics function.

Each step in the recruitment process has a cost component. HR professionals must work with the hiring managers to consider the cost of the different options in the process. For example, a job posting in the print edition of a newspaper generally costs more than the online edition. Using metrics, HR professionals should discuss the cost/benefit analysis of posting in either print, online or in both editions of the newspaper. Also relevant is the timeline assigned to each step in the recruitment process. While this could vary depending on how difficult it is to recruit for the specific position, the level of the position and the structure of the HR function in a nonprofit, each step in the recruitment process should be completed within a few weeks to ensure that the process is efficient and meets the need of the organization.

Summary

Recruitment is not only an important SHRM function, it is a survival function in nonprofit organizations. The unique challenges and opportunities in the environment of a nonprofit have created a context in which nonprofit HR professionals and hiring managers are constantly required to balance the need to recruit for the mission and competencies with the need of the current imperative such as what the funders want now. This chapter examines why it is important to understand the challenges and how they relate to recruitment. Since many nonprofits are small in size and have minimal resources, the recruitment function is sometimes less formalized and not aligned to the strategy of the organization. The recruitment methods and processes discussed in this chapter could provide basic how-to steps and strategies that nonprofit managers can use in their recruitment. As the gateway into the organization, recruitment sets the stage for the other HR functions such as training and development.

Discussion Questions

1. Explain the importance of values in the recruitment of employees in nonprofit organizations.
2. Your nonprofit organization is finding it difficult to attract new employees. You have been asked to look into the issue and offer recommendations. What are some of the factors you will consider in your analysis?
3. In the past year, a number of candidates have declined a job offer from your nonprofit organization because of salary concerns. What other factor(s) can you use to convince candidates that your organization is a good place to work?
4. What are some behavioral questions you will ask during an interview to ensure that there is a fit between a candidate and the culture of your nonprofit?

Notes

1 Berkshire, J. (2011) "As new graduates size up the job horizon, smart recruiting matters," *Chronicle of Philanthropy*. http://philanthropy.com/article/How-Charities-Can-Recruit-the/126956/. Retrieved April 3, 2011.
2 Information for this summary is based on an article in the *Chronicle of Philanthropy* and the Teach For America website.
3 Nye, D. (1988) *Alternative Staffing Strategies*. Washington, DC: Bureau of National Affairs.
4 Akingbola, K. (2006) "Strategy and human resource management in nonprofit organizations: Evidence from Canada," *International Journal of Human Resource Management*, 17(10): 1707.

5   Nye, *Alternative Staffing Strategies*, p. 1.
6   Akingbola, K. (2004) "Staffing, retention and government funding," *Nonprofit Management & Leadership,* 14(4): 453–465.
7   Mello, J. A. (2011) *Strategic Human Resource Management*, 3rd Edition. Mason, OH: South-Western Centage Learning.
8   Akingbola, K. (2013) "A model of strategic nonprofit human resource management," *Voluntas: International Journal of Voluntary and Nonprofit Organizations,* 24(1): 214–240.
9   Brown, W. A., & Yoshioka, C. (2003) "Mission attachment and satisfaction as factors in employee retention." *Nonprofit Leadership and Management,* 14(1): 5–18.
10 O'Neill, M., & Young, D. R. (1988) "Educating managers of nonprofit organizations," in M. O'Neill & D. R. Young (Eds.), *Educating Managers of Nonprofit Organizations* (pp. 1–21). New York: Praeger.
11 Akingbola, "Staffing, retention and government funding."
12 Scope of the Nonprofit Sector. Independent Sector. http://www.independentsector. org/scope_of_the_sector#sthash.JXfXkACh.dpbs. Retrieved November, 2013
13 Clark, J. (2007) *The UK Voluntary Sector Almanac.* London: The UK Workforce Hub at NCVO.
14 Barbeito, C. L., & Bowman, J. P. (1998) *Nonprofit Compensation and Benefits Practices.* New York: Wiley.
15 Handy, F., Mook, L., & Quarter, J. (2008) "The interchangeability of paid staff and volunteers in nonprofit organizations," *Nonprofit and Voluntary Sector Quarterly*, 37(1): 76–92.
16 Roeger, K., Blackwood, A. S., and Pettijohn, S. L. (2012) *The Nonprofit Almanac 2012.* Washington, DC: Urban Institute Press. http://www.urban.org/books/nonprofit-almanac-2012/
17 Nonprofit HR Solutions (2013) *Nonprofit Employment Trends Survey.* http://www. nonprofithr.com/wp-content/uploads/2013/03/2013-Employment-Trends-Survey-Report.pdf. Retrieved December, 2013.
18 Schwind, H., Das, H., & Wagar, T. (2007) *Canadian Human Resource Management*, 8th Edition. Toronto: McGraw-Hill Ryerson.
19 Nonprofit HR Solutions (2013) *Nonprofit Employment Trends Survey.*

7

TRAINING AND DEVELOPMENT

Learning Objectives

After studying this chapter, you should be able to:

1. Describe the basic concepts in training and development.
2. Discuss the strategic importance of training in nonprofits.
3. Gain understanding of what a training cycle is.
4. Explain types of training and relate them to the context of nonprofits.
5. Identify important trends in training and development.

London's Air Ambulance Value Training[1]

London's Air Ambulance takes training seriously. As the CEO Graham Hodgkin noted, the UK charity understands the need for nonprofits to find more innovative and cost-effective ways of offering training and development. Established in 1989 to provide emergency medical services to victims of serious injury in London, the charity has a mission to "provide patients with the world's most innovative and effective pre-hospital care." This mission puts training right at the core of what the charity is all about. However, similar to most nonprofits, there is minimal budget for training. With a total income of £3,524,804 in 2012/13 and a public service with high demand, the training budget of the organization for charity staff compared to doctors and pilots is low but growing. London's Air Ambulance leverages its network to provide training in specific areas. For example, it invites both corporate and individual supporters who have specialist skills in social networking, public affairs, business planning and marketing to provide training in these areas. In addition, staff, including the CEO, offer training to augment the training the organization pays for and the pro bono training provided by supporters.[2]

Introduction

The need to adapt to the unique drivers of change in the environment and develop the core competencies required for a nonprofit to achieve its strategic goals is critical to drive the mission of the organization. This requires managers to position the organization by investing in what is often the only asset of nonprofits, its human resources. Training and development are vital to the strategic goals and the mission of nonprofits. This chapter explains the strategic importance of training and development in nonprofit organizations. First, it introduces training and development starting with onboarding as an integral function for the development of human capital in organizations. This is followed by an examination of the role and types of training. Key activities and tools in training and development of employees are discussed from the point of view of the environment of nonprofits.

Onboarding

The need to ensure that employees have the knowledge, skills and abilities to perform the job includes the understanding of the culture, processes and systems in an organization. In Chapter 6, the concept of *onboarding* was introduced briefly as part of the recruitment process. Onboarding is a comprehensive process of facilitating new employees to learn not only about the job, the work unit and the organization, but also about performance expectations, resources and support that are available in the organization. It is designed to educate new employees about the organization as a system of interdependent job functions. The onboarding process for employees is a strategic partnership between managers, team members, HR professionals, work units and organizational stakeholders. A core element of onboarding is to facilitate employee engagement from the start, and align their goals with those of the organization. This is particularly important in nonprofits where it is critical to start to foster an understanding and linkage between the new employee and the values of the organization from the pre-employment stage.

Benefits of Onboarding

In broad terms, nonprofits and organizations in general need onboarding. It offers not an event but a process for kick-starting how the organization can facilitate the fit between an employee and the job, as well as building an engaging work environment. Hence, it serves a number of purposes for the nonprofit organization.

Make Employees Feel Welcomed from Day One

This enables new employees to get off to a good start. It also minimizes the initial challenges of a new work environment.

Enhance Employee Performance Sooner

A comprehensive onboarding program clarifies the performance expectations and provides opportunities for managers to coach employees as they transition into the new role. This helps to remove performance anxiety and contributes to the confidence of the new employee.

Enable Shared Values

The sooner employees understand and buy into the values of a nonprofit, the more likely they are to show greater motivation to contribute to mission of the organization. Research has indicated that employees are attracted to nonprofits because of their mission. Thus, one of the goals of onboarding for a nonprofit should be to confirm and consolidate the values the new employees have bought into before joining the organization.

Foster Quicker and Better Understanding of the Organization's Processes, Practices, and Policies

Due to the fact that it is more comprehensive than orientation, onboarding provides better opportunities for new employees to understand the processes, practices and policies of the nonprofit. It basically gives new employees more opportunities to ask questions.

Create a Performance Culture

Onboarding is a way of affirming the commitment of the organization to providing the resources and support new employees need to perform. It communicates that the organization fosters a culture in which performance is collaborative and supported through coaching and mentoring.

Create a Learning Culture

Similarly, onboarding contributes to a learning culture. The feedback discussion and learning needs that are identified in onboarding emphasize the importance of learning in the nonprofit. The investment of resources to onboarding would signal to the new employees that the organization takes learning seriously.

Lay the Foundation for Excellent Teams

Onboarding gives existing team members the opportunity to clarify their roles and explain formal and informal norms to new employees. This would likely reduce the likelihood of the avoidable conflict that tends to occur when new members join a team. The relationships that a new employee builds within and outside of the work unit would ease interaction after the onboarding is over.

Reduce Cost of Process Error

By providing a detailed clarification of performance expectations, coaching from a manager, and more opportunities to learn about processes over a longer period of time, onboarding helps to ensure that new employees are less likely to make costly errors. Perhaps they may be able to bring new insights that could help to increase efficiency.

Increase Retention

As indicated above, onboarding helps employees to transition to a new work environment, communicate performance expectations, and understand the culture of a nonprofit. These factors contribute significantly to reducing performance anxiety and providing a sense of belonging for the new employee. In turn, these factors reduce the likelihood that the new employee would consider resigning due to aspects of the job or the organization. New employees who are confident about their performance, clear about the role and perceive that they have the support of the manager and team members are less likely to quit their job.

Onboarding is a training function that must be designed in collaboration with line managers, recruiters and key organizational stakeholders. In small nonprofits, which often do not have a HR department, onboarding is coordinated between managers and frontline staff who collaborate to facilitate the transition of the new employees. It is also possible for nonprofits with an HR sub-committee of the board of directors to utilize the expertise of board members to develop the content of the onboarding program. Irrespective of the size of the nonprofit, onboarding should be embraced an as important process through which the organization can foster the fit between employees and its culture. Figure 7.1 shows an overview of a strategic onboarding program in a Toronto nonprofit hospital.

While research on onboarding in nonprofits is limited, one study on orientation of social workers advocated for onboarding long before it became a prevalent concept. According to Julie Abramson, "an acculturation model of orientation implies a process that takes place over time and, as such consumes more organizational resources than a brief orientation period."[3] She sees this as a way to address the dissatisfaction social workers indicated they feel when they join a new organization.

As a progressive HR practice, onboarding is being adopted as a tool to support performance management, to enhance an employee's comprehensive understanding of HR practices, and as a proactive channel for immersing the new employee in executing the strategy of the organization from day one. The training

Phase 1: Know and Connect	Phase 2: Learn and Assimilate	Phase 3: Perform, Give and Receive Feedback	Phase 4: Grow and Excel
Before start date	*Entry—first 2 weeks*	*3, 7 and 12 weeks post hire*	*1 year and ongoing*
• Introduce organization • Share culture and values • Communicate benefits • Describe locations • Discuss working environment	• Celebrate organization • Share department goals • Review expectations • Review resource, support and policies	• Share keys to success • Complete personal training needs assessment • Create performance and development plan • Perform probationary reviews *6 months post hire*	• Review progress over time • Follow up on learning • Review achievements and/or completed job-related projects • Discuss feedback, how to improve performance and build career

FIGURE 7.1 Strategic Onboarding Program Example

function starts at the onboarding stage for new employees in organizations. It is important for nonprofits to adopt onboarding as one of the frontline components of their HR strategy in order to maximize employee value contribution and foster employee engagement.

Training and Development

Training is always not far from the surface in most discussions about an organization's performance and effectiveness. At the strategic and operational levels of the organization, the keys to individual, team and organizational performance must at the least consider training. Training involves the acquisition of knowledge, skills and abilities to improve the performance of employees in their current positions.[4] It is essentially a planned intervention by an organization designed to help employees to elevate their performance now, not later in their career. Different organizations and professions have training that may be required as part of the compliance for the specific industry or for professional practice. For example, New York State requires certain healthcare professions to have infection control training every four years while employees in most organizations in the province of Ontario must complete workplace hazardous material information system (WHMIS) training. Training is extremely diverse. It could range from the acquiring of knowledge and skills of processes, tools and software to competencies such as negotiation and conflict management.

On the parallel side of training is *development*. Development entails the acquisition of knowledge, skills and abilities for the purpose of future job responsibilities, career path of the employee and goals of the organization. The focus of development is to support both the organization and the employee down the road as the employee's career advances.[5] As one would expect, many of the approaches used in training programs are relevant in development, albeit with a different goal. The objective of development is generally to prepare employees for management and senior leadership responsibilities.[6] Moreover, training and development feed into other HR functions. The knowledge, skills and abilities acquired in training feed forward into and complement the competencies acquired in development. For example, at the Canadian Red Cross, most of the knowledge and skills employees acquire in the volunteer management training program of the organization are critical in management and senior leadership roles.

Learning in organizations encompasses both training and development. It involves all the opportunities an organization provides for the acquisition of knowledge, skills and abilities to facilitate the behavioral change that will enhance the performance of the employee and the organization and, as a result, drive the achievement of the goals of the organization. Most of the learning in organizations could be classified under *non-formal* and *informal* learning as opposed to *formal* learning.[7] Formal learning generally refers to the educational ladder that starts from preschool to graduate studies. Non-formal learning refers to all organized education programs that take place outside the formal school system.[8] These are typically short-term and include many of the training and development opportunities offered by organizations. Informal learning occurs in spaces and places that are not necessarily governed by curricula, experts or timelines. It could be intentional, implied or simply through socialization.

Human resource development (HRD) is another relevant umbrella concept that is important to understanding training and development. HRD integrates the goals of training and development with organizational development, change and strategic management for individual, group and organizational outcomes.[9] One comprehensive definition describes HRD as "encompassing adult learning at the workplace, training and development, organisational development and change, organisational learning, knowledge management, management development, coaching, performance improvement, competence development, and strategic human resource development."[10] In addition to highlighting the wide-ranging purposes of HRD, this definition also demonstrates the links of training and development to the different aspects of HR and the functions of training and development in organizations including nonprofits.

Context of Training and Development in Nonprofits

At the core of training and development is the expectation of behavior change required to support goals of an organization. This central objective of training is similar to the core focus of nonprofits. As discussed in Chapter 1, the raising of awareness with the objective of driving change on social, political, health, education and economic issues is the stock in trade of nonprofits. Moreover, the raising of awareness, which happens to be the starting point of many nonprofits, is basically a training and development effort. As a result, training is inextricably connected to the mission, operations and performance of nonprofits in many ways.

First, employees and managers in nonprofits require unique competencies in addition to basic management knowledge, skills and abilities such as budgeting, planning and decision-making. For example, Herman and Heimovics identified eleven essential competencies for managing the operational challenge of non-profit organizations: (1) competency in new program development; (2) collaboration skills; (3) fundraising skills; (4) skill to establish (when) programs decline; (5) management skills; (6) lobbying skills; (7) skill to respond to human resource actions; (8) skill to manage relationship with government officials; (9) skill to lead accreditation efforts; (10) skill to interact with the board; (11) skill to develop human resources; and (12) employees' recognition skills.[11] The implication of these sector-specific competencies is that the training needs have reflected the importance of these capabilities. This is evidenced in the findings of a research study by the Nonprofit Leadership Alliance that showed the competencies in Figure 7.2 from the most important to the least important training needs of nonprofit jobs from entry level to mid-level managers and mid-level to senior leaders.[12]

Second, the routine operational activities of nonprofits are training related. Once new employees are aware of the mission of a nonprofit through recruitment and onboarding, the internal and external activities of the organization generally continue to reinforce the core objectives of the nonprofit. In effect, continuous learning about the culture and values and how to navigate the relationship with stakeholders is part of developing the competencies of a nonprofit employee. Training is used to identify, understand and integrate how employees learn about the values, the activities and the players in a nonprofit in order to better support the goals and mission of the organization.

Third, training is one of the HR practices that funders, including government, specifically ask nonprofits to provide as part of the requirements for funding. In addition to being part of the accountability requirements, nonprofit researchers have suggested that training is one of the ways funders exercise control and emphasize their interests and values on the activities and performance of nonprofits.[13] Since it is unlikely that the training developed to meet the requirements of one funder will also meet the demands of all other funders, this creates additional barriers in the effort of nonprofits to align the training they offer employees with other HR practices and the HR strategy of the organization. As illustrated in the example of London's Air Ambulance above and other examples below, financial resources for training are extremely scarce in nonprofits; competing demands for training by funders have implications for the meagre training dollars of nonprofits.

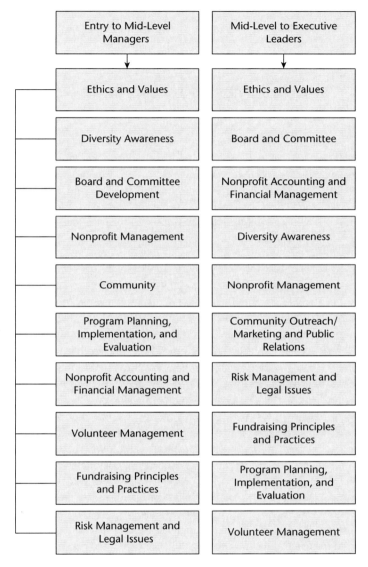

Entry to Mid-Level Managers	Mid-Level to Executive Leaders
Ethics and Values	Ethics and Values
Diversity Awareness	Board and Committee
Board and Committee Development	Nonprofit Accounting and Financial Management
Nonprofit Management	Diversity Awareness
Community	Nonprofit Management
Program Planning, Implementation, and Evaluation	Community Outreach/ Marketing and Public Relations
Nonprofit Accounting and Financial Management	Risk Management and Legal Issues
Volunteer Management	Fundraising Principles and Practices
Fundraising Principles and Practices	Program Planning, Implementation, and Evaluation
Risk Management and Legal Issues	Volunteer Management

FIGURE 7.2   Training Needs of Levels of Positions in Nonprofits

Fourth, the importance of training and development in nonprofits has also been heightened by the need to adapt to the constant and often unpredictable change in the industry environment of the organization. The era of contracting and increased dependence on government funding has necessitated the need to position the organization to be adaptive, innovative and strategic.[14] It is the ability to effectively manage and leverage this change that makes nonprofits competitive. This reality means that the organization must use training to continuously provide employees with new skills requirements. Box 7.1 highlights how the

New Jersey Society for Certified Accountants is using training both to enhance the skills of employees and to meet the changing needs of their students.

BOX 7.1 TRAINING AT NEW JERSEY SOCIETY FOR CERTIFIED PUBLIC ACCOUNTANTS

Training is a big deal at the New Jersey Society of Certified Public Accountants. The organization is small, with only 40 employees, "so there's not much room for advancement" which is one of the components covered in the Training and Development section of the survey, said Ellen McSherry, chief operating officer. That led the executive team to focus on "how we can help each individual advance his or her own skills, whether inside or outside the office."

The emphasis on training makes sense for practical reasons, as well as for improving employee morale, McSherry said. "The world is changing. What was a good skills set 10 years ago isn't necessarily a good skills set now."

The society does not want to solely rely upon the newcomers in technological areas, so long-time employees are being retrained. Every Thursday in February, for example, employees attended a 90-minute session on various elements of social media—Facebook, Twitter, etc. Each employee had a photograph taken by a new staff person who does all of the society's video work. The pictures will grace the employees' Facebook and Twitter accounts, through which they are encouraged to stay in touch with member CPAs throughout the state.

NJSCPA Outreach Coordinator Lauren Matullo said tips she picked up during the February social media training are already paying off, especially in her responsibilities as Next Generation Outreach Coordinator. She previously relied on mail, email and face-to-face contact. "I've been able to make more contacts with Twitter and LinkedIn," Matullo said. "When students get an email, if it doesn't catch their attention right away they delete it."

Before the social media training, "I was up-to-date with Facebook but more on a personal level," Matullo said. She learned such media as Twitter and Pinterest and discovered that "while I was on LinkedIn, I wasn't using it to the best ability." She's noticed an increase in students registering for those events after she announces it on LinkedIn. The training impressed on Matullo a sense that the NJSCPA managers see the benefit in letting staff "connect with society, use our social media to their advantage."

Source: Excerpt from Morton, G. (2013) "Small can come up big when it's employee relations," *The NonProfit Times Best Nonprofits to Work For*, 2013.

In all, training is essential to the effectiveness and survival of nonprofit organizations. Changing community needs and technology have also contributed to emphasizing why training is important in nonprofits. However, the challenges of training for nonprofits remain constant. On the one hand, the significant financial constraints of many nonprofits means they are not able to compete in terms of the compensation they offer to employees. On the other hand, nonprofits have used nonmonetary strategies including training not only to help employees to acquire knowledge, skills and abilities but also to retain their employees.[15] Although financial constraints limit the resources available to nonprofits for training, even very small nonprofits often use training to get their message across and to retain employees. In these small nonprofits, training is often the only formal HR function. Finally, to reinforce the importance of training in nonprofits, it has been suggested that nonprofit managers have a positive attitude towards training compared to managers in other sectors.[16]

Benefits of Training and Development

Related to the factors that contribute to the added importance of training and development in nonprofits discussed above, there are specific benefits for employees and the organization. The training investment nonprofits make benefits employees in a number of ways. One, employees acquire knowledge, skills and abilities for not only their job but also their overall competencies. This enhances their ability to advance their career within the organization or with other employers. Two, regardless of whether it is stated as such or not, training could be considered a form of benefit nonprofits provide to employees. This tacit benefit adds to the regular benefits offered by the organization. Three, some of the competencies employees acquire in training are transferable to community activities. In effect, nonprofit employees become informed and engaged community members through the training they receive in their organizations.

The benefits of training and development are extensive for nonprofits. First, consistent with the contributory factors discussed above, training is one of keys to the performance of nonprofits. Organizations that invest in training are better positioned to compete in the contract funding environment of nonprofits because of the skills employees acquire in areas such as the community outreach, marketing, program planning, implementation and evaluation. Second, training and development enhance the quality of the human resource pool available to the nonprofit. The diversity of skills of the human resource pool means greater flexibility for the nonprofit to deploy the competencies of the employees to adapt to change. Third, the training nonprofits provide enhances employees' motivation, which contributes to retention in the organization. Fourth, training contributes to the social exchange between employees and the nonprofit organization. From the discussions in Chapter 3, nonprofit employees could develop a reciprocal obligation to trust and be good to the organization because they perceive that the nonprofit has invested in them and has been good to them in its policies and practices. Fifth, training provides an opportunity to integrate the learning needs of employees into the planning and implementation of the strategy of a non-profit. Training needs determined during the strategic planning process feeds into knowledge and skills the nonprofit should plan to provide to the employees. This connection helps the employees to better understand the strategy of the non-profit. Finally, training is front and center of the strategy of nonprofits to adapt to the dizzying pace of the change in the environment. As nonprofits continuously scan the environment for current and emerging opportunities and threats, training is an important ingredient in the formulation of the goals and competencies required to achieve the goals.

Although nonprofits are under-resourced in terms of their ability to use professional HR expertise, research evidence appears to suggest that nonprofits understand the strategic importance and benefits of training for their organizations and their employees. For example, one UK study found that compared to the public sector, nonprofits provide a similar amount of off-the-job training to employees.[17] Similarly, a Canadian study also reported that nonprofits were more likely to provide training for their employees than for-profit business organizations.[18] The understanding of the importance and benefits of training in nonprofits has even been highlighted in situations where HR practices could be considered not to be strategic.[19] In other words, when nonprofits are not able to align HR practices with the strategy of the organization, at the least, they ensure that training is aligned with their business strategy.

Strategic Training Process

Training and development does not happen in a vacuum. It is a process that is guided by design models that are influenced by systems approach.[20] In effect, questions about strategy, who, what, when, where and how to train are critical to ensure the effectiveness of training for the nonprofit organization and the employee. Since training is competing with many other priorities in nonprofits, managers need to understand what exactly it could deliver in terms of outcomes and what are the specific processes involved in training. One prominent model of training and development is *instructional system design* (ISD). As illustrated in Figure 7.3, this model incorporates the key components of training and development.

Training Needs Analysis

Needs analysis is the first step in the strategic training model. It involves the determination of the organizational performance drivers, expectations and gaps that might exist. The analysis of the organizational context and any gap between the desired and actual performance are key to ensuring the effectiveness of training. The *organizational analysis* must carefully collect information about the needs for specific knowledge, skills and abilities in different functional areas in the organization. For example, nonprofits that provide disaster relief services such as

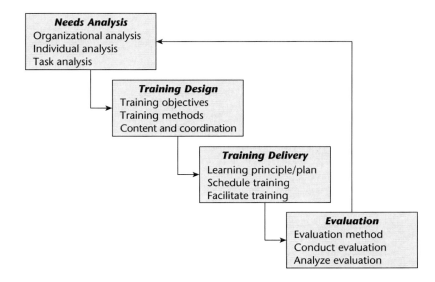

FIGURE 7.3   Strategic Training Model

World Vision in the US offer extensive training that covers different functions in disaster management relevant to their mission.[21] Due to the nature of disaster relief, World Vision also offers specific training on how to effectively respond in times of crisis to external organizational stakeholders. To pinpoint the training that should be provided, a *task analysis* must be completed to help managers to identify the jobs or roles that require the training.

Building on the example of World Vision, employees and managers in the disaster management department would be the primary target of the training on disaster relief and the "train the trainers" workshop that will enable them to train other stakeholders. Since it is unlikely that all employees in a specific job will have the gap between the desired and actual performance, an *individual* or *person analysis* should be completed to determine who needs the training. That involves determining the level of their knowledge and skills vis-à-vis the level required by the organization.

To collect the information required for needs analysis, the trainer will need to review documents, conduct interviews, and survey or observe employees to assess the level of their performance. Since it is often not possible to meet all the training needs of a nonprofit, it may be necessary to rank needs in order of priority and select the needs to be addressed.

Training Design

Once the needs analysis has been completed and it has been determined that there is a performance gap that can be addressed by training, the next step in the strategic training model is the *design* stage. The focus of training design is to outline a comprehensive plan that will include the objectives of the training, the instructional methods, content and coordination of the process. It ensures that the training process is seamless and that there is consistency across the phases of the training process. The training objectives connect the needs analysis to the content and the outcome of training. Box 7.2 shows some sample objectives from nonprofit training programs. The training method and content must consider the participants, what they need to learn, and how it will benefit their jobs. It is particularly critical to ensure that the content of the training meets the specific needs and priorities the organization has identified. Also part of the training design stage is the consideration of how the training will be evaluated. The design of the evaluation tool should be integrated into the training design process. Criteria for evaluation are determined and set out to measure the learning outcomes for the employees and the organization.

BOX 7.2 SAMPLE NONPROFIT TRAINING OBJECTIVES

The learning objectives of this half-day workshop are:

- Understand strategic human resources management.
- Examine various challenges with and strategies for managing human resources in community organizations.
- Learn strategies for providing HRM with or without funding.
- Explore progressive human resource management practices for community organizations.
- Align your organization with opportunities in today's changing operating environment.

Training Delivery

The *training delivery* stage of the model could be considered to be the action step of the process. This is where the employees get the opportunity to acquire the knowledge and skills outlined in the objectives through one or more of the many training methods. Training delivery includes the planning, scheduling and facilitation of the actual training using learning principles. In planning the training, the trainer must decide the method that is most effective for the participants (Box 7.3). Today, many training programs are blended; that is, they combine two or more methods to achieve the learning outcomes. For example, it is not uncommon to combine classroom training with e-learning to maximize the benefits of both methods. On-the-job training methods appear to be common in nonprofits. Scheduling must ensure that the timing of the training is suitable for the employees. Especially, it must avoid critical periods of the year when the organization is particularly busy with funding application deadlines.

BOX 7.3 TRAINING METHODS

- *Behaviour modelling*: An enactment of the desired behaviour. Participants practice behaviour.
- *Case studies*: In groups, participants analyze a problem situation, offer recommendations and action plan.
- *Critical incident*: Participants examine and analyze details of an incident as a basis for better understanding real problems.
- *Demonstration*: An illustrated lecture or presentation.
- *Lecture*: Teaching by an instructor which may incorporate visual aids.
- *Role-plays*: Participants re-enact situations which they face on the job, or which they will face in the future, or which they perceive to be job-like.
- *Simulations*: Participants pretend they are in a real work situation to solve problems.
- *On-the-job training*: Formal learning in actual work situations.

The ability of a trainer to facilitate the essentials of training contributes significantly to the effectiveness of the program. It has been suggested that any training session must include at least three basic components: presentation, practice and assessment. Presentation facilitates the understanding of the basic concepts, knowledge, skills and abilities that are related to the training objective, while practice provides a hands-on opportunity for training participants to engage in experiential activities that will reinforce the learning. As described below, assessment seeks to gauge the learning and the participant's perception of the learning experience. An effective trainer must encourage participation, use positive reinforcement, and react appropriately to cues from the participants.

Evaluation

The evaluation stage of the strategic training model is about assessing whether the expectations outlined in the training objectives have been achieved. It is also about feedback from the participants on the content, the trainer, the materials and other relevant aspects of the training. Evaluation basically focuses on three indicators: performance of the training, performance of the participants and content of the training. The previous stages of the training model provide the basis for and flow into evaluation. The end result of evaluation is continuous improvement. As a result, the information collected in evaluation will help managers, employees and the trainer to introduce improvements in the training and performance.

In practice, evaluation is the holy grail of training. While there are many models of training evaluation, one model that is perhaps more referenced than the others is the four levels of evaluation developed by Donald Kirkpatrick. The model suggests that evaluation should be completed at the following four hierarchical levels: reaction, learning, behavior and results.[22]

Reaction measures the positive and negative response of the participants to the training. They are asked to indicate their reaction to the learning, trainer, materials used in the training, classroom environment and, if applicable, the food served. It is the most common form of training evaluation. Since it is based mostly on the initial reaction of the participants, there is the possibility that the feedback could be subjective and weighted more against one factor than the others. For example, if the participants liked the facilitation style of the trainer, they may rate the learning higher than what they actually experienced.

Learning focuses on the question of whether a participant has actually gained new knowledge or skills. This measure can be operationalized by having a pre- and post-test in which the level of the knowledge and skills of the participants are tested before the training, followed up by a second test after the training. Improvement in the score is attributed the knowledge and skills participants acquire in the training.

Behavior ratchets the indicators of training to the level of action. Behavior measures whether the knowledge and skills acquired in the training are being transferred to the job. For managers, transfer of knowledge and skills to the job is one of the justifications for investing the resources of the organization in training. For transfer of learning to be effective, first managers must create an enabling work climate for the transfer. Second, the training must incorporate strategies employees can use to apply their new knowledge and skills on the job.

Results focus on the ultimate goal of training for the organization. It measures the actual contribution of the knowledge and skills acquired in the training to organizational performance. Results aim to show the specific benefits such as increased productivity and revenue that the organization has derived from the training. Results-related data can be obtained from the various performance metrics a nonprofit generates such as client satisfaction, volunteer participation and cost efficiencies.

Altogether, evaluation ensures that the value and contribution of training to organizational evaluation are emphasized. It also highlights the importance of training as a SHRM function. In addition, training evaluation provides many metrics that managers can use to support decision-making. Metrics are discussed in Chapter 13. Finally, the training evaluation feed forward into a new training process. In other words, the feedback and data collected during evaluation are analyzed as input to identify sources of potential training needs. It is a tool for the needs assessment to address other gaps between the expected performance and actual performance.

Trends in Training in Nonprofits

Training remains a critical SHRM function for nonprofits of different sizes. However, there are mixed signals on whether the need for training is being addressed in the sector.

Inadequate Training

According to the Nonprofit Times Best Nonprofits to Work For 2013, training and development was ranked lowest with 72 percent favourable rating among all participants in the nonprofit workplace survey, and 77 percent favourable rating among nonprofits that made "the best workplace to work for" list. Although the 72 favourable rating for all nonprofits could be considered to be acceptable in general, it is the lowest of the eight general categories which included leadership and planning, corporate culture and communications, role satisfaction, work environment, relationship with supervisor, training and development, pay and benefits, and overall employee engagement.[23] The undertone of this low rating points to concerns about the inadequacy of training in nonprofit organizations in the USA.

A similar concern about the inadequacy of training in nonprofits was evidenced in the recommendations of a commission established by the National Council for Voluntary Organizations in the UK. The Leadership 20:20 Commission recommended that all voluntary sector employees should get 40 hours of professional development.[24] The recommendation is one way of bridging the gap in training.

Resourcefulness and Training

Nonprofit are doing their best to ensure that employees are getting training regardless of the limited financial resources of the organizations. Many nonprofits are using creative and sometimes unconventional methods to provide training for employees. From nonprofit managers utilizing professionals in their network to provide training to asking business corporations to encourage their employees to volunteer their time to provide training to nonprofit employees, nonprofits are finding creative ways to provide training for employees. This is illustrated in the list of initiatives that some nonprofits indicated that they use in order to make training available to employees in an environment characterized by limited financial resources, and the specific examples of Make-a-Wish Foundation, Phoenix and RSPB (see Boxes 7.4, 7.5 and 7.6).

BOX 7.4 CREATIVE WAYS FOR A NONPROFIT TO PROVIDE TRAINING

- Provide training course.
- Use free or low cost existing courses.
- Focus training on only the essential skills.
- Ask volunteers to provide training.
- Enhance in-house training materials.
- Collaborate with other groups.

Source: Gault, K. (2011) "In a time of budget cuts, creativity is needed to training employees," *Chronicle of Philanthropy*, May 10, 2010.

BOX 7.5 TRAINING AT MAKE-A-WISH FOUNDATION, PHOENIX

(Excerpt from article by K. Gault)

A number of our chapter's CEOs and COOs provide training and developmental courses for their staffs at the local level. In addition to being cost-effective, providing training taught by our executives lets our chapters address issues that are specific to their regions.

Kurt Kroemer, Chief Operating Office

Source: Gault, K. (2011) "In a time of budget cuts, creativity is needed to training employees," *Chronicle of Philanthropy*, May 10, 2010.

BOX 7.6 TRAINING AT ROYAL SOCIETY FOR THE PROTECTION OF BIRDS (RSPB)

(Excerpt from article by Patrick McCurry)

The wildlife charity the RSPB has changed its approach to training over the past 10 years. It used to offer a large menu of courses but has reduced that and now delivers most of its training and development in-house, rather than using external providers.

David Hepburn, Head of Training and Development

Source: McCurry, P. (2013) "Charities seek a smarter way," *Third Sector*, July 30, 2013.

TABLE 7.1 Demand for Training

Strongest Demand	Strong Demand	Steady Demand	Emerging Demand
Board governance	Leadership	Cognitive	Succession planning
Grant seeking	Core managerial	behavioural therapy	Use of social media.
Proposal writing	skills	Conflict resolution	
Sustainability	Volunteer	Challenges of	
Fundraising	management	homeless	

Source: Canada HR Council for the Nonprofit Sector (2010) "Professional Development in the Nonprofit Sector What's the Demand?" *Trends & Issues*, http://hrcouncil.ca/labour/trends-issues.cfm.

Top Training Topics

It is conceivable to suggest that one of the outcomes of the limited financial resources for training is that nonprofits are increasingly learning the need to integrate training with SHRM. The link to the SHRM is how training adds real value in nonprofits. Hence, as evidenced in the unique and diverse competencies required in nonprofit organizations, the types of training provided in the sector vary. Although it is somewhat limited, research has given us some insight into the types of training that are particularly high demand in nonprofits. A study by Canada HR Council for the Nonprofit Sector classified the demand for training in nonprofits into four categories.[25] Table 7.1 shows that the training topics that are in high demand are consistent with the competencies identified previously in the chapter.

Summary

Training and development is perhaps the utmost tool for enhancing the quality of human capital and one of the critical ingredients of SHRM in nonprofits. The complexity of the social goods and services, the rate of change in the environment, and the imperious influence of funders on nonprofits emphasize the need for the knowledge, skills and abilities of employees to be constantly updated.

This chapter has examined training as a SHRM function in nonprofits. The discussion of the key concepts and training process highlights the important foundation for trainers and managers in nonprofits to understand how the acquisition of knowledge, skills and abilities is rooted in training and development. The challenges that underlie the environment and drive the strategy of nonprofits lead to the major training needs of the organizations and the trends in the sector. However, similar to the business sector, the role of training is continuously evolving in nonprofits, from a function to support creating awareness about the mission of a nonprofit, to a function used for accountability purposes by funders, and finally to an integrated strategic driver for investing in the human capital to gain competitive advantage in the unique social goods and services market. Since human resource is often the only asset of nonprofits, attracting, motivating and retaining employees by equipping them with the critical knowledge, skills and abilities is one of the best strategies for positioning the organization to adapt to the dizzying pace of change in the sector. In conclusion, more than any other indicator, the creativity these organizations have shown in providing training with meagre financial resources points to the strategic importance of training on the mission of nonprofits.

Discussion Questions

1. Explain the role of onboarding in the training strategy of nonprofit organizations.
2. Why should nonprofits consider the factors that influence training in the environment of the sector? If you consider these factors to be important, what should nonprofits do to manage the impact of the factors?
3. What are some of the factors that could influence the future direction of training in nonprofit organizations?
4. Should nonprofits invest more in training on advocacy or training that are relevant to current services?

Notes

1. Information for this summary is based on an article in the Third Sector, the website of London's Air Ambulance and the Royal Society of Medicine website, https://www.rsm.ac.uk/academ/air_ambulance.php.
2. McCurry, Patrick (2013) "Charities seek a smarter way," *Third Sector*, July 30, http://www.thirdsector.co.uk/news/1192947/Charities-seek-smarter/?DCMP=ILC-SEARCH
3. Abramson, J. S. (1993) "Orienting social work employees in interdisciplinary settings: Shaping professional and organizational perspectives," *Social Work*, 38(2): 152–157.
4. Saks, A. M., & Haccoun, R. (2007) *Managing Performance Through Training and Development*. Toronto: Nelson.
5. Mello, J. A. (2011) *Strategic Human Resource Management*, 3rd Edition. Mason, OH: South-Western Centage Learning.
6. Saks & Haccoun, *Managing Performance Through Training and Development*.
7. Livingstone, D. (1999) "Exploring the icebergs of adult learning: Findings of the first Canadian survey of informal learning practices," *Canadian Journal for the Study of Adult Education*, 13(2): 49–72.
8. Schugurensky, D., & Mundel, K. (2004). "Volunteer work and learning: Hidden dimensions of labour force training," in A. Datnow (Ed.), *International Handbook of Educational Policy*. New York: Kluwer Publishers.
9. McLagan, P. (1989) *Models for HRD Practice*. St Paul, MN: ASTD Press.
10. ESC Toulouse (2002) cited in McGuire, D. (2011) "Foundations of human resource development," in D. McGuire & K. M. Jørgensen, *Human Resource Development Theory and Practice* (pp. 1–11). London: Sage.
11. Herman, R. D., & Heimovics, R. D. (1989) "Critical events in the management of nonprofit organizations: Initial evidence," *Nonprofit and Voluntary Sector Quarterly*, 119: 132.
12. Nonprofit Leadership Alliance (2011) "The skills the nonprofit sector requires of its managers and leaders," www.nonprofitleadershipalliance.org. Retrieved December, 2013.

13 Hall, M., & Banting, K. (2000) "The nonprofit sector in Canada: An introduction," in K. Banting (Ed.), *The Nonprofit Sector in Canada: Roles and Relationships* (pp. 1–28). Kingston, ON: Queen's University School of Policy Studies.

14 Smith, R., & Lipsky, M. (1993) *Nonprofits for Hire: The Welfare State in the Age of Contracting.* Cambridge, MA: Harvard University Press.

15 Parry, E., & Kelliher, C. (2009) "Voluntary sector responses to increased resourcing challenges," *Employee Relations*, 31(1): 9–24.

16 Beattie, R., McDougall, M., & Solomon, S. (1994) "Scottish voluntary sector industry training organization – feasibility study." Scotland: SCVO and the Department of Employment.

17 Parry, E., Kelliher, C., Mills, T., & Tyson, S. (2005) "Comparing HRM in the voluntary and public sectors," *Personnel Review*, 34(5): 588–602.

18 McMullen, K., & Schellenberg, G. (2003b) *Skills and Training in the Non-Profit Sector* (No. 3). Ottawa: Canadian Policy Research Networks.

19 Akingbola, K. (2006) "Strategy and human resource management in nonprofit organizations: Evidence from Canada," *International Journal of Human Resource Management*, 17(10): 1707.

20 Quinton, R. (2011) "Organizational development and training," in B. J. Fried & M. D. Fottler (Eds.), *Human Resources in Healthcare: Managing for Success.* Chicago: Health Administration Press.

21 "Training." World Vision in the U.S., http://www.worldvisionusprograms.org/disaster_response_training.php

22 Kirkpatrick, Donald (1998) *Evaluating Training Programs: The Four Levels*, 2nd Edition. San Francisco: Berrett-Koehler Publishers.

23 Morton, G. (2013) "Best nonprofits to work for 2013," *Nonprofit Times*, www.thenonprofittimes.com.

24 Plummer, J. (2011) "Leadership 20:20 Commission publishes recommendations to improve quality of charity leadership," *Third Sector Online*, December 15, 2011, http://www.thirdsector.co.uk/news/1109489/Leadership-2020-Commission-publishes-recommendations-improve-quality-charity-leadership/?DCMP=ILC-SEARCH

25 Canada HR Council for the Nonprofit Sector (2010) "Professional development in the nonprofit sector: What's the demand?" *Trends & Issues*, http://hrcouncil.ca/labour/trends-issues.cfm.

8

PERFORMANCE MANAGEMENT

Learning Objectives

After studying this chapter, you should be able to:

1. Describe the basic principles of performance management.
2. Explain the methods and processes of performance appraisal.
3. Illustrates the connection between individual performance and organizational performance.
4. Explain the sources of performance information.
5. Describe the challenges and benefits of performance in nonprofits.

Performance Appraisal at Centre Francophone de Toronto

Performance management is first and foremost about providing employees the tools they need to achieve their performance objectives at the Centre francophone de Toronto. The nonprofit organization's mission is to support the full development of the Francophone community in all its diversity in the Greater Toronto Area. In this respect, it offers a number of services that are intended to enhance the well-being of the Francophone community including health, children and family, newcomer, employment and legal aid services. With 98 employees, the Centre francophone de Toronto focuses its performance management on the employee. Hence, the collaboration between the employee and the manager is critical to the process. The employee's self-appraisal is emphasized. Managers and employees understand that the performance management system is based on consensus. If there is no agreement between a manager and an employee about the performance ratings or other parts of the appraisal, the performance appraisal could be referred to the senior level of the organization.

Introduction

Simply put, organizations are established to achieve goals. Typically, to achieve the goals senior leadership has set for an organization, the management must foster and sustain a level of performance that will lead to this outcome. In essence organizational performance is the key to achieving the goals of the organization. As discussed in the review of the theories that underlie strategic human resource management (SHRM) in Chapter 2, all resources, systems and processes in the organization must work together toward the defined goals. Since human resource is the most critical resource that drives the performance of the organization, how employees perform and the systems and processes used to manage and drive improvement in their performance are vital to achieving the goals of the organization. This is the focus of performance management.

In this chapter, we examine performance management as a SHRM process in nonprofit organizations. The chapter presents the principles and methods of performance appraisal of employees in organizations. The chapter emphasizes how to drive performance improvement and behavior that will help the organization. The connection between individual and organizational performance and the role of the employee self-assessment are discussed. A process guideline for conducting effective performance appraisal is also provided.

Performance Management

Generally, *performance management* encompasses all the activities, systems and processes that are deployed to enable and support employees to contribute the maximum of their knowledge, skills and abilities to the organization. It also includes the organizational culture. As a strategic process, performance management is about engaging employees and leveraging their human capital in order to facilitate the performance of the organization. At the strategic and operational levels, it links organizational goals and operational objectives to employee performance and engagement. For this reason, performance management is a collaborative process that involves the manager, the employee and the senior leadership of the organization.

Importantly, performance management also links HR practices to the business strategy the organization is using to advance competitive advantage. All the critical interactions in HR are directly or indirectly related to performance management. The learning, motivation and retention of employees are made possible through performance management. Organizations also need it to manage the reward and recognition of employees. It is the centerpiece of SHRM because it is connected to and influences all HR practices of the organization. Figure 8.1 illustrates the interaction of performance management with key HRM functions. The HR professional works in partnership with employees and managers to ensure that the performance management system is effective.

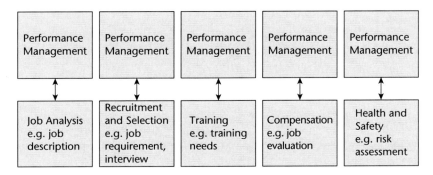

FIGURE 8.1 Performance Management and HRM Functions

As a system, performance management involves wide-ranging practices including goal setting, role clarification, performance monitoring, feedback, coaching and possibly mentoring. For example, the goal setting practice helps to facilitate a mutual understanding of the critical goals and expectations. An effective performance management system combines many of these practices to support the performance goals of employees. The system creates an environment in which continuous feedback is the norm.

Performance Appraisal

While performance management is an integrated system, *performance appraisal* is the key component that brings the practices that consitute performance management together. Performance appraisal is the formal systematic process of measuring employee performance, providing feedback and using ongoing communication to bring about performance improvement. Evidenced in this definition of performance appraisal is the importance of feedback and ongoing communication both of which we will discuss later in the chapter. What is relevant to note here is that performance appraisal is a process that is part of performance management. It is not simply an event that happens once or twice in a year between a manager and an employee.

Of course, there is the old school practice of performance appraisal during which employees meet and listen to the verdict of their managers about their performance over a period of time. The often anxious employees have little or no choice but to accept what the managers have been documenting in their file as the performance aberrations over the period the appraisal is supposed to cover. This often judgmental and one-sided event tends not leave room for employee self-assessment and focuses less on the learning, professional growth and development of the employees.

With contemporary performance appraisal, there is a two-way communication between the employee and the manager. This two-way communication ensures that employees are not only aware of the indicators that will be used to evaluate their performance, but that they are also encouraged to provide input on the performance measures. Performance appraisal helps the employees and their managers to understand the emphasis on information sharing about performance through regular feedback. Moreover, an effective performance appraisal process incorporates the needs and challenges of individual employees. The factors that drive employee motivation, contribution and how individual employees respond to the performance appraisal process require managers to draw on the partnership emphasized in appraisal in order to achieve the main goal of performance management, that is, to create a work environment in which people can perform to the best of their abilities. In short, performance appraisal captures a significant part of performance management especially in terms of the tools, process and interactions that are used to provide support that will aid the performance of an employee. Therefore, we will use the terms performance management and performance appraisal interchangeably in this chapter.

Purposes of Performance Appraisal

Performance appraisal system is an integral component of SHRM in nonprofit organizations. To this end, it serves a number of critical purposes. Fundamental to understanding the purposes of performance appraisal is to see it as a system that is interconnected not only to the HR functions but also to the operations of the nonprofits, especially the continuous improvement in service delivery. Accordingly, performance appraisal is about relationship between employees, managers and senior leadership as well as about maintaining focus on the operational effectiveness required to achieve the business goals of the nonprofit. The following are the specific purposes of performance appraisal.

- *Employee engagement.* Performance appraisal ensures that employees are involved in establishing performance goals and expectations. This enables employees to provide input into decisions about their jobs and facilitates ongoing dialogue with managers. The opportunity to contribute their perspectives improves employee motivation and raises the level of engagement.
- *Rewards and compensation.* The measures and information used in performance appraisal are key inputs in the determination of the appropriate level of compensation and rewards for employees. The content of compensation systems, including performance-based salary increases, bonus and incentive programs, depend on information provided by performance appraisal.
- *Legal mitigation.* An effective performance appraisal system helps the organization to objectively measure and document employee performance. This can be useful to mitigate complaints about discrimination in promotion or the opportunity to advance in the organization. The documentation is also relevant in situations in which claims about wrongful termination of employment arise.

- *Job design and evaluation.* Through performance appraisal, employees who are currently working in a particular job can provide up-to-date information that would enhance the design of the job. Such information also provides the main inputs for job evaluation through which the organization determines the relative worth of a job and creates the relative job hierarchy in the organization.
- *Performance feedback.* Performance appraisal is the primary channel through which employees and their manager discuss feedback and outline how to improve performance. For each employee, it provides an opportunity to discuss goals, the performance measures and competencies critical for achieving performance outcomes.
- *Training.* A key part of bridging the gap between the desired performance and the actual performance of employees is determining the training needs. Performance appraisal provides the information and the channel to determine the training needs for each employee. The performance feedback and training needs that employees and managers discuss can be aggregated to develop the training plan of the organization. Conversely, the knowledge and skills employees acquire in training is transferred into the overall performance appraisal management system to improve job performance.[1]
- *Career planning.* Performance appraisal facilitates career planning and development for employees and the organization. Employees can express interest in a specific career path, and discuss and outline a development plan with their managers.

In addition to the specific purposes above, performance appraisal can be used to collect information and provides support that would enhance employee well-being. Altogether, performance appraisal is one of the most important inputs and drivers of SHRM. It is central to HR planning and the implementation of HR strategy. Hence, both at the individual employee level and the organizational systems level, performance appraisal is an imperative influence on organizational performance.

Performance Management and Nonprofits

At the core of organizational performance in nonprofits are the contributions of employees and volunteers, both frontline and governance. As discussed in Chapter 3, the personal nature of the social goods and services that nonprofits provide, coupled with the values that shape the essential characteristics of these organizations, means that individual performance is critical to the mission. The corollary is that nonprofit managers must understand the importance of performance management. When nonprofit managers support the performance needs and challenges of individual employees, they are directly influencing the performance of the organization.

While the link between individual employee performance and organizational performance is not unique to nonprofits, the influence of the context on the design and implementation of performance management system is unique. Consistent with the alignment perspective introduced above, on one hand, each nonprofit must consider the contextual factors to ensure that there is a linkage between performance management and core HR practices such as compensation, training and recruitment. On the other hand, performance management must be aligned with the mission and strategy of the nonprofit through the HR strategy developed to attract, motivate and retain employees for the organization. From both viewpoints, the contextual factors, especially the interpersonal transaction-heavy operation of the nonprofit enterprise and the different drivers of motivation and values of nonprofit employees, set up the context of performance management differently for managers. These are the complexities that shape performance management in nonprofits.[2]

Importance of Performance Management for Nonprofits

It is with the complexities of the context and the characteristics of employees in mind that we consider the importance of performance management for the employees and the nonprofit organization.

Keeps the Focus on Nonprofit Mission

In the beleaguered world of nonprofits, many of the contextual factors we discussed in Chapter 3, such as government contracting funding, could de-emphasize the focus on the mission of the organization. In addition to the risk of mission creep, unrelated short-term project funding may inhibit the ability of employees to link their performance to the mission of the organization. Performance management could be used to align the objectives of the projects and link them to the mission of the nonprofit.

Helps to Reinforce Performance Linkage

Similar to organizations in other sectors, performance management is imperative to how nonprofits reinforce the performance "big picture." However, the need to reinforce the link between employee performance and organizational performance in nonprofits is made more pronounced by the fact that social objectives are often not easily measurable. Hence, performance management is a critical process to help employees understand how their performance link directly to the performance of the organization.

Facilitates Goals and Accountabilities of Individual Employees

An outcome of focusing on the mission and the linkage between employee and organizational performance is that performance management helps nonprofits to set specific goals and accountabilities for individual employees. By clarifying the expectations and accountabilities, employees are better able to focus their knowledge and skills on the performance goals that benefits the organization.

Provides Input for Hard-to-Measure Social Objectives

Although the performance of nonprofits in terms of the social objectives that define their organization is often not easily measurable, employee performance management could enhance what is measured. By setting goals and objective assessment of individual employee performance through the performance management process, concrete performance outcomes could be rolled up to the organizational level.

Provides Opportunity for Objective Assessment of Employee Performance

An effective performance management enables the organization to objectively assess the performance of individual employees. The goal setting, clarification of expectations and other elements of the performance appraisal enables the organization to objectively measure the performance of the employee.

Provides Opportunity for Conversation on Employee Progress

Employees need to know how they are doing in terms of their performance. This is even more so for nonprofit employees who are more likely to be attracted to the organization based on intrinsic factors such as the mission and values rather than extrinsic factors such as compensation.[3] Discussion between managers and employees about progress towards performance goals, areas for improvement and available support would help the employees to know whether they are performing and what they need to improve.

Encourages Employee's Commitment and Continuous Development

By constantly reminding employees about organizational goals and the importance of their contribution, performance management facilitates employee commitment to the mission and strategic goals of the nonprofit. The process reinforces the connection of employees to the mission and values of the organization. Moreover, when there are performance discrepancies, the process helps employees seek out training opportunities. This enhances the continuous development of employees.

Provides Opportunity for Employees to Provide Feedback

As noted above, performance management is a two-way street. In nonprofits where the feedback from stakeholders is particularly important, performance management provides an opportunity for employees to offer feedback to managers and the organization. For managers, the feedback from employees helps them to improve their supervisory practices and management style. Employee feedback also ensures that the organization can elicit information for continuous improvement of organizational practices. Information from the frontline about service delivery could be channeled through the performance management process to senior management of nonprofits for strategy formulation and implementation.

Enables Manager to Formally Recognize the Employee's Achievements

Similar to employees in other sectors, nonprofit employees need to be recognized for their performance and commitment to the organization. This need for recognition is heighten by research findings that suggest that not only is compensation lower in nonprofits, it is often not related to performance.[4] Performance management is therefore an important process that provides the opportunity to duly recognize the performance achievements of employees in nonprofits. As evidenced in Box 8.1, the importance of performance appraisal extends to senior leaders of the organization.

BOX 8.1 PURPOSE OF EXECUTIVE DIRECTOR (ED) PERFORMANCE APPRAISAL

- Supports organizational effectiveness by holding the ED accountable for her/his individual and organizational performance.
- Ensures that ED's work plan supports the strategic direction of the organization.
- Tightens the link between strategic objectives and day-to-day actions.
- Provides a formal structure for communication between the board and ED to clarify and record performance expectations.
- Provides ongoing feedback on performance.
- Captures the Board's perception on ED's strengths and provides satisfaction and encouragement to the ED via constructive feedback.
- Establishes plans for improving performance as necessary; assesses training and development needs and opportunities.
- Informs reward decisions.
- Provides legal documentation.
- Career development tool for the ED.

Source: "Effective Practices for Non-Profit Agencies" (2011) United Way of York Region, Ontario, Canada.

In all, performance management is mission critical and an important SHRM process for any nonprofit that wants to motivate and retain employees.

The ability of a nonprofit to effectively manage complex social transactions, support strategy and the mission of the organization significantly depends on the performance of employees. Performance management is the prime process for invigorating employees towards the goals of the nonprofit. On a positive note, research suggests that performance appraisal is widely in use in nonprofits and that managers understand its benefits.[5] However, due to the many challenges of the sector, it has been suggested that nonprofit managers are somehow failing to manage the performance for employees and volunteers. The remainder of this chapter provides an overview of the basic process in performance appraisal and how to ensure that performance management is a continuous process.

Who Should Provide Performance Information?

A central question in performance management is "Who is responsible for the appraisal?" Is the employee's immediate supervisor the right person to conduct the appraisal and provide the information? As discussed previously, in traditional performance management, the immediate supervisor of the employee evaluates the employee's performance and provides the information to document how the employee performed over a period of time. Typically, the *supervisor's appraisal* is completed using the evaluation tool the organization has developed for this purpose. However, the immediate supervisor-based appraisal system is beset by various problems. First, the nature of nonprofit jobs is complex. Hence, it is difficult for one person to accurately provide objective insight on the performance of the employee who is performing a job.[6] Second, the immediate supervisor may also lack continuous and close interaction with the employee to comprehensively assess the latter's performance. The nature of nonprofit organizations means that the employee and the supervisor may work at different locations. Many nonprofit employees work on the streets and return to their offices a couple of times a week. Third, again as noted earlier, this traditional approach is one-sided and does not provide adequate opportunity for the employee to provide feedback and self-assess. Fourth, it provides less opportunities for the employee to learn, grow and develop in their job. These limitations have necessitated a rethink and led to calls for a more balanced approach to performance appraisal.

Self-appraisal is one of the more balanced approaches to performance appraisal. It involves employees completing a detailed evaluation of their own performance as part of the performance appraisal system that will normally include the immediate supervisor's assessment of each employee's performance over a period of time. Essentially, it is a joint effort between the employee and the immediate supervisor. There are a number of advantages. One, for a typical nonprofit employee whose work is characterized by emotional transaction with clients, the self-appraisal is essential to provide a first-hand account of the reality of the job and her or his performance. The information the nonprofit will provide about their performance will likely be better than what supervisor, who may not be directly involved in service delivery, will provide. Two, the self-assessment gives the nonprofit employee a voice in the evaluation of his or her own performance. This is consistent with the social objectives and egalitarian values of organizations in the sector. Three, as a result of the voice, especially the fact that the nonprofit is actualizing its values, the employee is better motivated to improve his or her performance. Four, self-appraisal also provides the nonprofit a window into the challenges of frontline jobs. The performance appraisal therefore becomes a key part of the continuous improvement process. However, self-appraisal is not without its limitations. First, it is obviously the subjective opinion of the employee. Second, the relationship between the employee and the immediate supervisor could hinder the ability of the manager to counteract the employee's subjective rating of her or his own performance.

For a nonprofit manager, the limitations of supervisor's and self-appraisal can be tempered with insights from their subordinates. *Subordinate appraisal* is a system in which employees provide feedback on the performance of their immediate supervisor or manager. Typically, such an appraisal is focused on aspects of the role of the manager that subordinates can objectively and relatively evaluate such as communication style and interpersonal skills. One advantage of subordinate appraisal for the manager and the nonprofit is that it is a good source of information for training needs. The manager can build on the skills that are below par from the evaluation of the employees. Another advantage of this appraisal for a nonprofit is that it can provide information on leadership skills the organization needs to acquire and/or develop. The aggregate information could have patterns that should guide HR planning. A disadvantage of subordinate appraisal is that it could easily become a popularity contest. For example, managers could make decisions on the basis of employees perceiving them in positive light and not in the best interest of the nonprofit organization. The opposite of this is another disadvantage of subordinate appraisal. When managers make decisions that are in the best interest of the organization but perceived negatively by employees, the employees could use subordinate appraisal to rebuke the managers for not making decisions that favours them. Since nonprofits have social objectives and advocate for social causes, it is possible that divergence in value orientation between managers and employees will be reflected in subordinate appraisal.

Since nonprofits tend to be small and employees work closely together, *peer appraisal* could be useful to the organization. In this type of appraisal, employees who work together are asked to provide feedback on the performance of one another.[7] Of course the appraisal should focus on behaviors in the job that colleagues are able to evaluate objectively such as contribution to the team and interpersonal skills. It is important to limit such an appraisal to the primary team that work closely together. For example, a worker in the community health program of YMCA-YWCA of Greater Victoria, Canada, is not likely to have a good insight on the performance of a colleague in the health and fitness program. Although less frequently used compared to appraisal conducted by the immediate supervisor, peer appraisal could provide valuable frontline or actual job-level information on the performance of the employee. Peer appraisal could enhance teamwork by fostering collaboration among colleagues. However, it is not advisable to use peer appraisal in work situations in which employees are in direct competition, such as sales.[8] To use peer appraisal, nonprofits must provide training for employees about the goals and the specific use of the feedback that is collected in order to avoid creating an adversarial employee relations environment.

Peer appraisal could be incorporated into a *team appraisal system* or vice versa.[9] The focus of team appraisal is the performance of the entire team as a collective. Hence, it is the performance of the team that is measured and evaluated. The adoption of team appraisal has implications for nonprofits. Similar to business and public sector organizations, it reinforces the importance of teamwork.[10] Particularly in nonprofits, team appraisal emphasizes the collective values of many of the organization. Moreover, it is inevitable for team level performance-based compensation, which, as we will discuss in the next chapter, could be an option for nonprofits. One major drawback of team appraisal is the difficulty in separating out individual high performers and performance loafers. This is a consequence of the free-rider problem which is characterized by people not contributing proportionately to team performance but benefiting equally from the rewards.[11] To address this limitation, it is generally advisable to combine team appraisal with other sources of appraisal.

Providing quality client service is critical in order for nonprofits to achieve their mission. In effect, the feedback from clients plays an important role in the overall performance management system of nonprofits. As important stakeholders and the market for the social goods and services provided by nonprofits, clients have a direct impact on the performance of nonprofits. *Client appraisal* is essential for nonprofits. The feedback provided by clients is an important input for performance management and the core HR functions in the organization. It is devoid of many of the political limitations discussed in the other sources of appraisal information. Most importantly, it is a continuous improvement tool that should be used constructively in performance appraisal to help employees bridge any real gaps in performance.

Bringing two or more of the sources of the performance appraisal information together is inherently difficult. However, it provides a more comprehensive and multidimensional picture of employee performance. This is the goal of *360-degree performance appraisal* or multirater feedback. The 360-degree appraisal collects performance feedback from multiple sources including supervisor, peers, subordinates and clients. It has been described as "boundaryless appraisal" because it combines elements of top-down appraisals, upward appraisals and reflects the philosophy of boundaryless organization.[12] The basic selling point of 360-degree is the recognition that the performance of an employee is reflected in the interactions that are part of the job both internal and external to the organization. Although it has been suggested that the use of multirater feedback has increased significantly,[13] there is limited evidence of its use in nonprofit organizations. However, a study on performance management in nonprofits found that many of the organizations implemented a comprehensive system including formal and informal feedback.[14] Although there continues to be controversy about whether to use 360-degree feedback for performance appraisal that is tied to administrative purpose such as compensation or simply for employee development, the potential uptake of this multirater feedback in nonprofits would depend on some of the following advantages and disadvantages.[15]

Advantages

- The diversity of sources of feedback provides a comprehensive insight on the performance of the employee.
- A consistent pattern in the feedback can reinforce the identification of performance gaps.
- The information can provide more specific input for HR planning, training and development.
- It can help employees to better understand the impact they have on various people they interact with on the job.

Disadvantages

- Multirater feedback is not necessarily more objective than supervisor's feedback. If one rate is subjective, nothing stops the other raters from being subjective.
- It is costly and it takes more time to implement.
- Criteria may not be commonly understood by employees and those doing the appraisal.
- Employees do not generally have any involvement in the formulation of criteria.
- If those providing feedback know that it will affect someone's employment, they are less likely to provide candid feedback.[16]

The source of performance appraisal is inextricably linked to the issue of account-ability in nonprofits.[17] Whether a nonprofit links the performance of employees to the mission of the organization from the top down or adopts a flexible system that incorporates top-down, bottom-up and horizontal source of feedback will influence who provides the information for performance appraisal. The types of initiatives that are implemented, such as the ones in the example of the American Heart Association shown in Box 8.2, are part of ingredient for effective performance management.

BOX 8.2 IMPROVING PERFORMANCE AT THE AMERICAN HEART ASSOCIATION

The mission of the American Heart Association is building healthier lives, free of cardiovascular diseases and stroke. With head office in Dallas, Texas and close to 2,800 employees nationwide, Nancy Brown the CEO of AHA set a goal of improving cardiovascular health of all Americans by 20 percent while also reducing deaths from heart disease and stroke by 25 percent by 2020.

Two examples of strategies for improving performance at AHA are:

- Employee engagement

  o CEO created employee think-tank to help her find new ideas for the business.
  o Annual employee engagement survey which AHA has been able to tie to lower turnover and higher productivity.

- Sponsorship of the American Heart University

  o The AHU provides support to employees to improve their performance through online classes and in-person workshops.

Sources: Morton, G. (2013) "Flexibility and ties to mission keep employees loving their jobs," *The NonProfit Times Best Nonprofits to Work For*, 2013; O Hara, K. J. O. (2011) "How Nancy Brown engages employees to improve the American Heart Association," *Smart Business*, May 31, 2011. http://www.sbnonline.com/component/k2/7-dallas-editions/20192#.U0a7NPlSZWY. Retrieved November, 2013.

What Should Be Appraised

To effectively deploy performance management systems, nonprofits must first understand the idiosyncrasies of the existing methods of performance appraisal, how they fit the employee and organizational contexts of their nonprofit and how to go about implementing whichever method management has decided to adopt. In particular, understanding the methods of performance appraisal would ensure that nonprofits are measuring the performance indicators that are critical to their organization. To actualize the benefits of performance management, the knowledge of the methods of performance appraisal is imperative. This section discusses the main methods of performance appraisal.

Similar to other major organizational practices, the methods of performance appraisal have evolved considerably over the past decades. Nonetheless, there are three main methods of measuring performance that have consistently been examined in the literature. These are measures of performance that are based on employee traits, employee behaviors, and the results or outcomes that the employee attains. Each type of measure indicates the type of information that the performance appraisal will emphasize.

Traits

The focus of trait measures in performance appraisal is on the characteristics of the employee. This could be either physical or psychological characteristics. Examples of traits include resourcefulness, imagination, sociability and conscientiousness. These are used to determine whether the employee has the traits that are essential for performance on the job. Although research has found that some traits such as conscientiousness, agreeableness and openness to experience have moderate impact on job performance,[18] there are significant questions on the validity and reliability of trait measures. For one, traits mean that performance is based on the personality or aspects of the physical attributes of the employee. Besides, none of the measures of traits that have been found to have a modest link to job performance can be considered to be a reliable measure of how an employee performs. Since trait measures assess who the employee is, the importance of the job is somewhat deemphasized. Even if traits can be linked to what the job is about, the objectivity of the measure and the process of measurement are open to questions.

Importantly, the subjectivity of trait measures raises questions that touch on a fundamental characteristic of nonprofit organizations. The focus on characteristics or personality is particularly inconsistent with the egalitarian values of many nonprofits. For example, trait measures could provide the opportunity for discrimination based on the characteristics of the employee. Similarly, the issue of procedural and distributive justice could also arise if trait measures are used as the basis of administrative decision-making such as pay for performance, transfer and assignment to a special project. Regardless of their limitations, trait measures are common within and outside of the nonprofit sector.

Behaviors

Behavior measures that are used in performance appraisal are a significant step up from trait measures. Behavior measures are focused on what employees do. In other words, they measure the job related actions of employees. The opportunity to objectively identify and assess the specific actions that are deemed to contribute to job performance is beneficial to the employee, the manager and the organization. For example, since the behaviors that exemplify effective customer service are reasonably observable, a manager can provide specific feedback. The employee is in a better position to modify the behavior that needs improvement and the organizations benefits from the performance and efficiency in the process. Moreover, behavior measures of performance appraisal are more suitable for improving team performance through job rotation designed to enhance task proficiency of team members.[19]

The focus on behaviors is important for nonprofits where employees are engaged in work characterized by interpersonal transactions. Observable behaviors including verbal and non-verbal communication are part and parcel of the work roles of employees in nonprofits. In addition, nonprofits must show that the social services they provide to clients are reliable and consistent. When clients walk through the door of a nonprofit, they expect a certain level of service in the interaction with the employee of the nonprofit. This is measurable in terms of the action or behavior of the employee. For example, the work roles required to provide support to vulnerable women and children who receive support from Care International in disaster relief and development programs can be measured in terms of actions involved in the distribution of food and emergency supplies, providing access to education and raising awareness. The duties and responsibilities of a Livelihood Specialist shown in Box 8.3 illustrate the behaviors that are assessed in the performance of the job.

BOX 8.3 CARE INTERNATIONAL LIVELIHOOD SPECIALIST

Duties and Responsibilities of a Livelihood Specialist

- Train women in skills related to agricultural production.
- Implement gender and value chain approaches to linking women producers and business owners to market opportunities.
- Assist women in achieving greater agricultural productivity through more and higher-level access to agricultural inputs, tools, and techniques, thereby lessening their physical and time burden.
- Provide women with financial literacy.
- Support women's asset management activities.
- Implement gender-transformative approaches to agricultural production, contributing to changed gender norms within producer associations, among business owners, and in farming communities.
- Encourage sustainable women's employment among community leaders.

Source: Care International Careers, http://ch.tbe.taleo.net/CH05/ats/careers/requisition.jsp;jsessionid=1201E751229EBAB8FFD11808CFC5C73D.NA10_primary_jvm?org=CAREUSA&cws=1&rid=2255.

Outcomes/Results

Another method of measuring performance is to focus on the outcomes or results achieved in the work role. Outcomes are focused on the deliverables outlined in the duties and responsibilities as well as the specific strategic and operational goals achieved in the job. In simple terms, outcomes are about what is accomplished in the job and not about the characteristics of the employee (traits) or what the employee does (behaviors). A performance appraisal that is based on outcomes is a win-win for the organization and the employee because it is about goals which are defined at the beginning and assessed at the end of the performance period. Apart from clarity of goals, the organization and the employee are better able to pinpoint the impact of the specific job. Hence, on paper, it could be argued that this is perhaps a logical and uncomplicated basis for measuring performance on the job. This position is particularly appropriate for routine tasks because they are more likely to be well defined, specific and have quantifiable criteria.[20] However, when the tasks in a job are non-routine, outcomes can be more complex, not easily defined in advance, take longer to achieve and can even be indeterminate.[21] In essence, the limitations of outcome measures of performance are pronounced jobs that have non-routine tasks.

Outcomes are relevant to the emphasis on accountability in nonprofits. By using outcomes-based measures in performance appraisal nonprofits are able to directly link the performance of employees to the outcomes that funders have set for the organization. Also, outcomes would reinforce and enhance the motivation and commitment of nonprofit employees to the mission of the organization. However, the implementation of outcomes-based measures of performance appraisal could encounter significant limitations. First, the social and often complex factors involved in the mission of nonprofits suggest that outcomes are not easily measurable.[22] Second, when outcomes are measurable, they are more likely to be achieved over a longer period of time that is beyond one or two years. Third, the tasks that make up many jobs in nonprofits are non-routine transactions. While the interactions between an employee and different clients may be similar, the body of knowledge and skills required to provide support to the clients are diverse and often unique to nonprofits.[23] The limitations do not invalidate the use of outcomes-based performance appraisal nonprofit. Rather, they highlight important considerations managers should address in the development and implementation of the performance appraisal system.

Both behaviors and outcomes measures of performance in particular have attributes that nonprofits can incorporate and use in their appraisal systems. To a lesser extent, some traits measures such as a conscientiousness and openness to experience could be used to provide specific feedback to employees. Essentially, it is possible to have a performance appraisal that combines features of the three types of measures. What is evaluated in performance appraisal should be what is important to the SHRM of the organization.

What Are the Methods of Performance Appraisal?

Knowing what to measure in performance is the basis of the method and tool that is developed to do the actual appraisal. Although there are differences in performance appraisal methods and forms, one key feature of any form or tool is that it must clearly demonstrate the differences in the levels of performance. The following are commonly used forms or tools in performance appraisal.

Graphic Rating Scales

The *graphic rating scale* is a performance appraisal method that uses rating continuum to evaluate how well an employee meets the performance standard required in a job. Although it is sometimes considered as a measure of traits, graphic rating scales are also used to measure behaviors and outcomes. Due to its simplicity, flexibility and adaptability, it is perhaps the most widely used instrument for performance appraisal. The levels of the continuum are used to indicate the different levels of the performance of employees on the continuum or scale. For example, a scale could be 1 (below performance expectation) to 5 (above performance expectation). Figure 8.2 is an example of *graphic rating scale*. Graphic rating scales could meet the needs of nonprofits, especially the ability to use the form for different jobs. However, nonprofits must pay particular attention to the problem of subjectivity in the rating. Training managers on performance appraisal and using a form with comments such as in the example could help in this regard.

Ranking

Ranking is a performance appraisal method that requires the manager to evaluate each employee's performance using a scale from best to worst. The outcome of

Performance Expectations	Check Rating					Comments
Demonstrates Initiative	1 □	2 □	3 □	4 □	5 □	
Knowledge of Systems & Procedures	1 □	2 □	3 □	4 □	5 □	
Meets Deadlines	1 □	2 □	3 □	4 □	5 □	
Interactions with Colleagues	1 □	2 □	3 □	4 □	5 □	
Interactions with Patients	1 □	2 □	3 □	4 □	5 □	

1. Unsatisfactory (Performance clearly below acceptable level. Corrective action required)
2. Needs Improvement (Performance that partially meets expectations)
3. Meets Expectations
4. Occasionally Exceeds Expectations
5. Regularly Exceeds Expectations (Performance that frequently exceeds expectations)

FIGURE 8.2 Example of Graphic Rating Scale

ranking is that the manager is able to differentiate employees based on their performance. Generally, such differentiation facilitates administrative decision-making such as promotion, salary increase and layoff. Although ranking is considered a simple method, it has a number of limitations that counteract its advantages. First, a common issue with ranking is that it could be subjected to halo effect in which the manager focuses only on one aspect of the employee's performance to determine how to rank their overall performance. Second, the manager may also base the performance appraisal on the most recent interaction with the employee at the expense of performance over the entire period.[24] Third, it is not practical to rank a large number of employees without employing subjective factors to differentiate between them. Fourth, ranking is not suitable for providing feedback to enhance the development of employees.[25]

Forced ranking is a form of ranking in which managers are asked to place employees in a performance category or cluster. The idea is that a certain percentage of employees must be placed in the different categories that are based on their performance, which is similar to grading students on a bell-shaped curve. For example, 10 percent of the employees could be categorized as excellent, 20 percent as above average, 40 as average, 20 percent as below average and 10 percent as poor. One key selling point of forced ranking is that the organization is better able to identify and reward employees who are performing at the excellent level. Another selling point is that it is also used to separate out employees for promotion and development opportunities. Of course, the opposites of these selling points also apply. Employees who are performing below average are not rewarded and if in the "poor performance category," they may require performance improvement plans which can lead to termination of employment. Employees in the latter group are likely to be part of voluntary or involuntary exits from the organization.

Forced ranking remains a controversial performance appraisal method. Critics have suggested that it is subjective, lacks fairness, undermines trust, teamwork and demotivates employees.[26] Although many organizations have used forced ranking, and some including Lending Tree, GlaxoSmithKline and AIG still use it,[27] perhaps the most commonly cited example is how it was used by General Electric (GE) under former CEO Jack Welsh. The GE approach required managers to cluster employees into three groups: the top 20 percent; the middle 70 percent and the bottom 10 percent. Employees in the top 20 cluster were rewarded and those in the bottom 10 percent had to improve or exit the organization.[28] There is minimal evidence of whether nonprofits are using forced ranking.

Behavioral Anchor Rating Scale (BARS)

BARS is a performance appraisal method in which behavioral descriptions are linked to a continuum or levels of employee performance. The levels or continuum of performance are represented in scales that include numbers. The goal of BARS is to assist managers to better observe behavior, use the meaning of that behavior to evaluate performance, and to record the performance on a continuum of effectiveness for specific dimensions of behavior.[29] In effect, it improves upon the subjectivity limitation of graphic rating scales by providing descriptive standards for the rating and the observed performance.[30]

Table 8.1 provides an example of BARS. In addition to improving the subjectivity limitation, the description of the performance levels provides a common frame of reference of the importance of the rated tasks for both the employee and the manager. This ensures that there is better understanding, buy-in and self-assessment of performance from employees. BARS also provides more accurate information for training and development and HR planning. It facilitates the communication of organizational policy and extension of the domain of evaluated performance.[31] However, a nonprofit organization would need to devote significant resources to develop BARS performance appraisal forms. Since each job would require a customized performance appraisal form, HR and job-specific expertise are essential. Depending on the number of jobs, to develop BARS may take significant work and time. Resource-challenged nonprofits may find the requirement difficult.

Behavioral Observation Scale (BOS)

BOS is basically an extension of BARS. In this type of performance appraisal method, managers are asked to indicate the observed occurrence rates of the identified behavior that characterize the desired job performance. The assumption is that there is a constant degree of performance sufficiency regardless of the behavior that is used to describe it.[32] Since BOS focuses specifically on the ideal behavior, managers are simply looking for how often an employee demonstrates the behavior. Figure 8.3 illustrates a BOS for a nonprofit frontline position.

Narrative

Narrative is a performance appraisal method that involves the manager writing a statement to describe the performance of an employee. Typically, the manager is required to succinctly capture how well the employee is meeting the performance expectations. The use of competencies and areas for improvement are also typically highlighted in narrative performance appraisal. Depending on the type of job and the level of a position, the narrative could be an open format in which the manager can simply write their comments about the performance of the employee. It could also be a structured format with questions to guide the manager's comments. However, the narrative method is often used to complement the rating methods in the form of a comments section as illustrated in Figure 8.2.

TABLE 8.1 Example of Behavioral Anchor Rating Scale

Performance Expectations	Scale	Behavior Description
Job Knowledge	1 Exceeds Expectations	Consistently demonstrates excellent knowledge of the job, applies effective techniques to job tasks, determines the care required to accomplish tasks appropriately, coaches others on the knowledge, skills and abilities required for the job when needed
	2 Meets Expectations	Demonstrates the knowledge, skills and abilities to do the job effectively, efficiently and safely, completes assignments to departmental standards independently
	3 Needs Improvement	Demonstrates lack of knowledge, skills and abilities to do the job effectively, maintains consistent daily performance level
Communication	1 Exceeds Expectations	Consistently demonstrates effective communication skills, superior ability to communicate and clarify difficult information and excellent comprehension of oral and written materials
	2 Meets Expectations	Demonstrates professional communication skills, conveys information concisely and clearly, free of error, and incorporates active listening
	3 Needs Improvement	Demonstrates average written and oral communication skills. Written communications are sometimes unclear, have grammatical and spelling errors
Teamwork	1 Exceeds Expectations	Consistently emphasizes team goals above personal goals, supports team members to solve work problems, accepts constructive feedback in a cooperative manner, regularly contributes to improve team performance
	2 Meets Expectations	Supports achievement of team goals, contributes a fair share of responsibilities, collaborates with and supports team members and understands the importance of the team
	3 Needs Improvement	Lacks understanding of the importance of team performance. Does not assume fair share of team responsibility. Expects team members to complete most tasks and does not support team colleagues

Behavioral Observation Scale	Almost Never				Almost Always
	1	2	3	4	5
Determines the care support required by client immediately after assessment	____	____	____	____	____
Communicates difficult information clearly	____	____	____	____	____
Collaborates with team members to solve work problems	____	____	____	____	____
Willing to accept new assignments	____	____	____	____	____
Uses own judgment to organize work	____	____	____	____	____
Demonstrates concern for safety of self, clients and others	____	____	____	____	____

FIGURE 8.3   Example of Behavioural Observation Scale

The narrative method provides an excellent opportunity for a manager to present rich qualitative insights on the performance of the employee. The manager has significant leeway in terms of what and how to describe the employee's performance as well as the importance attached to the different aspects of the performance. A brief review of relevant literature suggests that the combination of how specific the comments provided are, the number of comments provided and the valence of comments explained, to a small extent, improvement in individual performance.[33]

Although there is no evidence of research that has specifically examined the narrative method of performance appraisal in nonprofits, on the surface it appears to fit with the qualitative characteristics of services of nonprofits. To meet the accountability demands of nonprofits, overcome the limited HR expertise and the resources challenges of organizations in the sector, a narrative method would need to be combined with a rating method to be effective. One major drawback of the narrative method is that it is dependent on the written and communication skills of the manager completing the appraisal. The ability to accurately capture the key performance highlights of the employee and provide relevant feedback at the same time in brief statements may be difficult.

Critical Incident

Critical incident is a performance appraisal method in which the manager is expected to document or keep record of the employee's positive and negative performance. It is a collection of descriptive accounts of critical incidents that are relevant to provide a detailed insight into the performance of the employee, including all parts of organization's system impacted by or that impact the employee's performance.[34] It is typically an open-ended method that is simply based on the record in the manager's notes or files for each employee. Therefore, there are no particular guidelines, format or questions that the manager must follow.

Critical incident is an important way of addressing some of the challenges that many managers encounter, the need to keep relevant records of critical incidents and job interactions involving those incidents such as feedback, coaching and follow up with employees. Since the critical incidents are continuing throughout the performance appraisal period, this method is a good way of reinforcing positive performance and providing constructive feedback for negative performance. However, the need to regularly document critical incident might be too onerous for some managers because of the heavy workload of their job. It would also be impractical for managers with a large number of direct employees and those who do not have the opportunity to directly observe incidents in the course of the employee performing her/his job.

Nonprofits might find the critical incident to be valuable if it is combined with another performance appraisal method, such as management by objectives (MBO), which is discussed below. The limitations noted above are particularly relevant to nonprofit managers in organizations of different sizes and scope.

Management by Objectives

Management by objectives (MBO) is a performance appraisal method that is based on mutually agreed performance goals set by the manager and the employee, regular feedback to the employee and the evaluation of whether the goals were achieved. The method attempts to link performance appraisal directly to the strategy of the organization. It emphasizes that strategic goals should be the source of or at the least influence the performance goals agreed upon by the manager and the employee. In addition, negotiation is important in MBO because the goals should be mutually agreed upon. Also important are the regular feedback and the measures of the goals.

As a performance appraisal method, it has been suggested that MBO focuses on cognitive constraints (i.e. understanding and learning), interpersonal oriented development and both intrinsic and extrinsic motivation because it aims to satisfy the expectations of the employee and the manager.[35] In effect, it is added that the accountability for attaining goals in MBO is public because it involves both the employee and the manager. The participation of the employee in setting the goals not only motivates and directs efforts toward the goals, it could enhance the ability of the employee to plan, self-assess progress and identify opportunities for development. MBO attempts to increase the communication between the employee and the manager which further helps to enhance the shared perception between the players and the organization.

MBO may not be suitable for some types of jobs and organizations. Jobs with minimal autonomy and decision-making may not be particularly ideal for MBO because employees are less likely to have discretion on the work process.[36] In effect, using MBO for non-professional jobs could be a challenge. Also, since employees will have different objectives, MBO would take time and resources to coordinate.

For nonprofits, the use of MBO in performance appraisal would ensure that there is a focus on client-centered outcomes. It would enhance the process for continuous communication not only between the manager and the employee but also with the clients. The employee and the manager may need to elicit feedback from clients to provide input for the regular feedback meeting that is part of MBO. Although not recent, previous research has identified MBO as one of the often-used methods of performance appraisal in child welfare organizations.[37] Pecora and Hunter specifically noted that MBO would be more useful to child welfare organizations because it is results-oriented and it allows professional judgment and specialized skills. They explain the advantages and disadvantages of MBO and offer guidelines on how to determine whether MBO would work for an organization.

Basically, the MBO process would include the following steps:

1. *Define objectives.* First, the employee and the manager meet to discuss and outline the objectives the employee will focus on during the year. The meeting would involve the negotiation of the goals. It is critical that the manager and the employee have a shared understanding of the goals

2. *Create performance measures or indicators.* The manager and employee work together to outline the specific indicators or measures that will be used to evaluate the performance of the employee.

3. *Establish process for periodic feedback and work progress review.* This regularly scheduled meeting will enable the manager to keep abreast of the progress of the employee. It would also enable the manager to provide feedback and offer guidance on the need for modification of the objectives if necessary.

4. *Record and reward performance accomplishments.* The performance-appraisal cycle is incomplete without evaluating the performance of the employee to determine whether goals have been achieved. What is done here is to match the indicators to the objectives with consideration for extenuating factors that might be beyond the control of the employee. Whether goals are achieved or not are tied to the opportunity to receive rewards in the MBO performance appraisal method.

In a way, MBO encapsulates some of the key elements of performance appraisal, goals setting, employee involvement, ongoing feedback, performance goals that are aligned to the strategy of the organization, and indicators that are outlined at the start of the performance period.

The Performance Appraisal Meeting

As noted previously in this chapter, performance appraisal is an ongoing communication between employees and their managers. An important part of this communication is the appraisal meeting. For this reason, it is relevant to look at preparatory concerns and key considerations for the meeting. This section describes a generic guideline for preparing for and conducting the performance appraisal meeting in nonprofits. Although it should be noted that there are different ways of facilitating this very important meeting, for nonprofits in particular, the meeting is yet another opportunity to demonstrate the values of the organization.

How to Prepare for the Performance Review Meeting

Prepare the Employee

Plan ahead. The manager should start planning for the performance appraisal meeting in collaboration with each employee. This should involve a discussion about the purpose, date and time of the meeting. Some of the important considerations that should be factored in setting up the meeting include the timing of major departmental and corporate projects the employee is involved in and the stage of completion of tasks that are likely to weigh significantly on the performance of the employee. For nonprofits, the funding application period is likely not an ideal time for performance appraisal.

Review objectives. If applicable, the employee should review the performance objectives that were outlined at the beginning of the performance appraisal period. If there are no set performance objectives, the employee should review the job description and relevant performance indicators. The manager should encourage the employee to reflect on her/his work and contribution in relation to the expectations of the position.

Access forms and resources. The manager should advise the employee on where to access the performance appraisal forms and resources. Since many organizations now have an intranet or online performance management system, the HR department should ensure that the online tools provide employees with detailed guidelines, resources and access to the performance appraisal forms. If the nonprofit does not have an intranet or an online performance management system, the manager should provide the employee with a copy of the performance appraisal form to review.

Complete self-appraisal. A key step in the preparation of the employee for the performance appraisal meeting is self-appraisal. The employee should complete a *self-appraisal* before the meeting with the manager based on a candid evaluation of his/her own performance. If there are performance objectives and indicators, the employee should use such objectives and indicators to guide the self-appraisal.

Prepare Yourself (the Manager)

Review indicators. The first step that should be undertaken to prepare the manager for the performance appraisal meeting with the employee is to review the performance goals and indicators that will be used to evaluate the performance of the employee. This preparatory review should also consider relevant organizational factors that could have contributed to delay in the achievement of the goals.

Consider values. The nonprofit manager should also consider how the values of the organization apply to the employee's job and responsibilities. This could help to frame the discussion about how the behavior of employee aligns with values of the organization.

Solicit feedback. If applicable, the preparation phase is also the time to solicit and obtain feedback from other sources such as clients and colleagues. If the nonprofit does not use a 360-degree or peer appraisal system, the manager should review relevant feedback from clients if the employee's job is a frontline position. The notes from feedback and coaching discussions with the employee during the performance appraisal period should be reviewed.

Review past appraisal. It is also pertinent for the manager to review the employee's previous performance appraisal. This is particularly important to provide a basis for comparing current and previous performance of the employee. The manager should also review the job description to prepare for discussions about the training and development needs of the employee.

Review form. A critical step in the preparation for the performance appraisal meeting is the review of the actual appraisal tool or form. Many of the online performance management systems have examples for managers to peruse before using the system. If it is a new system the manager is not familiar with, it is advisable to conduct a trial appraisal for a fictional employee in a real position. As part of this step, the manager should also review the performance appraisal resources which are made available by the HR department or staff of the organization.

Conducting the Meeting

Make the employee feel at ease. The manager should make all possible effort to ensure that the employee feels at ease right from the start of the meeting. This will help to reduce the tension and anxiety that is associated with appraisal meetings.

Outline the purpose. The manager and the employee should briefly discuss the purpose of the meeting and how the discussion will proceed. The employee should be encouraged to speak and offer his/her insight.

Emphasize coaching. It is important for the manager to emphasize his/her role as a coach and not a judge in the performance management system. The manager should reiterate his/her support and assistance, by saying something like, "During this discussion, I'd like to offer any assistance I can and answer any questions you may have. I'm here to help you succeed in your position."

Discuss employee self-appraisal. The employee self-appraisal is a centerpiece of an effective performance system. The manager should facilitate a detailed discussion of the performance achievements and the concerns that the employee has highlighted in the self-appraisal. The discussion should also include the employee's suggestion on how to address the performance concerns.

Discuss your feedback. The manager should discuss his/her own specific feedback with the employee. It is important to focus the discussion on performance behavior and reinforce the feedback with specific examples. Similarly, the manager should clearly recognize the employee's good performance and discuss concerns the employee did not mention. The manager's suggestions on follow-up actions should be an important part of the discussion. The manager may also explore a development plan with the employee.

Discuss rating. In a rating-based performance appraisal method, the manager should avoid emphasizing the performance ratings at the expense of providing feedback. The manager and the employee should discuss any point of disagreement in the self-appraisal completed by the employee and the manager's rating with the aim of reaching a consensus.

Summarize plan. To end the meeting, the manager and the employee should summarize the major highlights of the performance appraisal meeting including any follow up action. It is important for the manager to remind the employee about available resources and support. If the employee's performance needs significant improvement, the manager may schedule a follow up meeting sooner to assess progress towards a competent level of performance.

Summary

Performance management remains the epicenter of SHRM and critical HR functions. It is perhaps the most important system link between employee performance and organizational performance. The most important goal of performance management, which is to support the strategy of the organization, should be clear to employees, their managers and the senior leadership of the organization. Both the administrative and developmental functions of performance appraisal should be driven by the goals of the organization. Employees as individuals and as members of teams should be able to connect their work roles to the strategic direction of the organization through performance management. Managers should be able to provide clear focus on the behaviors that are consistent with the performance indicators. Managers should also be able to use performance management to determine how well the performance of the employees match the indicators and what types of follow up actions are needed to address performance gaps.

A modern performance management system could enhance the adaptive capability of the organization. The participation of employees in the performance appraisal process could provide important input and insight that could help the organization to better position itself and adapt to change in the operating environment. In addition to the contribution of performance management to organizational performance and the role of managers, it ensures that there is a focus on the employee. The focus on employees and their collaborative role in the appraisal process contribute to the quality of human capital in the organization.

Nonprofits are especially predisposed to derive the benefits of performance management at the different levels of the organization discussed in this chapter. However, the essential purpose of nonprofits, the complexity of the operating environment and the characteristics of employees incorporate additional dimensions to the performance management system. On the one hand, these exigencies could add additional challenges to the process of implementing an effective performance management system. On the other hand, the exigencies further accentuate the importance of performance management. It has been suggested that high-impact nonprofits find a way to implement performance appraisal regardless of the challenges.[38] All in all, these pressures explain why performance management is a mission critical system for nonprofits.

Discussion Questions

1. What are some of the benefits of integrating employee performance appraisal with organizational performance in nonprofits?
2. Some employees in your nonprofit organization have indicated that they are open to the introduction of peer appraisal to complement supervisor's appraisal. What are the potential downsides to the use of peer appraisal?
3. You have been asked to consider the implementation of a 360-degree performance appraisal system in your small nonprofit with 20 employees. What are some of the challenges and opportunities of adopting this system in a small organization?
4. How can nonprofits use MBO to advance advocacy activities?

Notes

1 Mello, J. A. (2011) *Strategic Human Resource Management,* 3rd Edition. Mason, OH: South-Western Centage Learning.
2 Becker, K., Antuar, N., & Everett, C. (2011) "Implementing an employee performance management system in a nonprofit organization," *Nonprofit Management & Leadership,* 21(3): 255–271.
3 Devaro, J., & Brookshire, D. (2007) "Promotions and incentives in nonprofit and for-profit organizations," *Industrial and Labor Relations Review,* 60(3): 311–339.
4 Ballou, J. P., & Weisbrod, B. A. (2003) "Managerial rewards and the behavior of for-profit, governmental and nonprofit organizations: Evidence from the hospital industry," *Journal of Public Economics,* 87(9–10): 1895–1920.

5 Selden, S., & Sowa, J. (2011) "Performance management and appraisal in human service organizations: Management and staff perspectives," *Public Personnel Management,* 40(3): 251.

6 Fried, B. (2011) "Performance management," in B. J. Fried & M. D. Fottler (Eds.), *Human Resources in Healthcare: Managing for Success.* Chicago: Health Administration Press.

7 Belcourt, M., Singh, P., Bohlander, G., & Snell, S. (2014) *Managing Human Resources,* 7th Canadian Edition. Scarborough, ON: Nelson.

8 Belcourt, Singh, Bohlander, & Snell, *Managing Human Resources.*

9 Fried, "Performance management"; Belcourt, Singh, Bohlander, & Snell, *Managing Human Resources.*

10 Fried, "Performance management."

11 Ibid.

12 Waldman, D. A., & Bowen, D. E. (1998) "The acceptability of 360 degree appraisals: A customer supplier relationship perspective," *Human Resource Management,* 37(2): 117–129.

13 Maylett, T. (2009). "360-degree feedback revisited: The transition from development to appraisal," *Compensation & Benefits Review,* 41(5): 52–59.

14 Selden & Sowa, "Performance management and appraisal in human service organizations."

15 van der Heijden, B. I. J. M., & Nijhof, A. H. J. (2004) "The value of subjectivity: Problems and prospects for 360-degree appraisal systems," *The International Journal of Human Resource Management,* 15(3): 493–511; Maylett, "360-degree feedback revisited."

16 Maylett, "360-degree feedback revisited"; van der Heijden & Nijhof, "The value of subjectivity."

17 Curran, C. J. (2002) "Performance management: Help or a burden to nonprofits?" *Journal for Nonprofit Management,* Summer, 3–17.

18 Hurtz, G. M., & Donovan, J. J. (2000) "Personality and job performance: The Big Five revisited," *Journal of Applied Psychology,* 85: 869–879; Thoresen, C. J., Bradley, J. C., Bliese, P. D., & Thoresen, J. D. (2004) "The Big Five personality traits and individual job performance growth trajectories in maintenance and transitional job stages," *Journal of Applied Psychology,* 89(5): 835–853.

19 Scott, S. G., & Einstein, W. O. (2001) "Strategic performance appraisal in team-based organizations: One size does not fit all," *Academy of Management Executive,* 15(2): 107–116.

20 Scott & Einstein, "Strategic performance appraisal in team-based organizations."

21 Ibid.

22 Sowa, J., Selden, S. C., & Sandfort, J. (2004) "No longer unmeasurable? A multidimensional integrated model of nonprofit organizational effectiveness," *Nonprofit and Voluntary Sector Quarterly,* 33: 711–728.

23 Akingbola, K. (2012) "A model of strategic nonprofit human resource management," *Voluntas: International Journal of Voluntary and Nonprofit Organizations,* 24(1): 214–240.

24 Schwind, H., Das, H., & Wagar, T. (2007) *Canadian Human Resource Management,* 8th Edition. Toronto: McGraw-Hill Ryerson.

25 Fried, "Performance management."

26 "Forced Ranking in Performance Management," http://archive.unitetheunion.org/pdf/%28JN3144%29%20Performance%20Management%20Briefing.pdf.

27 Kwoh, L (2012) " 'Rank and Yank' Retains Vocal Fans," http://online.wsj.com/news/articles/SB10001424052970203363504577186970064375222

28 Ibid.

29 Bernardin, H. J., & Smith, P. C. (1981) "A clarification of some issues regarding the development and use of Behaviorally Anchored Rating Scales (BARS)," *Journal of Applied Psychology*, 66(4): 458–463.

30 Jacobs, R., Kafry, D., & Zedeck, S. (1980) "Expectations of Behaviorally Anchored Rating Scales," *Personnel Psychology*, 33: 595–640.

31 Rick, K., Kafry, D., & Zedeck, S. (1980) "Expectations of Behaviorally Anchored Rating Scales," *Personnel Psychology*, 33(3): 595–640.

32 Kane, J. S., & Bernardin, H. J. (1982) "Behavioral observation scales and the evaluation of performance appraisal effectiveness," *Personnel Psychology*, 35: 635–641.

33 Brutus, S. (2010) "Words versus numbers: A theoretical exploration of giving and receiving narrative comments in performance appraisal," *Human Resource Management Review*, 20(2): 144–157.

34 Twomey, D. F., & Twomey, R. F. (1992) "Assessing and transforming performance appraisal," *Journal of Managerial Psychology*, 7(3): 23–32.

35 Campbell, D. J., & Lee, C. (1988) "Self-appraisal in performance evaluation: Development versus evaluation," *The Academy of Management Review*, 13(2): 302–314.

36 Huang, K., Chen, K., Huang, C., & Yien, J. (2011) "Performance appraisal-management by objective and assessment centre," *American Journal of Applied Sciences*, 8(3): 271–276.

37 Pecora, P. J., & Hunter, J. (1988) "Performance appraisal in child welfare: Comparing the MBO and BARS methods," *Administration in Social Work*, 12(1): 55–72.

38 Crutchfield, L. R., & Grant, H. M. (2008) *Forces for Good: The Six Practices of High-Impact Nonprofits*. San Francisco: Jossey-Bass.

9

COMPENSATION AND BENEFITS

Learning Objectives

After studying this chapter, you should be able to:

1. Explain why compensation and benefits are important.
2. Discuss the concept of total reward strategy and basic principles of compensation.
3. Clarify the types of compensation and benefits.
4. Describe methods of job evaluation.
5. Explain concerns about incentive pay in nonprofits.
6. Illustrate the importance of compensation and benefits to SHRM in non-profits.

Strategic Compensation at The Redwood

The Redwood is about adding value to the lives of the vulnerable women and their children who access the services of the nonprofit. With a mission to support women and their children to live free from domestic abuse by providing safe, accessible services that will help them reach their goals, this Toronto-based nonprofit understands the critical role of employees. Redwood is small with about 30 employees but it serves a significant number of clients each year. In 2013, it answered over 500 crisis calls, provided over 35,000 meals and provided shelter for 117 women and children. The compensation challenge was huge. However, the limited resources did not deter a mission-aligned compensation strategy. When survey results consistently showed that their employees who are part of the sandwich generation were having challenges and compensation was part of the issue, The Redwood initiated a strategic compensation review. Similar to most nonprofits, funding was a challenge but large turnover would be a major threat to the organization. The result of the strategic compensation initiative was that the organization was able to use a mix of benefits and salary increases over two years for the counselling team to stay relatively competitive.

Introduction

Evidently, compensation is one of the important tools an organization can use to influence the behavior of employees. The need to influence the behavior of employees, especially by attracting them to work for the organization, motivating them to focus their work effort on the needs of the organization, and rewarding their performance, is essential in order to achieve the goals of the organization. In effect, compensation is central to the ability of the organization to attract, retain and motivate employees who will contribute to the strategic goals of the organization. From the point of view of employees, compensation is the return on the investment in their education, training, and the labor input they have contributed to the organization.[1] It is a form of quid pro quo of their employment relationship with the organization. In essence, an effective compensation system serves a critical purpose for the organization and the employee at different levels.

This chapter discusses compensation as a strategic human resource management (SHRM) function in nonprofit organizations. The opening part of the chapter describes the elements of total rewards, the purpose of compensation and the method of job evaluation. The middle section briefly examines compensation in nonprofits and the case for and against incentive pay in the nonprofit sector. The final part of the chapter examines benefits and non-monetary incentives. The importance and role of compensation as part of an integrated SHRM system is emphasized throughout the chapter.

Compensation

Compensation can be defined as the cash and non-cash payment employees receive from their employers in return for the service rendered to the organization. In a basic sense, compensation is a primary legal obligation of the organization to its employees. This legal obligation underlies the employment relationship. But there is a lot more to compensation than a legal obligation. Compensation includes other elements of pay (e.g. variable pay) that an organization offers an employee in recognition of his or her performance. Following from the introduction above, compensation is integral to the SHRM system and should be integrated with the business strategy of nonprofits. It is vital to the efforts of nonprofits to attract, motivate and retain employees they need to achieve their mission. Moreover, compensation is often the largest percentage of the total operating budget of nonprofits.[2]

Compensation is a key component of total rewards strategy in nonprofits. The construct of total rewards encapsulates the key elements that drive the ability of an organization to attract, motivate and retain employees. In addition to compensation, the other elements of total rewards in the WorldatWork model of the construct are benefits, work-life, performance and recognition, development and career opportunities.[3] Total rewards strategy emphasizes the importance of the context of the organization, a point that is particularly relevant to understand compensation in nonprofits. It also underscores the link between compensation and the core HR practices in tandem with a clear focus on SHRM. Another valuable insight from total rewards strategy is the explanation of its outcomes for employees. Basically, total rewards strategy includes a focus on what employees will derive from the efforts of the organization to attract, motivate and retain them.[4] The point here is that an effective total rewards strategy will result in higher level of engagement and job satisfaction among employees which in turn drive the performance of the organization. However, the most important new thinking from total rewards strategy can be explained in terms of how it reinforces the connection between mission, strategy and SHRM from the perspective of compensation and benefits. It broadens our understanding of how to effectively use compensation in SHRM.

Objectives of Compensation

Compensation serves different but often overlapping purposes for the organization, teams and employees. However, it is not uncommon for the purpose of compensation at one level of the organization to conflict with the purpose at another level. A common example is the hiring manager wanting to pay a competitive salary that is based on the current market pricing for a position in order to recruit an experienced job candidate. However, due to other factors, some of which will be discussed later in the chapter, this might raise concerns about *internal equity* in compensation for long-serving employees of the organization. The goal of attracting and recruiting an experienced employee from the standpoint of compensation in this common example is clearly in divergence with the internal equity purpose of compensation.

Attract and recruit employees. Compensation should help the organization to attract and recruit the employees the organization needs to achieve its strategic goals. Although there are other factors that contribute to the ability of a nonprofit to attract and recruit new employees, compensation ensures the competitiveness of the organization.

Motivate and retain employees. Compensation is also designed to motivate employees to perform in their jobs and foster desirable behavior to meet the expectations of the nonprofit. It plays a role in the decision of employees to remain with or exit the organization.

Facilitate internal equity. A common objective of compensation is to ensure that there is comparable pay for jobs of similar value to the nonprofit. Since compensation is an indication of the relative worth of a job, any significant disparity in pay between similar jobs could raise concerns among employees.

Reward employees. Compensation is also intended to reward employees for a job well done. It reinforces the performance and behavior that meet the expectations of the organization.

Align employee's job and organizational outcomes. Related to the reward objective, compensation helps the organization to underscore the connection between the job role of the employee and the outcomes of the nonprofit. This would help the employee to better understand how her/his contribution impacts the outcomes of the organization.

Ensure legal compliance. As noted previously in the chapter, an organization has a legal obligation to pay the employee for her/his labor. Compensation is the means through which the organization meets the requirement of this legal obligation.

Facilitate affordability. There is no point in a compensation structure that a nonprofit organization cannot afford. The compensation system should ensure that the budget for salaries and wages is financially affordable to the nonprofit.

Facilitate efficiency. Compensation should be efficient to administer and understandable to employees of the nonprofit. The day-to-day administration of a compensation system should not be particularly difficult for HR staff to manage. Also, employees should understand the basics of the compensation system such as how salary increases are determined.

Types of Compensation

Broadly, a compensation system can be categorized into the following two main types: *direct* and *indirect* compensation.

Direct Compensation

Direct compensation can be divided into fixed and variable pay. *Fixed pay* is generally the percentage of an employee's compensation that does not vary based on job performance or outcome.[5] Rather, it is tied to the element of time in the sense that the employee is required to work a certain number of hours per week or month. This type of compensation is also known as base pay. A *wage* is a form of base pay that is determined by the number of hours worked by the employee while a weekly or monthly time period is used to calculate a *salary*.

Variable pay is the portion of direct compensation that is determined by the achievement of specific performance objectives or outcomes, or at the discretion of the management.[6] Although examples of variable pay include different types of incentive pay such as bonus, commission and stock options, in nonprofits variable pay is mainly in the form of bonus. This is due in part to the fact that nonprofits do not distribute profit. Many US nonprofits provide incentive pay for top executives based on performance, tenure on the job or combination of both.[7] A research study found that executive compensation in nonprofits is only modestly affected by CEO performance.[8] However, the same study suggested that free cash flow contributed to the level of compensation of nonprofit CEOs. Regardless of the level of the pay, the issue of incentive pay is generally a contentious issue in nonprofits. The issue is discussed later in the chapter.

Indirect Compensation

Indirect compensation includes mostly *non-monetary benefits* and *perquisites* provided to employees by the organization. The goal of indirect compensation is to help to meet some of the needs of employees, which may be related or unrelated to their job.[9] Although benefits and perquisites are often incorrectly considered to be an add-on to compensation, they are generally part of the total compensation package. There is a real cost to the organization to provide benefits for employees. Generally, indirect compensation can be classified into three main types: protection programs, employee services and pay for time not worked.[10] Many of the protection programs are mandated by legislation. Benefits will be discussed in detail later in this chapter.

The components of compensation provide a nonprofit organization the options of what to emphasize in its *compensation strategy*. It also provides the information on how to determine the mix of base pay, variable pay and benefits to offer employees (see Figure 9.1). For example, a nonprofit would need to decide whether to spend more on benefits that are important to employees and reflective of the values of organization, increase direct pay, offer some form of incentive pay, or a combination of the three options. Whatever combination is adopted is a matter that should be determined by the compensation strategy of the nonprofit.

Compensation Strategy

The most critical questions about what an organization would do about compensation should be addressed in the compensation strategy. It includes questions about both the financial, non-financial and socio-psychological rewards the organization would like to emphasize. In other words, compensation strategy raises and addresses questions about extrinsic and intrinsic rewards. These questions are further accentuated by the unique environment of nonprofits and the characteristics of nonprofit employees which are discussed below.

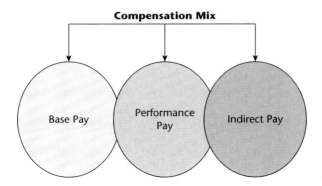

FIGURE 9.1 Compensation Mix Choices

Source: Adapted from Long, R. & Ravichander, H. S. (2006) *Strategic Compensation: A Simulation.* Scarborough: Nelson.

Hence, compensation strategy is fundamental to the ability of a nonprofit to attract, recruit and motivate employees.

Compensation strategy is about the compensation mix choices made by the organization. Basically, it outlines the mix of choices included in the compensation system, explains why the organization decided to deploy the specific choices, and how the organization will administer the compensation system. The compensation strategy has implications for the effective use of human resources in the organization.[11] It includes the guiding principles, design, implementation and the day-to-day administration of the compensation system in an organization.[12] Compensation strategy also signals the pay policy and informs the key processes in compensation such as pay for performance, annual increases and bonuses. All the relevant base pay, performance pay and indirect compensation offered to employees of the organization are outlined in the compensation strategy.

It is important to emphasize that not only must the compensation strategy be congruent with other HR practices and be a critical component of SHRM, it must also be aligned with the business strategy of the organization. The fit between compensation and the business strategy is one of the ways of directing individual performance towards the strategic objectives of the organization.[13] Compensation is also a tool for communicating and reaffirming the importance of the strategy of the organization. Bearing in mind the total rewards strategy discussed above, compensation is a visible and integrated SHRM tool.

Closely related to compensation strategy is the concept of *compensation philosophy*. It outlines the fundamental beliefs of the organization about compensation. The compensation philosophy statement lays bare the values of the organization pertaining to what employees are paid and how they are paid. This typically includes how the organization will compete in terms of pay for employees. The philosophy guides the design of the compensation system in terms of choices of what is included and emphasized, and the difficult balance between competing priorities. For example, it gives an indication of whether pay increases will be based on performance or years of service or both. Nonprofits must ensure that their compensation philosophy reflects the core values that define the organization.

Together, compensation strategy and philosophy provide a specific direction on compensation in the organization. The compensation strategy helps nonprofit managers to identify and effectively communicate the focal points of the organization's compensation system. This could help to enhance the employee engagement efforts of managers. The ability of the organization to attract and recruit new employees is also enhanced with a clear compensation strategy that is consistent with the business strategy of the nonprofit.

Compensation in Nonprofits

Compensation is a particularly touchy topic in most organizations. It is even more so in a nonprofit with a heightened level of competitive environmental factors such as accountability and public scrutiny. It is therefore not a surprise that compensation is consistently identified as a concern in most nonprofits.[14] Although the environment of nonprofits in each country is different, the evidence of nonprofit compensation challenges in the US,[15] Canada,[16] and the UK[17] appears to have a similar pattern. As a result, while the general objectives of compensation and the importance of compensation strategy discussed above are relevant, there are specific drivers and elements of compensation in nonprofits.

Intrinsic versus extrinsic rewards. The need to balance between the choices available to nonprofits in the design of the compensation system starts with the question of whether to emphasize intrinsic or extrinsic rewards. Intrinsic rewards are generally the psychological rewards or outcomes that employees derive from doing the job. Examples of intrinsic rewards include meaningfulness, participation in decision-making, and autonomy. In nonprofits, research has shown that employees value the opportunity to contribute to the public good that underlies the mission of nonprofit organizations.[18] Nonprofit employees are motivated by the causes and good deeds in which their organizations are involved.

Extrinsic rewards are the tangible rewards that employees receive from the organization in return for their employment and performance on the job. The common forms of extrinsic rewards include pay increases, bonuses, benefits and payments for time not worked. Extrinsic rewards help organizations to meet the basic needs (hygiene needs) of employees.[19] It is not the be all and end all of employee satisfaction, but it helps the organization to avoid losing employees because they not satisfied. Although extrinsic rewards continue to play an important role in how employees are compensated in organizations, the value of intrinsic rewards in employee motivation and retention is more important than ever before.

The question about the choice between intrinsic and extrinsic rewards in compensation in nonprofits is relevant because nonprofit employees have inherent intrinsic motivation. The fact that employees are attracted to and identify with the mission of nonprofits[20] emphasizes the need for managers to seriously consider the SHRM importance of intrinsic rewards in the design of their compensation system. Nonprofit managers must deploy intrinsic rewards to build on the inherent characteristics of their employees. It is an essential component of the compensation system that contributes to the effectiveness of SHRM in nonprofits.

Non-distribution constraint. One of the basic characteristics of nonprofits is that they do not distribute net earnings to individuals who control the organization such as members, officers, directors or trustees.[21] This basic characteristic impacts compensation at different levels of the organization. At the very least, it plays into the choices available to nonprofit managers in terms of what can be included in the compensation mix of the organization. Generally, non-distribution constraint suggests that there is a limit to what type of compensation nonprofits can offer employees. For example, nonprofits do not generally offer stock options in their compensation. Also, non-distribution constraint means that there are limited financial resources available to nonprofits to use in compensation. When nonprofits are able to generate net earnings, it does not necessarily mean that portion of such earnings can be used to enhance compensation.

Goods and services. The nature of the goods and services provided by nonprofits is inextricably linked with compensation. The provider of social goods and services characteristic of nonprofits plays into compensation mainly through the market value attached to some types of human services and benevolent jobs. While these jobs are highly valued in society, the compensation market pricing of the jobs tends to be lower. As discussed below, the relative worth of nonprofit jobs in the job-worth hierarchy is influenced in part by the human service characteristics of the jobs and the skills required for those jobs.

Pay for performance or not? The question of whether incentive pay or pay for performance is appropriate is a particularly divisive issue in nonprofits. Since pay for performance links compensation to the performance of the individual, team, and/or the organization, it is supposed to align the goals of the organization with those of the employees. For managers, it addresses some of the problems in agency theory. Pay for performance melds the interests of managers to those of the board of directors. Nonprofits are increasingly using pay for performance as a core component of their compensation system, especially for top executives.[22] Although the introduction of pay for performance could enhance the ability of nonprofits to attract, retain and motivate employees, there are concerns about its appropriateness. Box 9.1 outlines the specific concerns about the use of pay for performance in nonprofits. However, recent research has found that nonprofits use pay for performance in their compensation system to address perceived individual performance differences and to enhance their ability to gain influence in their competitive environment.[23] Generally, many of the challenges can be addressed with clear guidelines spelling out rewards for performance that have the potential of minimizing shirking and enhancing performance of employees.[24]

BOX 9.1 CONCERNS ABOUT PAY FOR PERFORMANCE IN NONPROFITS

- Mission Concern
  Pay for performance could take the focus of employees away from the mission.
- Donation Concern
  Donors and the general public would have concerns if they perceive that their donation is used to pay for bonuses.
- Performance Indicator Concern

Since it is a challenge to define an objective performance indicator in nonprofits, the basis of pay for performance is complicated.
- Change in Services Concern
  Due to government contract funding, nonprofits change services to adapt to the funding environment. This could make it difficult to adopt pay for performance.
- Executive Compensation Concern
  Pay for performance for nonprofit executives may come at the expense of other employees.

Source: Barbeito, C. L., & Bowman, J. P. (1998). *Nonprofit Compensation and Benefits Practices*. New York: John Wiley; McMullen, K., & Schellenberg, G. (2003a). *Job Quality in Nonprofit Organizations*. Ottawa: Canadian Policy Research Network; Akingbola, K. (2004) "Staffing, retention and government funding: The Canadian Red Cross, Toronto Region," *Nonprofit Management and Leadership*, 14(4): 453–467.

Lower pay. A key comparative element of compensation in nonprofits is that pay is generally lower in the sector. Studies have shown that the average pay of many nonprofit jobs is lower than similar jobs in other sectors.[25] This difference in pay is accentuated for management and professional jobs. The question of the comparatively lower pay in nonprofits is a multifaceted issue. On the one hand, one perspective suggests that the lower pay issue has been attributed to the non-distribution constraint characteristic of nonprofits discussed previously. In addition to the factors above, it reduces the budget and sources of cash available for compensation. Also relevant is the funding challenges discussed in Chapter 3. Funding affects the compensation system of nonprofits both directly and indirectly. The direct impact is in the form of the compensation costing and level in the funding contract, while the indirect impact is often through the institutional effect of the funder on the nonprofit. In fact, it has been suggested that nonprofit managers accept lower wages to indicate their fiduciary role to the funding organization and patrons.[26] Funding further limits the competitiveness of compensation in nonprofits.

On the other hand, another perspective suggests that lower pay could actually be an important factor in the HR branding of nonprofits. In this sense, employees are attracted to the fact that the goals of nonprofits are not related to profit maximization.[27] The willingness of employees to work in the sector with the knowledge of the lower pay means that employees essentially donate their labor for the purpose of the mission of the organization.[28] This is called the donative labor hypothesis.[29] Employees are somewhat similar to volunteers in this respect.

The low pay issue inhibits the ability of nonprofits to attract and retain employees. In effect, it curtails the competitiveness of nonprofits with other sectors. The 2013 Nonprofit Employment Trends Survey reported that most of the organizations indicated that inability to pay was their greatest retention challenge. Similarly, over half of the organizations have difficulty competing with other sectors based on salary.[30] However, low pay is not uniform across nonprofits. Some nonprofits pay their managers better wages than other organizations. Variability in pay across types of nonprofits has been found to relate to size and whether organization type, managerial quality and industry types are fixed to government grants.[31]

Together, these nonprofit-specific factors further emphasize the importance of the unique drivers of compensation in nonprofits. Of course the drivers overlap. They add to the general organizational factors such as size to shape compensation systems in nonprofits. Since most nonprofits are small, size is a particularly important organizational factor in these organizations. It does play a critical role in compensation because of the small budget and assets of nonprofits.[32] Research suggests that financial capacity issues emanating from funding have a significant influence on other capabilities including HR.[33] The bottom line is that nonprofit managers must pay particular attention to balance these drivers as challenges in the design of compensation systems. Compensation is at the forefront of the SHRM challenges of most nonprofits. Compared to other sectors, nonprofits have different compensation challenges. But the need to align their compensation systems to SHRM in the organization is not different from other sectors.

Job evaluation

Job evaluation is the systematic process and tool for determining the relative worth of jobs in an organization. It is at the center of the design and implementation of an effective compensation system, especially the base salary structure. The job-worth hierarchy is the key outcome of job evaluation.[34] Job evaluation is based on three key assumptions:[35] (1) it is logical to pay the best salaries for the jobs that are most critical to achieving the goals of the organization; (2) people will feel there is equity if the salaries that are paid are based on the relative worth of their jobs; (3) a job structure that is based on this promotes the goals of the organization.[36]

In a broad sense, job evaluation encompasses the entire formal process of determining basic pay. This process has four main components: job analysis, job evaluation, pay structure, and maintenance.[37] Job evaluation uses the information provided by *job analysis* to compare jobs based on what each job is worth to the organization. As discussed in Chapter 6, *job analysis* is the systematic process through which information collected to define the nature of the job and the knowledge, skills and abilities required to perform the job are determined. As a key component of HR planning, the information provided by job analysis is intended to clearly define the job responsibilities and the job specification. The job evaluation phase in the broader process outlines what the job is about—what the characteristics of the job are. *Pay structure* creates salary ranges and levels for positions in an organization, while the maintenance involves the regular updating of salary information based on changes in the organization and the market.

Job evaluation is a rational process that draws on specific measures or standards to group jobs into a hierarchy. It does this by analyzing the job content in terms of its intrinsic value to the organization as well as relevant market data for the job. In essence, job evaluation is about relationships.[38] The relationship between jobs and employees, between jobs and the organization and between jobs and the market are analyzed and monetized through job evaluation. Although rational, it is a process that is dependent on discretion and decision-making.[39] Managers and HR professionals who design compensation systems make strategic decisions about pay for the organization. Thus, there is a risk that job evaluation could be more subjective than objective. This risk is mitigated by the need for job evaluation to lay the foundation of internal equity and external competitiveness, a topic to be discussed later in the chapter. For now, we provide a brief overview of the methods of job evaluation.

Ranking

Job ranking is a simple job evaluation method that uses basic information to rank jobs from highest to lowest based on their relative importance to the organization. It is a possibly subjective method that involves the review of the job responsibilities followed by comparison with other jobs. Since jobs are compared to other jobs at a high level, detailed analysis of the content of each job is not part of the process used to determine the overall ranking. In addition to the fact that it could be subjective, ranking is not practical for organizations with large numbers of jobs.

Ranking also downplays the relative differences between jobs in terms of their importance to the organization.[40] For example, Table 9.1 presents a hypothetical ranking of five real jobs at Belmont Housing Resources for Western New York.[41] Similar to other jobs in the ranking, it does not reflect the actual relative difference between Housing Rehab Programs Manager and Family Self Sufficiency Program Coordinator. It is possible that the latter is three times as important as the former.

TABLE 9.1 Ranking of Jobs at Belmont Housing Resources for WNY

Jobs	*Rank*
Maintenance Assistant	1
FSS/Homeownership Coordinator	2
Family Self-Sufficiency Program Coordinator	3
Housing Rehab Programs Manager	4
Vice President, Housing Programs	5

Classification

Job classification is an evaluation method in which jobs are slotted into pre-determined classes or levels (Table 9.2). The key factors that are used to determine the level of a job are the job requirements, job specification and working conditions. Although job classification is a significant step up from job ranking, it also involves the comparison of jobs. However, in job classification, the job description is thoroughly analyzed and compared to a role profile that summarizes the class or level.

To create a job profile, most job classification systems cluster relevant skills, knowledge, abilities and tasks together to define levels.[42] Hence, they foster efficiency and enhance HR practices, including selection, performance appraisal and training for the organization. Regardless of the system, two main decisions are fundamental in job classification. The first is the defining of the type and number of job profiles, while the second is the method that will be used to group job classes or levels.[43] Typically, the higher the class of a job in a job classification, the higher level of responsibility, job specification and salary range. However, achieving internal equity is a goal as it is in the other methods of job classification. To a lesser extent, job classification could be susceptible to the problem of subjectivity, especially if the criteria for slotting jobs into a class are not clearly defined.

TABLE 9.2 Sample Job Classification

Title	Annual salary range minimum	Annual salary range maximum
Grade 1	$31,881	$36,505
Admin Assistant Data Entry Clerk Receptionist		
Grade 2	$34,991	$40,174
Community Services Coordinator Membership Support Coordinator Communication Coordinator		
Grade 3	$38,420	$45,200
Volunteer Coordinator Community Outreach Coordinator HR Coordinator		
Grade 4	$42,178	$49,620
Assistant Program Supervisor Grant Writer Development Associate		
Grade 5	$43,578	$54,473
Community Consultant Project Coordinator II Program Supervisor		

Market Pricing

Unlike the other methods of job evaluation, market pricing looks to the external market as the primary benchmark to create salary structure for an organization. This is not to suggest that job content evaluation is not considered. On the contrary, job content evaluation which includes the job requirements and job specification provides the basis for the market pricing. Job content is the starting point that provides the information the designer of the compensation system would use to identify the relevant market comparators and benchmark jobs. However, the key distinguishing factor of market pricing in the creation of job hierarchy for an organization is the emphasis on external compensation data.[44]

Similar to other methods of job evaluation, the effectiveness of market pricing depends on the quality of available compensation data, data collection and the analysis of the data. These factors are especially important in market pricing to ensure that there is a match between the jobs of the organization and the market comparator jobs. A WorldatWork course manual offers four questions that are important to any organization that is considering market pricing as a method for job evaluation (Box 9.2).[45]

BOX 9.2 QUESTIONS FOR MARKET PRICING

- Is the organization capable of collecting data on a majority of its jobs?
- Are the data sources reliable?
- Are the sources representative of the relevant labor markets?
- What is the best way to analyze and use the data collected?

Source: WorldatWork. Course Manual.

In addition to the issues raised by the questions above, market pricing has other limitations. First, the use of market pricing could influence designers of compensation systems to rely on just the job titles to determine the comparators for the jobs of the organization. Although good market salary surveys generally encourage a thorough analysis of the job profiles of the comparator and benchmark jobs, the job title is the first information that is compared. Second, market pricing could compound internal equity due to the emphasis on market competitiveness and the differences in the market for jobs within an organization. Third, some jobs are difficult to benchmark because each organization within the same sector adapts the content of them differently.[46] Bearing in mind that most nonprofits are small organizations with limited resources, the questions and limitations should be considered carefully before adopting market pricing.

Point System

The point system is a quantitative method of job evaluation that determines the value of a job by assigning points to core elements of the job, known as compensable factors.[47] There are four main ideas with corresponding processes in the point system. First is the concept of compensable factors. Jobs are defined by compensable factors. These are basically elements of the job such as knowledge, skills, experience, ability, responsibility, accountability and working conditions derived from the job analysis.[48] The second idea is that there are different levels of compensable factors in each job. For example, a job may require different levels of education and experience. The allocation of points is the third idea. Points are assigned or allocated to each compensable factor based on the nature of the factor and its contribution to the desired outcomes of the job. The fourth idea is the total points. The job is evaluated by calculating the total points of all the compensable factors.[49] This determines the value of the job.

Typically, the result of the point system is a relatively objective job and salary structure with salary ranges. The point system enables the HR compensation specialist or the job evaluation committee to clearly define, measure and analyze the compensable factors of a job in detail. The comparative differences between jobs are better reflected and understandable to managers and employees. This facilitates internal equity in the organization. The use of compensable factors and the systematic process deployed in the point system are a considerable improvement over the ranking and the job classification systems. Moreover, the point system is easy to revise and new jobs can be added as required.[50] However, the point system has a number of limitations. It requires significant time and resources to set up. Also, it often serves to reinforce the hierarchy that exists in organizations which could reflect more of the salary survey data than job evaluation.[51] There are also many judgment calls involved in the process, which apparently enhance the quality of the system.[52]

The following overview outlines a generic process for implementing a point system method of job evaluation.[53] It summarizes the generally similar steps that have been presented in the academic and practitioner compensation literature with some variations to the context of nonprofits.[54] It is important to note that the process can be customized to meet the needs of the organization.

Step 1: Select Compensable Factors

As discussed above, compensable factors are the key elements of the job, such as knowledge, skills, experience, ability, responsibility, safety, accountability and working conditions. Nonprofits must ensure that the selected compensable factors are measurable. Also, each factor must be present to a varying degree in all jobs.

TABLE 9.3 Level Definitions for Education

Degree	Definition
1	At least high school diploma
2	Attain trade or career certificate
3	Attain associate degree
4	Attain undergraduate degree
5	Attain graduate degree

Step 2: Determine Factor Degrees or Levels

Since all jobs do not have the same degrees for all compensable factors, the non-profit must determine the different degrees for a given factor. The levels indicate the relative importance of each factor across jobs as well as the sub-factors within each factor, if applicable. Hence, it is important to have an adequate number of degrees in order to highlight the differences between jobs. But the number of degrees should be determined by the nature of each factor. Table 9.3 illustrates the definition of degrees or levels for education.

Step 3: Assign Points to Compensable Factors

The next step is to assign points to the factors based on their relative importance to the organization. The points are assigned to the factors consistent with the number of degrees in a given factor. Before assigning points, the specific weight of the factors must be determined to indicate the relative value of each factor. For example, the weights could be assigned as follows: experience 30 percent; education 20 percent; effort 15 percent; responsibility 20 percent; and working conditions 15 percent. Of course, each nonprofit could customize the weights consistent with the needs and operational realities of the organization. This emphasizes the fact that assigning points often involves judgment calls by the Compensation Analyst or the Job Evaluation Committee. Even when points are assigned using statistics, judgment calls must be made on how to use the statistics to reflect the relative value of the job. The reality is that points are more easily assigned to some factors than others. For example, experience can be assigned points based on the number of years while the sub-factors of responsibility must be defined.

Step 4: Assign Points to Compensable Sub-Factors

As illustrated in Table 9.4, points must also be assigned to the sub-factors in each factor to reflect the relative value of the sub-factors. The points assigned to the factor are divided among the sub-factors. Generally, the highest level sub-factor is assigned a point first followed by the other sub-factors based on the judgment call of the Compensation Analyst or the Job Evaluation Committee.

TABLE 9.4 Point System

Factors	Minimum Points	Maximum Points	Weight	Points
Responsibility			40%	400
Service Delivery	20	200		
Business Leadership	10	100		
Planning	5	50		
Continuous Improvement	5	50		
Knowledge & skills			30%	300
Core Knowledge	10	170		
Analytical Skills	8	80		
Customer Service Skills	5	50		
Supervision			15%	150
Supervision	0	150		
Effort			15%	150
Mental Effort	10	100		
Physical Effort	5	50		
Total Points				1000

Step 5: Evaluate the Jobs

The job is now ready for evaluation. With points assigned to the factors and sub-factors, the jobs can be evaluated with the new point system. It is advisable to evaluate the key or benchmark jobs first. The evaluation process involves the analysis of the job description of the benchmark jobs in terms of the levels, the compensable factors and the points. The goal of the analysis is not only to evaluate the benchmark jobs but also to test the validity of the point value assigned to the compensable factors. If there is a match between the new point system and the benchmark jobs, the outcome is the points of the sub-factors of the benchmark jobs.[55] The evaluation of the benchmark jobs is completed by adding all the points of the sub-factors together to calculate the total points of each of the benchmark jobs.

Step 6: Create Salary Structure

The difference between the total points of the benchmark jobs is the basis of the salary structure of the organization. The jobs are positioned on a scale to indicate the job-worth hierarchy based on their total points. The development of the salary structure includes the creation of salary grades and ranges. To create a salary, jobs that have similar total points are clustered into salary grades.[56] New jobs are evaluated and based on their point values, and the jobs are slotted into the salary grades.

Factor Comparison

Factor comparison is a job evaluation method that shares some of the elements of ranking and the point system. As the name suggests, the key concept of the method is factor comparison. First, the compensation analysts must determine the compensable factors of certain jobs in the organization that will be used as key compensable factors. This is done by comparing compensable factors against other comparable factors directly. Unlike the point system, the emphasis is on the compensable factors and not the jobs per se for this phase of the process. Second, following the determination of the key compensable factors, benchmark jobs are assessed based on the compensable factors.[57] Typically, the compensable factors that are used are mental effort, skill, responsibility, physical effort and working conditions. Third, a factor comparison scale is created to evaluate other jobs. Basically, the compensable factors of the jobs to be evaluated are compared to the compensable factors of the benchmark jobs on a factor-to-factor basis.

Although it is rarely used, factor comparison can better be adapted to the organization. It also clearly shows better comparison between jobs because the emphasis is on the comparable factors. However, the complexity of the method makes it difficult to implement. Moreover, the method could overemphasize the benchmark jobs.

In all, regardless of the method of job evaluation a nonprofit adopts, a major goal in addition to grouping jobs into levels or grades is to achieve internal equity. The question of internal equity is evidently a major concern for nonprofits due to their social mission and values. Although external competitiveness is similarly a concern, the operating environment of nonprofits has rendered their ability to address this particular challenge essentially a long shot. Since most nonprofits are small organizations, it is not clear how valuable recent innovations in job evaluation such as competencies and broad banding will benefit the organization. Moreover, research on the use and type of job evaluation in nonprofits is negligible.

Benefits

To understand total rewards in nonprofits, one must also examine and have a relative understanding of the state of employee benefits in the sector. Benefits are a key component of total compensation that is neither base pay nor pay for performance.[58] It can broadly be defined as any type of reward, inducements or services provided by an employer to employees that is apart from direct compensation.[59] Employers use benefits to supplement the cash compensation and meet the needs of employees.

Benefits are an important component of a total rewards strategy. Employee benefits play a significant role in a nonprofit's ability to attract, retain and motivate employees. Moreover, the cost of benefits is a source of concern for managers in many organizations because it constitutes a significant portion of the organization's compensation cost.[60] According to recent data, benefits account for about 30 percent of the total compensation cost of US organizations.[61] Bearing in mind that compensation cost accounts for between 60 and 80 percent of the operating cost of many nonprofits, the cost of benefits in nonprofits would be considerable. The unique characteristics and the changing needs of employees require a focused SHRM that incorporates benefits. Hence, it is imperative to understand the diverse strategies in benefits and how to effectively communicate the content of benefits and changes to employees in nonprofit organizations.

Type of Benefits

The basic forms of benefits that employers provide to employees can be classified into three main categories: legally required, voluntary benefits, services and perquisites.[62] Although there is significant variation in the national and state/provincial legislation as well as HR practices of nonprofits in the US, the UK and Canada, this broad categorization includes the main types of benefits provided to employees.

Legally Required Benefits

As the name suggests, legally required benefits are generally those benefits that employers are legally required to provide to employees. In the US, employers and employees are required to contribute to social security, Medicare and unemployment insurance. Most states also require employers contribute to workers' compensation, which provides income to employees who are unable to work due to workplace injury or illness.[63] Social security is a public benefits program that provides retirement income, disability income and survivorship benefits to families of workers who die.

Employers in the UK are required to make payments to the National Insurance Contributions (NICs). The national insurance contributions qualify employees for certain public benefits including state pension, contribution-based jobseeker's allowance, bereavement allowance, contribution-based employment and support allowance.[64] Employees also contribute to national insurance. Canadian employers are required to contribute to the Canada and Quebec pension plans, workers' compensation and employment insurance. Some Canadian provinces also require employers to contribute to public health insurance plans.

Voluntary Benefits

These are benefits that employers have a choice to provide or not provide. However, most employers provide some form of voluntary benefits to facilitate their SHRM goal of attracting, motivating and retaining employees. In addition, voluntary benefits help the organization to mitigate potential risks to productivity from employee personal and family well-being issues. The major forms of voluntary benefits are healthcare, insurance, retirement and reimbursed time off.

Healthcare Benefits

Healthcare benefits generally cover prescription drugs and medical care including surgery. Most healthcare benefits also provide coverage for vision and dental care.

Insurance

Employers provide opportunities for employees to have insurance coverage for life and short-term and long-term disability. Some also provide long-term care insurance and travel insurance.

Retirement Benefits

Retirement benefits are intended to provide income for employees when they retire. The two basic types of retirement benefits are defined benefit and defined contribution plans. In a defined benefits plan the employee receives a guaranteed pension based on his or her length of service to the organization, salary and age. Defined contribution plans can be based on the employer's contribution only—known as non-contributory plan[65]—or on contributions by both the employee and the employer. The pension that the employee receives will depend on the total contribution and the investment income. Increasingly, employers are adopting defined contribution plans more than defined benefit plans.

Reimbursed Time Off

These types of benefits are related to payments by the organization to employees when they are not actively at work. Reimbursed time off includes holidays and vacation pay, which is legally required for most full-time employees. Other types of reimbursed time include paid leave, personal days, sick leave and jury duty.

Services and Perquisites

Services and perquisites are other forms of benefits that are not within the categories of traditional benefits that employers offer employees. Often, services and perquisites are tailored to meet the specific needs of the employees. Common examples of services include employee assistance program (EAP), wellness programs, education allowances and membership at fitness clubs. Perquisites could be tied to the level of a job and could include executive coaching, use of a car provided by the organization, and membership of exclusive clubs.

Benefits in Nonprofits

Benefits are particularly important to nonprofits. Foremost, it is a way of high-lighting the concerns of the organization for the well-being of employees from a purely altruistic perspective. What the organization is saying is that we care for our employees not only because of our employment relationship but also because of our fundamental values. The point here is that nonprofits can live their values through the types of benefits they offer employees.

Although this implicit expectation is lofty if one should consider the complex challenges in the operating environment of nonprofits, it is a no-brainer based on the primary characteristic of these organizations. The good news is that research has found some evidence that nonprofits are actually providing benefits based on their concern for the well-being of their employees.[66] This good news is further reinforced by a significant body of evidence that suggests that nonprofits do generally provide benefits that compare favorably with those of both the public and business sectors in terms of the range of benefits.[67] In fact, nonprofits are more likely to include more generous benefits such as paid leave, vacation and family leave in their total compensation package than for-profit organizations.

Box 9.3 provides an excellent overview of what organizations are doing and the direction of employee benefits in nonprofits in the US. The insight on innovative practices further reinforces how nonprofits are using social mission and values to drive the benefits they offer to employees.

BOX 9.3 INNOVATION IN BENEFITS IN US NONPROFITS

- Most large nonprofits on this year's list show flexibility in benefits that allow them to, in essence, practice what they preach.
- WWP's compassion fatigue workshop is one example.
- Other examples include:
  - o five days annual leave for elder care offered by the Alzheimer's Association;
  - o wellness programs by the American Heart Association; and,
  - o a discount on Patagonia apparel, described as "an ecoconscience brand that makes great clothes," offered to employees of the Natural Resources Defense Council.

Source: Morton, G. (2013) "Small can come up big when it's employee relations," The *NonProfit Times Best Nonprofits to Work For,* 2013.

In Canada, a significant number of nonprofits are increasingly providing innovative benefits to employees. Many nonprofits offer flexible time, compressed work week, and travel costs.[68] Compared to a decade ago, when most nonprofits did not provide benefits,[69] 80 percent of nonprofits in a 2013 nonprofit compensation and benefits survey offered health and education benefits to employees.[70] However, these benefits are more prevalent in large nonprofits. Also, retirement benefits are offered only in about 50 percent of the participating nonprofits.

However, the picture of benefits in nonprofits is not all rosy. There are many facets of the challenges of benefits in nonprofits. First, there are still a minority of nonprofits that are not able to offer benefits due mainly to the small size of the organization. With many nonprofits having only a few employees, the ability to buy benefits coverage at competitive rates is limited. Second, the impact of contract funding that has resulted in the increased use of temporary and part-time staff means that there are groups of nonprofit employees who are not eligible for benefits available to full-time employees.[71] Three, the costs of benefits is a particular challenge to nonprofits because of the very limited financial resources of most organizations in the sector. Nonprofits have to adopt on-going cost containment strategies to ensure that benefits are affordable within the meagre resources of the organization. Table 9.5 outlines some generic cost containment strategies that have been adopted in nonprofits and organizations in other sectors. Finally, it has been suggested that nonprofits offer generous benefits to counter the challenges of low salaries in the sector. Benefits featured prominently as one of the options nonprofits are leveraging to compete with other sectors in their effort to attract, motivate and retain employees.[72] While this is not an issue per se, it cast a shadow on the point that benefits are offered based on the social mission and values of nonprofits.

TABLE 9.5 Cost Containment Strategies

Strategy	Detail
Education and Communication	Communicate cost of benefits
	Educate employees on the how they can help to manage costs Control costs
	Educate employees on how costs impact their contributions
Manage Plan Design	Manage and review eligibility
	Encourage coordination of benefits with spouses
	Explore flexible spending account/health spending account
	Consider plan options: fully insured plan; self-insured plan (ASO); flexible plan (Cafeteria)
Manage High Risk and Over-usage	Introduce system to manage high-risk users
	Introduce process to manage over-usage
Use Analytics	Use analytics to project usage and experience
	Project cost increases and decreases
	Introduce mitigating strategies
Promote Wellness	Introduce wellness programs
	Incentivize wellness activities

Source: Some of the strategies are adapted from *Stretching the Health Benefits Dollar*. A report by the Advisory Board HR Investment Centre.

Summary

Compensation and benefits are critical to the effectiveness of SHRM in nonprofits. The need to offer competitive compensation and benefits is driven not only by the SHRM goal of attracting, motivating and retaining the highly qualified and committed employees the organization requires to achieve its strategic objectives, but also of actualizing the values of the organization. In addition, the context of compensation and benefits is further complicated by the unique characteristics of the employees and the operating environment of nonprofits. For employees of nonprofits, compensation is not and cannot be about extrinsic rewards. Nonprofit employees want more than a good compensation package. They want to be compensated by the intrinsic reward of doing their public good jobs, by actualizing the values that attracted them to the organization, and most of all, by seeing the real impact of these in the lives of the clients of their organizations.

The operating environment poses significant challenges to the development and implementation of an effective compensation system. Managers must analyze and understand how these drivers and the internal environment coalesce to shape compensation and benefits. Regardless of the content of the compensation mix adopted and the process used to develop and communicate compensation and benefits, continuously scanning the environment means that nonprofits are positioned to adapt and manage the need for change in compensation and benefits.

Discussion Questions

1. Explain the importance of compensation in the ability of nonprofits to attract and recruit qualified employees.
2. Since most nonprofit organizations cannot compete with for-profit businesses and the public sector in terms of compensation, how can benefits be used to enhance the total compensation in nonprofits?
3. Incentive pay is controversial in nonprofits. What can nonprofits do to address the concerns about incentive pay?
4. A human service nonprofit organization in Chicago asked a consultant to conduct a salary survey on its behalf. What are some of the factors the consultant must consider?

Notes

1 Lawler, E., III (2000) *Rewarding Excellence: Pay Strategies for the New Economy.* San Francisco: Jossey-Bass.
2 Barbeito, C. L., & Bowman, J. P. (1998) *Nonprofit Compensation and Benefits Practices.* New York: John Wiley.
3 Rogers, S., & Marcotte, S. (2010) *Communicating Total Rewards.* Scottsdale, AZ: Worldat Work Press.

4 Ibid.

5 WorldatWork (2008) *Job Analysis, Documentation and Evaluation*. Scottsdale, AZ: WorldatWork Press.

6 Ibid.

7 Hrywna, M. (2009) "Exec's salary becomes a funding problem," *Nonprofit Times*, September 1, 2009, http://www.thenonprofittimes.com/news-articles/exec-s-salary-becomes-a-funding-problem/. Retrieved December, 2013; Schorsch, K. (2011). "NW hospital CEO's payday: Harrison leads parade of non-profit health system execs with $10 million," *Crain's Chicago Business*, 34(47), http://www.chicagobusiness.com/article/20111119/ISSUE01/311199974. Retrieved December, 2013.

8 Frumkin, P., & Keating, E. K. (2010) "The price of doing good: Executive compensation in nonprofit organizations," *Policy and Society*, 29(3): 269–282.

9 Long, R., & Ravichander, H. S. (2006) *Strategic Compensation: A Simulation*. Scarborough: Nelson.

10 Ibid.

11 Gomez-Mejia, L. R., & Welbourne, T. (1988) "Compensation strategy: An overview and future steps," *Human Resource Planning*, 11: 173–189.

12 WorldatWork, *Job Analysis, Documentation and Evaluation*.

13 Cumming, C. M. (1994) "Incentives that really do motivate," *Compensation & Benefits Review*, 26: 38–40.

14 Jobome, G. (2006) "Management pay, governance and performance: The case of large UK nonprofits," *Financial Accountability & Management*, 22(4): 331–358.

15 Nonprofit HR Solutions (2013) *Nonprofit Employment Trends Survey*, http://www.nonprofithr.com/wp-content/uploads/2013/03/2013-Employment-Trends-Survey-Report.pdf. Retrieved December, 2013.

16 The HR Council (2011) "Money matters: Compensation in the nonprofit sector," http://www.hrcouncil.ca/labour/trends_compensation.cfm. Retrieved June, 2013.

17 Dearden-Phillips, C. (2013) "Charities must pay proper money to attract and keep good chief executives," *Third Sector*, August 19, 2013, http://www.thirdsector.co.uk/news/1207826/Craig-Dearden-Phillips-Charities-pay-proper-money-attract-keep-good-chief-executives/?DCMP=ILC-SEARCH. Retrieved December, 2013.

18 Roomkin, M., & Weisbrod, B. (1999) "Managerial compensation and incentives in for-profit and non-profit hospitals," *Journal of Law, Economics, and Organisations*, 15: 750–781.

19 Herzberg, F., Mausner, B., & Snyderman, B. B. (1959) *The Motivation to Work,* 2nd Edition. New York: John Wiley & Sons.

20 Brown, W. A., & Yoshioka, C. (2003) "Mission attachment and satisfaction as factors in. employee retention," *Nonprofit Leadership and Management*, 14(1): 5–18.

21 Hansmann, H. B. (1980) "The role of nonprofit enterprise," *The Yale Law Journal*, 89(5): 835–901.

22 Theuvsen, L. (2004) "Doing better while doing good: Motivational aspects of pay-for-performance effectiveness in nonprofit organizations," *Voluntas: International Journal of Voluntary and Nonprofit Organizations*, 15(2): 117–136.

23 Brandl, J., & Güttel, W. H. (2007) "Organizational antecedents of pay-for-performance systems in nonprofit organizations," *Voluntas: International Journal of Voluntary and Nonprofit Organizations*, 18: 176–199.

24 Barbeito, C. L., & Bowman, J. P. (1998) Nonprofit Compensation and Benefits Practices. New York: John Wiley; McMullen, K., & Schellenberg, G. (2003a) *Job Quality in Nonprofit Organizations*. Ottawa: Canadian Policy Research Network;

Akingbola, K. (2004) "Staffing, retention and government funding: The Canadian Red Cross, Toronto Region," *Nonprofit Management and Leadership*, 14(4): 453–467.

25 McMullen, K., & Schellenberg, G. (2003a) *Job Quality in Nonprofit Organizations*. Ottawa: Canadian Policy Research Network.

26 Hansmann, "The role of nonprofit enterprise."

27 Roomkin & Weisbrod, "Managerial compensation and incentives in for-profit and non-profit hospitals."

28 Hallock, K. F. (2002) "Managerial pay and governance in American nonprofits," *Industrial Relations,* 41: 411–428.

29 Preston, A. (1989) "The nonprofit worker in a for-profit world," *Journal of Labor Economics*, 7(4): 438–463.

30 Nonprofit HR Solutions, *Nonprofit Employment Trends Survey*.

31 Hallock, "Managerial pay and governance in American nonprofits."

32 McMullen & Schellenberg, *Job Quality in Nonprofit Organizations*.

33 Hall, M. H., Andrukow, A., & Associates (2003) *The Capacity to Serve: A Qualitative Study of the Challenges Facing Canada's Nonprofit and Voluntary Organizations*. Toronto: Canadian Centre for Philanthropy.

34 WorldatWork, *Job Analysis, Documentation and Evaluation*.

35 French, W. L. (1987) *The Personnel Management Process*, 6th Edition. Boston: Houghton Mifflin. Cited in Gupta, N., & Jenkins, D. G. (1991) "Job evaluation: An overview," *Human Resource Management Review*, 1(2): 91–95.

36 Ibid.

37 Kilgour, J. G. (2008) "Job evaluation revisited: The point factor method," *Compensation & Benefits Review*, 40(4): 37–46.

38 Chaneta, I. (2014) "Effects of job evaluation on decisions involving pay equity," *Asian Social Science*, 10(4): 145–152.

39 Kilgour, "Job evaluation revisited."

40 Schwind, H., Das, H., & Wagar, T. (2007) *Canadian Human Resource Management*, 8th Edition. Toronto: McGraw-Hill Ryerson.

41 Belmont Housing Resources is an affordable housing nonprofit that offers housing-related services including rental assistance, promoting home ownership, educating renters and landlords.

42 Peris-Ortiz, M., Rueda-Armengot, C., & Pechuan, I. G. (2012) "Job classification for the purpose of making optimal decisions concerning management control," *Canadian Journal of Administrative Sciences*, 29(3): 231–241.

43 Pearlman, K. (1980) "Job families: A review and discussion of their implications for personnel selection," *Psychological Bulletin*, 87(1): 1–28; Peris-Ortiz, Rueda-Armengot, & Pechuan, "Job classification for the purpose of making optimal decisions concerning management control."

44 Smith, H. L., Fried, B. J., van Amerongen, D., & Laughlin, J. D. (2011) "Compensation practices, planning, and challenges," in B. J. Fried & M. D. Fottler (Eds), *Human Resources in Healthcare: Managing for Success*. Chicago: Health Administration Press.

45 WorldatWork, *Job Analysis, Documentation and Evaluation*.

46 Smith, Fried, van Amerongen, & Laughlin, "Compensation practices, planning, and challenges."

47 Kilgour, "Job evaluation revisited."

48 Lawler, E. (1986) "What's wrong with point-factor job evaluation," *Compensation & Benefits Review*, 18(5): 20–28.

49 Ibid.

50 Smith, Fried, van Amerongen, & Laughlin, "Compensation practices, planning, and challenges."

51 Lawler, E. (1986) "What's wrong with point-factor job evaluation."

52 Kilgour, "Job evaluation revisited"; Smith, Fried, van Amerongen, & Laughlin, "Compensation practices, planning, and challenges."

53 Bergmann, T. J., & Scarpello, V. G. (2001) *Point Method of Job Evaluation in Compensation Decision Making.* New York: Harcourt College Publishers; Chaneta, "Effects of job evaluation on decisions involving pay equity."

54 Kilgour (2011) offers a recent comprehensive review of the point system and provides the key reference for process discussed in this section.

55 Schwind, Das, & Wagar, *Canadian Human Resource Management.*

56 Kilgour, "Job evaluation revisited."

57 Smith, Fried, van Amerongen, & Laughlin, "Compensation practices, planning, and challenges."

58 Long & Ravichander, *Strategic Compensation.*

59 Bureau of Labor Statistics (2005) *Employee Benefits in Private Industry.* U.S. Department of Labor.

60 Conference Board (2007) *Employee Benefits: Second Generation Wellness and Productivity.* New York: Conference Board Institute.

61 Bureau of Labor Statistics (2014) *Employee Benefits in Private Industry.* U.S. Department of Labor.

62 Kanungo, R. N., & Mendonca, M. (1997) *Compensation: Effective Reward Management.* Toronto, ON: John Wiley.

63 Jones, E. (2005) "An overview of employee benefits," *Occupational Outlook Quarterly,* 49(2): 19.

64 HM Revenue & Customs (2013) "National Insurance – the basics." http://www.hmrc.gov.uk/ni/intro/basics.htm#3. Retrieved December, 2013.

65 Peris-Ortiz, Rueda-Armengot, & Pechuan, "Job classification for the purpose of making optimal decisions concerning management control."

66 Chen, X., Ren, T., & Knoke, D. (2014) "Do nonprofits treat their employees differently? Incentive pay and health benefits," *Nonprofit Management & Leadership,* 24(3): 285–306.

67 Pitt-Catsouphes, M., Swanberg, J. E., Bond, J. T., & Galinsky, E. (2004) "Work–life policies and programs: Comparing the responsiveness of nonprofit and for-profit organizations," *Nonprofit Management and Leadership,* 14(3): 291–313; Charity Village (2013) *Canadian Nonprofit Sector Salary & Benefits Study.*

68 Charity Village, *Canadian Nonprofit Sector Salary & Benefits Study.*

69 McMullen & Schellenberg, *Job Quality in Nonprofit Organizations.*

70 Charity Village, *Canadian Nonprofit Sector Salary & Benefits Study.*

71 Akingbola, K. (2004) "Staffing, retention and government funding: The Canadian Red Cross, Toronto Region," *Nonprofit Management and Leadership,* 14(4): 453–467.

72 Nonprofit HR Solutions (2013) *Nonprofit Employment Trends Survey.*

10

LABOR RELATIONS

Learning Objectives

After studying this chapter, you should be able to:

1. Describe the basic concepts in labor relations.
2. Explain why employees join unions.
3. Discuss union representation in nonprofits.
4. Outline strategies for building countervailing labor relations.
5. Illustrate the role of managers in the negotiation and administration of collective agreements.

Values-Based Strike: Southern California Red Cross Worker on Strike[1]

When Red Cross workers in Southern California walked off the job on April 30, 2007, the strike was unique. The goal was to highlight that staffing is a safety issue and impacts donors. According to the LA Times, *the workers insisted that blood supply must not be affected. Management also identified with the issue that necessitated the strike.*[2]

Introduction

In this chapter, the nature and characteristics of unionized nonprofit organizations is explored to explain how managers and employees work together in this environment. One key goal of the chapter is to provide a basic understanding of the concepts of labor relations. Hence, the chapter starts with what it means to be unionized. The chapter also includes a brief overview of relevant labor relations legislation, issues in labor-management relations and why nonprofit employees join unions. The opportunities and challenges that managers should understand as part of managing unionized employees are examined in the chapter.

Labor Relations: SHRM and Basic Concepts

The question of labor relations in nonprofits is almost nonexistent in management discourse in the sector. In fact, the nonprofit literature has so scarcely and sporadically explored the question that one might think that there are no unionized nonprofits. For the numerous unionized nonprofits, managing employees and working with union representation is an operational reality of the organization. The opening case illustrates the unique way labor relations could manifest in nonprofits. Hence, it is not only worth discussing, it is also important for managers and employees in nonprofits to understand labor relations.

Labor relations describe the interaction or relationship between employees, represented by a union as their bargaining agent, and the management of the organization. It is a critical factor in the effectiveness of SHRM because the relationship between employees, union and management could influence the ability of the organization to motivate and retain employees as well as the overall state of employee relations in the organization. The need to align labor relations with HR practices and, in particular, the strategy of the organization with SHRM practices does not differ in nonprofits. Rather, it is accentuated by the unique characteristics and context of nonprofit organizations.

Typically, to be unionized, a group of employees must join an existing union or organize a union. The union organization for a specific workplace is usually referred to as a local within a larger labor organization, for example, Local 49 of the Service Employees International Union (SEIU) or Local 23 of the Canadian Union of Public Employees or (CUPE). Generally, it is unusual for a workplace that is unionizing to form an independent union. A *union* is any type of labor organization that is formally or informally recognized to represent the interests of employees in a specific organization.[3] It is important to note that union locals are nonprofit mutual associations. They are member-based associations in general and operate according to the principle of one member one vote and they elect an executive from their membership to represent the local.

Unions are basically intermediaries between the organization and the employees as a collective as well as individuals. Unions advocate for the rights of employees, protect and support their interests in collective bargaining. Specifically, unions exist to improve the economic well-being and the conditions of employment of the employees who are their members. The purpose of unions includes health and safety and, often, broader political goals that are aligned with the interests of employees. The key process in labor relations for facilitating discussions and negotiation is called collective bargaining.

Some organizations have associations that are not unionized, but are recognized by the employer to represent employees in bargaining. The University of Toronto Faculty Association (UTFA) is an example. The labor relations jurisdictions in the US, the UK and Canada all have some form of voluntary recognition. In Canada, non-unionized workplace associations cannot strike, and they range in extent of their rights from those that are particularly active to those, like UTFA, that are relatively independent and that negotiate a collective agreement that is binding and that have agreements for mediation and arbitration.

Collective bargaining is a system and a process through which the labor union representing the interests of the employee and the management of the organization negotiate the terms and conditions of employment. As a system, collective bargaining has components and interactions that are connected to create an outcome. The interaction is extensive and multifaceted including the connection of the organization to the labor market, principles and legislations, as well as the interactions of the organization with players such as the government, union organization and, possibly, the public. As a process, collective bargaining involves a series of steps that are completed to achieve the goal which is a collective agreement. Collective bargaining is a cyclical process because collective agreements are renewed over a specified period of time normally two or more years.

As noted above, *collective bargaining agreement* is the goal of collective bargaining. It includes the key terms of employment and provisions or clauses to govern the relationship between the employees, the union and the management of the organization. A standard clause in most collective agreements is the means through which grievances are discussed and settled, otherwise known as the *grievance procedure*. The *grievance procedure* clause could also outline the terms under which the union can embark on a strike or the management can lock out employees. Two other standard clauses of a collective agreement are the management rights and the union recognition clause. The management rights provision summarizes the exclusive decision purview and autonomy of the management that are beyond the provisions of collective bargaining agreement. Typically, such a clause would include the right of management to run the day-to-day operations of the organization. The union recognition clause defines the bargaining unit represented by the union. In other words, it states the positions that the union represents and are covered the collective bargaining agreement.

Overview of Unionization

To provide a broad context on unionization, it is relevant to highlight the trends across the countries in which the examples of nonprofits in this book are based. The overview provides the context for the discussion of the opportunities and challenges of unionization in nonprofits.

United States

Generally, the rate of unionization—the percentage of wage and salary workers who are members of unions—has been declining in the US for many years. Up to the 1970s, union membership was around 30 percent of the US labor force.[4] According to the Bureau of Labor Statistics, by 1983, the first year for which comparable union data are available, the union membership rate was 20.1 percent of wage and salary workers.[5] The 1990s saw a steep decline in union membership with about 13.9 percent of workers in unionized jobs in 1999. By 2013, the number of unionized wage and salary workers has decreased further to 11.3 percent of the labor force. The Bureau of Labor Statistics data show that workers in the public sector are more likely to be unionized with 35.3 percent of this group having union membership. This is compared to union membership of 6.7 percent among private sector workers.

Currently, the rate of unionization in nonprofit organizations in the US is unclear because nonprofits are likely to be reported across many occupations in the Bureau of Labor Statistics data. However, it is estimated that less than 6 percent of nonprofit employees are unionized.[6] Based on this number, one can assume that the sector has a low rate of unionization. However, it has been suggested in the past that the rate of unionization will increase in nonprofits due to many of the factors discussed in Chapter 3.[7] The change and the challenges in the environment, including the relationship with the government, have been offered as drivers of unionization in nonprofits. The key factors are reviewed later in this chapter.

United Kingdom

In the UK, the rate of unionization, which is defined as trade union membership, remained relatively stable between 1995 and 2007 at between 28 percent and 29 percent.[8] Although there was a slight increase in trade union membership between 2011 and 2012, the increase was consistent with overall increase in UK employees. The level of union membership in 2012 was stable at 26 percent of the labor force. The National Statistics on trade union membership indicated that most of the increases in membership were in the public sector up to 2010 with the private sector numbers decreasing over the same period. Due to the aftermaths of the recession in 2008 and 2009, the trend in union membership reversed with the public sector experiencing a sharp decline in 2010 and 2011 but stabilizing in 2011 and 2012. The rate of union membership in the private sector increased in the same period. In 2012, 56.3 percent of the union members were in the public sector.

Similar to the US, the voluntary sector data in the UK appears to be reported across many occupations and industries. Hence, it is difficult to indicate the specific level of unionization in the sector. However, research has highlighted the increased efforts of unions to represent employees in the voluntary sector and the relative success and challenges of unionization campaigns.[9] Although there appear to be opportunities for unionization in the voluntary sector, it is not clear what the future holds.

Canada

The rate of unionization in Canada has also decreased significantly since the 1980s. However, the decrease in the rate of unionization has hovered around 31 percent for most of the past decade.[10] After some fluctuation in the downward trend, the rate of union members decreased from 33.7 percent in 1997 to 31.5 percent in 2007. The rate of unionization remained at 31.5 percent in 2012. Significantly more employees in the public sector, 71.4 percent, are unionized compared to the private sector.[11]

In Canada, there is some evidence that unionization increased specifically in nonprofits in the late 1990s. The report, based on Statistics Canada's 1999 Workplace and Employee Survey (WES), indicated that 40 percent of employees in nonprofits were covered by a collective agreement.[12] However, subsequent reports are yet to be analyzed to see whether the trend has continued over the past decade. Research has addressed unionization based on case studies.

Unionization and Nonprofits

Nonprofits are unique settings for HR practices and SHRM. The uniqueness of the sector is perhaps best exemplified in terms of unionization and labor relations. When nonprofits are unionized, there are critical contextual factors that are likely to have been at play for unionization. Also, these factors are likely to influence how the organization interacts with the union and the outcomes employees expect from union membership. To put it simply, nonprofits employees are likely to unionize not just for the sake of joining or forming a union, they are likely to have been influenced by sector-specific factors. Underlying this proposition are the basic characteristics of nonprofits and the employees of nonprofits, especially the importance of the mission and values. Since the contextual factors impact nonprofits in different ways, it means that unionization may be an advantage or disadvantage.[13] Fortunately, research has explored the drivers of unionization, the challenges and how nonprofit managers are responding to unionization.

Why Nonprofit Employees Unionize

Similar to employees in other sectors, nonprofit employees are likely to unionize if they deem that unionization will bring about certain benefits and influence the work environment in ways that meet their expectations. In effect, the general factors that encourage employees to join or form a union, which can broadly be classified as economic, social, organizational and political factors, also apply to nonprofit employees. However, there are important nonprofit angles in each factor. On economic factors, there is evidence that nonprofit employees have embarked on unionization drive to improve wages and conditions of employment.[14] Box 10.1 provides an insight into the factors that contributed to the unionization drive of employees of Larkin Street Youth Service in San Francisco. The employees were concerned about benefit cuts, increased workload and high turnover. However, consistent with the literature on positive response from some nonprofit employers,[15] there are two nonprofit twists to the unionization drive at Larkin Street Youth Services. First, the management appeared to be supportive, once the vote was successful. Second, employees appeared to see unionization as an opportunity to partner with management on social justice.

BOX 10.1 LARKIN STREET YOUTH SERVICES EMPLOYEES VOTE TO JOIN UNION

(Excerpt from an article by Corey Hill)

When employees of Larkin Street Youth Services in San Francisco began talking about unionizing earlier this spring, their concerns centered on issues familiar to workers of all stripes: understaffed departments, increased workloads, benefit cuts, high turnover. . . .

Nearly all the nonprofit's staff participated in the election, and when the vote was counted on June 6, the outcome was clear: By a margin of 67 to 17, Larkin Street workers voted to unionize with representation through SEIU 1021, a labor organization that represents employees of local governments, healthcare organizations, and school districts throughout Northern California.

Whatever the case may have been beforehand, after the vote, Larkin Street's management expressed support for the measure. "We look forward to working collaboratively with SEIU to improve the lives of the youth served by Larkin Street and to insure that Larkin Street is a great place to work," said Sherilyn Adams, executive director of Larkin Street Youth Services.

Source: Hill, C. (2013) *East Bay Express*, August 7, 2013. http://www.eastbayexpress.com/oakland/unionizing-nonprofits/Content?oid=3675593 Retrieved January, 2014.

Nonprofit employees also form or join a union in order to gain or enhance their voice in the organization. Again, this political rationale for unionization is not unique to nonprofit employees. Research has shown that for-profit and public sector employees have cited gaining a voice in the management and decision-making process of the organization as a factor in their unionization drive.[16] For nonprofit employees, the need to gain a voice is more than just management and internal decision-making. Research has found that nonprofit employees unionize to gain a voice in planning, service delivery and evaluation, as well as public policy and community development.[17] In short, nonprofit unionization could be about gaining a voice to support and enhance the mission and values rather than the economic benefits to employees.

There is also evidence that nonprofit employees are deciding to join or form a union as a way to address the challenges that result from government–nonprofit relations, especially contracting, funding and accountability issues. It has been suggested that nonprofits that depend more on government funding appear to be more likely to unionize than those with less government funding.[18] The role of government–nonprofit relations on unionization is a multifaceted issue. In terms of pay, government could be directly and indirectly contributing to the uncompetitive and low level of pay in nonprofits through contracting and pressure on nonprofits to reduce costs. The variability in pay level has been found to relate to government funding among other factors.[19] The reality is that when services are downloaded by the government to nonprofits, the level of pay for the jobs attached to the services is often not comparable to the compensation in the public sector.[20] Nonprofit employees see this disparity and consider unionization as an option to address the gap.

The downloading of public services aspect of government–nonprofit relations could also contribute to the decision of nonprofit employees to unionize. The reasoning here is that since a large percentage of public sector employees are unionized and public services are contracted out to nonprofits, it is expected that nonprofit employees will be encouraged to form or join a union because of the close affinity between some types of nonprofits and the public sector.[21] Similar to public sector employees, nonprofit employees are generally white-collar workers and they provide similar types of services, hence the similarities could encourage employees to desire to unionize in order to closely reflect the characteristics and ethos of the public sector.[22]

Another factor that has been offered to explain the potential for employees to form or join a union in nonprofits is the opportunity for the employees to partner with unions to achieve social justice and advocacy objectives.[23] From this perspective, nonprofit employees—and managers in some cases—perceive unions as important allies who could add more resources and capabilities to the issues and causes that are important to the employees and the nonprofit organization. In some instances, employees know that unions could provide an important voice and social legitimacy to their advocacy initiatives. Especially in this environment of government contracting to nonprofits, employees are undoubtedly aware that unions could assist to put significant pressure on the government. Together, the opportunity to enhance advocacy activities to government and promote the egalitarian values that attract employees to nonprofits has contributed to the motivation of employees to form or join a union in the sector. Box 10.2 shows an example in which a union played an important role to save a nonprofit hospital from demise.

BOX 10.2 UNION AND NONPROFIT PARTNERSHIP

Powerful Partnership

(Excerpt from an article by Jennifer Berkshire)

Lately, some unions and charities have been joining forces not only to try to organize nonprofit workers, but also to defend social services in tough budgetary times. When unions and charities work together, argues Rand Wilson, a spokesman for Service Employees International Union Local 285 in Boston, they can be more powerful than as individual advocates.

In Boston, where Local 285 represents members who work in hospitals and nursing homes, the union teamed up in 1999 with a nonprofit hospital in Quincy, MA, that was on the verge of bankruptcy. "The union was able to work with the mayor, the Legislature, and hospital administrators to make sure that emergency appropriations were made," says Mr. Wilson. Today, the hospital not only remains open, but it also has since affiliated with a large Boston hospital, giving it added financial and clinical support.

Source: Berkshire, J. C. (2002) "Nonprofit groups turn to unions to organize workers and collaborate on common causes," *Chronicle of Philanthropy*, November 21, 2002, http://philanthropy.com/article/Nonprofit-Groups-Turn-to/52443/. Retrieved January, 2014.

On the organizational front, nonprofit employees could decide to join or form a union if they are unhappy with the management of the organization. Similar to the for–profit and the public sectors, the disgruntlement of employees could stem from the basic management style in the organization. In nonprofits, employee disgruntlement has been linked to increased workload and accountability requirements imposed by funders, which has in turn led to the adoption of lean management practices.[24] The working conditions make employees isolated and overburdened by routine tasks and unsupportive management that emphasize processes over people. A consequence of such working conditions is the desire to join or form a union if the opportunity should present itself.

A conclusion one can draw from this review of the reasons why nonprofit employees join or form a union is that nonprofit-specific social, political and organizational factors appear to underlie unionization in the sector more than the typical "bread and butter" issues of wages and conditions of employment. This is not to suggest that nonprofit employees do not care about economic matters. To the contrary, they do. However, the studies cited have found that concern about economic factors is intertwined with mission, values and the advocacy goals that are important to the employees. As Baines[25] noted, "bread-and-butter" union issues remained important to the research participants but were inextricably linked to having a voice in social justice initiatives within and beyond the workplace. Besides the apparent importance of the characteristics of nonprofit employees in the decision about unionization, the other major factor is government–nonprofit relations, particularly contracting. This suggests that both the strengths and challenges of nonprofits coalesce to drive unionization in the sector. The body of research to date suggests that union status could ensure collaboration between management and employees to enhance the mission and mitigate the impact of the environment, particularly the government.

Labor Relations Law

Before, during and after employees form or join a union, they must understand and work within the provisions of the law enacted to govern the labor relations activities, processes and interactions. Labor law regulates activities of the employees, the unions, employers and the relationship between the parties. From the perspective of employees, labor law generally emphasizes their collective rights to form or join a union and to engage in collective bargaining. The discussion in this section provides an overview of the primary labor law with a focus on the process through which employees join or form a union to negotiate and represent their interests. The process is known differently as union recognition, representation or certification.

United States

The National Labor Relations Act (NRLA), also known as Wagner Act, was enacted by the US Congress in 1935 to provide legal backing to employees to form or join a union and to engage in collective bargaining with their employers. Of course, the act has been amended numerous times over the years. The NRLA is the law that regulates federal labor relations including the rights of employees and employers and the curtailing of labor management practices that are detrimental to employees, businesses and the US economy.[26] In addition to the protecting the rights of employees to unionize and engage in collective bargaining, the NRLA also includes provisions on unfair labor practices. The act requires employers to negotiate in good faith with the union certified to represent the employees.[27] The National Labor Relations Board (NLRB) manages and implements the provisions, the activities and processes that are related to the Act, including the unfair labor practice process.

Perhaps a brief overview would provide insight into one of the key roles of the NRLB. For an employee, a group of employees, an individual, or a labor organization acting on behalf of the employees, interested in forming or joining a union, the first step is to petition the NRLB.[28] This step of the process essentially indicates that the group of employees would like to gain union representation. A critical part of the recognition process is the submission of authorization cards signed by at least 30 percent of the employees in the proposed bargaining unit. The authorization cards confirm that employees in the proposed bargaining unit would like to be represented by a specific union. For the next step, the NLRB will determine the appropriateness of the bargaining unit. This involves ascertaining that the group of employees are similar in terms of nature of work, skills, wages, working conditions and professional community of interest. For example in nonprofit hospitals, nurses and housekeeping employees have different bargaining units. If an election is to be conducted, the verification of the appropriateness of the bargaining unit is followed by the certification election conducted by the NRLB. A successful certification election is when a simple majority of the voters, defined as 50 percent plus one, votes in favour of the certification. It is important to note that employers can voluntarily recognize the union when at least 30 percent of the employees in the proposed bargaining unit have signed the authorization card. In this case, the petition to the NRLB for a representation vote could be avoided.

The process outlined above provides a summarized overview of the NRLB representation process. For a comprehensive outline of the process and relevant resources, please see the NRLB website.[29]

United Kingdom

The Employment Relations Act 1999 provides the statutory framework on how employees in the UK can be represented by a union. The Act basically clarifies existing law and introduced a new system through which a union could be recognized as the bargaining agent for a group of employees.[30] However, this procedure will only kick in if the employer and the union are not able to reach a voluntary agreement on recognition of the latter as the bargaining agent for the employees. Specifically related to union representation, the Act provides that an individual employee has a right to be accompanied by a trade union representative of their choice in disciplinary and grievance procedures.

To be recognized as the bargaining agent to represent a group of employees, the union that is seeking the recognition must make a request for recognition to their employer. It is relevant to note that the employer must have 21 or more employees. If the parties agree, the union becomes the bargaining agent of the group of employees. As a result, the recognition process is completed. However, if the employer does not accept or fails to respond to the request, the process will continue. To learn more about the steps, please see explanatory notes on the legislation.[31] The Employment Relations Act 2004 further clarifies the provisions of the 1999 Act. Among other provisions, it added statutory protection for employees in relations to their activities with the union.

Canada

Although the specific provisions and details in the law governing labor relations in the US and Canada are somewhat different, there are some parallels. In fact, the Wagner Act has been noted to have influenced Canadian labor relations policy.[32] The rights of employees to form or join a union and to engage in collective bargaining were first enacted in law in Ontario in 1943. Wagner-style labor relations laws were later introduced by most of the provinces and the federal government after the wartime regulations repealed in 1948.[33] Most importantly, the Rand formula was introduced in 1946. The formula stipulates that all employees in a unionized workplace must pay union dues regardless of whether they join the union or not. The reasoning was that everybody benefits from the outcome of bargaining including those who opt not to join the union. Depending on the industry, the legal jurisdiction for labor relations could be at the Provincial or the federal level. The Canada Labour Code is the name of the primary labor relations law at the federal level, while a similar law is called the Labour Relations Act or Code at the provincial level. The Labour Relations Board implements the provisions of the Act or Code.

A union is required to submit an application for certification to the Labour Relations Board (the board) in order to start the process to become the bargaining agent for a group of employees. The application to the board is preceded by the delivery of the certification application package to the employer within two days before it is submitted to the board. Once the board confirms with the employer that the application for certification has been received, the employer is required to immediately post the application and notice for the employees. Also, the employer must respond to the certification application. The employer's response must be sent to both the board and the union. If 40 percent of employees in the proposed bargaining unit have signed the union membership cards, the board will initiate a representation voting.

The two-step certification process summarized above is based on the law in Ontario and a number of other provinces. Some jurisdictions in Canada including the Federal Labour Code allows automatic certification if majority of the employees in the proposed bargaining unit have signed membership cards.

Nonprofits

The certification process is a key part of the labor relations law which also includes provisions on collective bargaining, how to resolve disputes and the role of the labor board. Understanding and working within the provisions of the law is a prerequisite for an effective labor relations environment. Nonprofits in particular have to view the law not only in terms of their legal obligations to enable employees to exercise their rights, but also in terms of the values of their organization. However, there is research evidence from the UK that some non-profits could be counteracting the opportunity provided by labor relations law for employees to form and join a union.[34] In fact, one study found that nonprofits had double the level of cases at industrial tribunal than those of private and public sector organizations.[35] Similarly, in Canada the research, though limited, has suggested that some nonprofits use unethical behavior to avoid collective bargaining.[36] Based on a review of the literature, there is currently little recent research on how nonprofits in the US are responding to unionization drives by employee groups.

Collective Bargaining

Collective bargaining is the centerpiece of labor relations. It is the critical process that actualizes the rights of employees to negotiate the terms and conditions of employment collectively with management through their union. The US NRLA 1935 defines the obligation to bargain collectively:

> For the purposes of this section, to bargain collectively is the performance of the mutual obligation of the employer and the representative of the employees to meet at reasonable times and confer in good faith with respect to wages, hours, and other terms and conditions of employment, or the negotiation of an agreement, or any question arising thereunder, and the execution of a written contract incorporating any agreement reached if requested by either party, but such obligation does not compel either party to agree to a proposal or require the making of a concession.

The principle that employees should be able to influence the conditions under which they work underlies collective bargaining.[37] The terms of employment and working conditions including wages, working hours, benefits, health and safety as well as the interaction between employees and the organization are important to most employees. However, most of these terms and conditions cannot always be negotiated by individuals. Hence, collective bargaining is about employees having a voice not only as individuals but more importantly as a collective. The idea is that employees would participate and this would help to relatively balance the significant gap between the power of the individual employee and the employer in negotiation.

How does collective bargaining really work? Although the answer to this question could be varied, especially between North America and parts of Europe, there are some common grounds. Once the union has been certified as the representative or bargaining agent for a group of employees, the stage is set for collective bargaining to commence. The union and the nonprofit must initiate the process by agreeing how and when they would exchange proposals on terms and conditions of employment that each party hopes will become the content of the collective agreement. As noted previously in the chapter, the collective bargaining process is a recurring process and the negotiations typically involve modifications to an existing contract.

Typically, the items in the bargaining proposals are wide ranging. In North America, the custom is that the initial proposal of the union would include significantly more items than they realistically expect to become part of the collective agreement.[38] Conversely, management will typically include only a minimal number of items, that is, much less than it is prepared to settle for. The objective of this strategy is to ensure that both parties have sufficient room for bargaining, which generally requires some elements of give and take. Adams contrasted this approach to the European (e.g. the UK) approach to collective bargaining proposal in which items are more realistic, less extensive and closer to the settlements the parties expect to achieve.[39] The exchange of collective bargaining proposals will also include the setting of dates for formal negotiations.

Generally, the items that can be considered in collective bargaining are somewhat extensive. The NRLB classifies bargaining items into three main categories. These are mandatory, permissive or illegal items.[40] Mandatory items are issues that the employer and the union are required to negotiate in bargaining such as wages, hours of employment and other conditions of employment. Permissive or non-mandatory items are issues that are lawful for the parties to bargain but they are not required. These items are unrelated to wages and conditions of employment, they are considered to be voluntary items. Examples of permissive issues include benefits for retirees, the board of directors of the organization, and the union's internal matters. Illegal or prohibited items are issues that the party cannot negotiate as part of collective bargaining. Discrimination against particular groups is a common example of a prohibited item the parties in collective bargaining may not negotiate.

During the actual collective bargaining, the parties are represented by their respective teams. The management team may include one or more executives of the organization, a member of the board of directors, the HR Director/Manager. It is not uncommon to have a professional negotiator as part of the management team. The organization may also include an individual who will provide research support in the team. The union team would typically include members of the union executive, a few employees, and a national representative of the union if the union is a local one.

Collective bargaining takes time. Both the management and the union will typically have bargaining priorities and goals. These are determined during the preparation for collective bargaining which may include a survey or other forms of consultation with stakeholders. Also, the parties will review terms of the current collective bargaining agreement, if applicable, and the collective agreement in similar organizations. A major part of the preparation for collective bargaining is a comprehensive analysis of the external environment to determine the trends that could play into and impact the outcome of bargaining. The external environment factors include economic indicators, the labor market and government policy.

Beyond the specific items, the collective bargaining process involves different elements that are characterized and shaped by individual and group dynamics. In other words, the formal process and items in collective bargaining are mixed up with personality and group dynamics to determine the tenor and outcome of collective bargaining.

The individual and group factors are mitigated by the duty to bargain in good faith. If collective bargaining is the centerpiece of labor relations, the duty to bargain in good faith is at its heart. The parties must bargain with the intention of reaching an agreement. Hence, there must be sincerity and a reasonable effort to facilitate the goal of having a collective bargaining agreement. For example, the NRLA requires the employer to provide "relevant and necessary" information to the union in order to enable them to bargain wages, hours and other conditions of employment from an intelligent position. Essentially, the duty to bargain in good faith is about being real and reasonable.

If successful, the outcome of collective bargaining is an agreement. The collective bargaining agreement will stipulate the terms and conditions of employment of employees in the bargaining unit. The failure to reach an agreement could mean that the employees are in a legal strike position. The right of employees to engage in a strike and the right of an employer to lock out employees are provisions of the NRLA and labor relations legislation more generally. However, if there is a collective bargaining impasse, the first step is to try and reach a settlement with the help of a third party. As a result, the collective bargaining impasse is referred to as mediation or arbitration for resolution. Both mediation and arbitration involve a third party (or parties) who will examine the issues and the positions of both the union and employer. In mediation, after reviewing the issues and the positions of the union and the employer, the mediator will offer recommendations on a settlement. However, the recommendations are nonbinding. The arbitrator also reviews the issues and the positions of the parties before making a binding decision on how to resolve the impasse.

Managing Unionized Employees

Depending on your perspective, managing employees who are members of a union could mean a mix of specific challenges and opportunities for managers and nonprofit organizations. For the HR manager and team, the collective bargaining process and the administration of collective bargaining agreement require a different but important emphasis to facilitate an effective labor relations environment. The challenges and opportunities that result from managing unionized employees would necessitate decisions on strategic choices and how to maximize the resources and capabilities of a nonprofit. For that reason, managers must understand the challenges and opportunities.

From a theoretical standpoint, the challenges and opportunities discussed below summarize the contrasting positions of the neoclassical and institutional perspectives respectively.[41] While the neoclassical perspective posits that managing unionized employees negatively impacts organizations, the institutional perspective emphasizes the positive contribution of unionization to the organization. However, the two perspectives agree on one issue. Similar to the neoclassical perspective, the institutional perspective acknowledges that unionization could lead to increased wages for employees.[42] The institutional perspective adds that the positive effects of unionization counteract the union wage premium.[43] In other words, the advantages of unionization to the organization outweigh the disadvantages.

It is important to note that although research, especially in the US and Canada, is yet to thoroughly examine the challenges of managing unionized nonprofit employees, the characteristics of the sector could provide an insight into how the challenges and opportunities will play out and the role of managers.

Challenges

It has been suggested that unionization could affect decision-making because it impinges on the rights of management to run the day-to-day operations of an organization.[44] This perspective notes that such interference would at the least affect delay decision-making and the ability of managers to be responsive to the needs of clients in a timely manner.

The advocacy activities of the union within and outside of the organization could negatively impact the ability of the organization to efficiently deploy the human capital of the employees. In simple terms, the suggestion here is that advocacy activities could take the focus of unionized employees away from performing their job. Since seniority is emphasized, employees would rely more on seniority than their performance.

Managers may have limited flexibility to deal with employee issues because they have to work within the provisions of the collective bargaining agreement. A common example often cited in this regard is that it is more difficult and time consuming to deal with problem employees in unionized organizations. This is because the grievance procedure may include a progressive disciplinary process.

The processes that are outlined in the collective agreement to manage unionized employees could result in managerial inefficiencies. For example, managers are expected to respond to information requests and work with the union on issues related to the administration of the collective bargaining agreement. The thinking is that the labor relations responsibilities take managers away from their core duties and could make them less effective.

Ultimately, the combination of the challenges of managing unionized employees could affect the performance and bottom line of the organization. On the whole, the direct and indirect cost of labor relations could be a burden on the organization. Moreover, the resources and capabilities deployed by the organization to manage unionized employees could be considered to be productivity and efficiency losses because they do not contribute to the market competitiveness of the organization.

Labor Management Partnership

Before examining the opportunities, it is important to emphasize that these challenges can be managed with an effective labor management strategy. One such strategy is to build a partnership with the union in the organization. Building a partnership is not going to come about overnight. However, it is critical for the senior executives and managers to have a partnership mental model to work effectively with the union. Our mental model, which can be described as the perception, beliefs, experience or meaning that guides our behavior,[45] influences how we relate with unions. For example, if managers have a mental model that the challenges above impact the organization's performance, this would affect their ability to collaborate with the union and leverage the opportunities described below. Box 10.3 outlines some general recommendations on how to build effective labor management relations.

BOX 10.3 INGREDIENTS FOR BUILDING LABOR MANAGEMENT PARTNERSHIP

- Make an effort to know and understand the union.
- Expect and be open to different perspectives.
- Develop and maintain an atmosphere of respect.
- Keep informal dialogue pipeline open and ongoing.
- Voluntarily seek input and share problems.
- Engage union in business process improvement.
- Have an excellent understanding of the collective agreement.
- Build a partnership with the union.
- Leverage the bond developed in the collective bargaining process.

Adapted from: Akingbola, K. (2010) "Three critical ingredients for effective labour relations environment," Presented at the Annual Conference of the Human Resources Professional Association, Toronto; Painter, B. & Ponak, A. (2005) *Beyond Collision: High Integrity Labour Relations*. Calgary: Modern Times Productions, University of Calgary.

Opportunities

As noted above, employees join or form a union in order to enhance their voice in the organization. This enhanced collective voice can be leveraged by management to facilitate improved productivity. This perspective suggests that management style must encourage employee participation and input in order to benefit from the voice employees gain through unionization.

Employee voice could also contribute to quality and continuous improvement in the organization. Unionized employees who interact directly with customers have insights on customer experience and issues the organization could use to improve customer service. Collective employee voice is reflected in how front-line employees operationalize management strategy in their interactions with customers. It can help to reinforce the specific practices and values that management has decided to foster in the organization.

Employees who are unionized tend to have a lower rate of turnover. This means that the organization would have reduced recruitment-related costs. Also, a high rate of employee retention means that the organization can implement strategies to better engage employees and provide training to improve performance. Similarly, retention provides the opportunity to equip the employee with enhanced knowledge and skills that are needed to manage the internal systems and processes of the organization. The opportunities derived through retention also include helping employees to grow and develop a career path with the organization.

Unionized employees can help to monitor managerial behaviors that are detrimental to managers and the organization. The assumption here is that managers are not immune from unilateral decisions and behaviors that are inconsistent with the best interest of the organization as well as their own interests. Hence, through the institutional support of the union, unionized employees can provide checks and balances that are difficult for an individual employee who is acting alone.

Coupled with the impact of monitoring, the grievance procedure provides a formal governance structure to bring the unionized employees and management together to address issues. Not only is the governance structure a more efficient way to address organizational issues than managing individual employees, it provides a relative channel for the average employee to have their issues addressed.

From the point of view of the opportunities, the combined effect of the factors above, especially the collective voice and the possibility for enhanced engagement, could motivate employees to exercise discretionary effort in their job. In effect, the opportunities highlight the ways the impact of unionized employees could benefit the organization, the manager and the employee.

Although the basis of much research that underlies the challenges and opportunities of managing in a unionized organization are related to productivity, employment growth and the financial performance of the organization, many of elements of the challenges and opportunities are relevant to the context of nonprofits. The opportunities offered by the processes and interactions in unionized organizations are particularly consistent with the values of nonprofits such as participation and the social good. The challenges outline the barriers to organizational effectiveness that could stem from unionization. As nonprofit managers try to figure out how to overcome the above challenges including how they coalesce with the other challenges in the sector, the managers must also understand and leverage the opportunities that come with unionization. The nonprofit managers must be prepared to balance the challenges and the opportunities not only to neutralize the effect of the former, but also to operationalize the latter as an integral part of the values-based orientation of their organization.

Summary

To many nonprofit organizations, the need to manage labor relations is a daily operational reality. These nonprofits work within the effects of managing unionized employees. There is relatively less research on unionization in nonprofits than other aspects of management in the sector. Although research on labor relations in nonprofits is scant in the US and Canada, research from the UK has offered some insight, especially on the question of the unionization efforts of nonprofit employees, how nonprofit organizations are responding to unionization and the future prospect for unionization in the sector. It is unclear how labor relations are playing out in nonprofits that are unionized. The little research there is has provided some insights, but we are far from understanding the complex dynamics that are evolving in the relationship between employees, the union and management in these organizations.

Discussion Questions

1. Beyond economic factors, what are some of the reasons why nonprofits' employees may want to form or join a union?
2. This chapter suggests that unions collaborate with nonprofits on social justice issues. How can nonprofit organizations best leverage the opportunities to work in partnership with unions?
3. What is your opinion about unionization in nonprofits? Do you expect unionization to increase or decrease in nonprofits? Why?
4. What are the most difficult challenges for unions and nonprofits in their relationship?

Notes

1 Mathews, J. (2007) "Red Cross walkout targets staffing," *Los Angeles Times*. May 1, 2007, http://articles.latimes.com/2007/may/01/local/me-redcross1. Retrieved November, 2013.
2 Labour Law Casebook Group (Eds.), *Labour and Employment Law: Cases Materials, and Commentary*, 7th Edition. Toronto: Irwin Law.

3 Kehoe, F. and Archer, M. (2007) *Canadian Industrial Relations,* 11th Edition. Oakville, ON: Century Labour Publications.

4 Mello, J. A. (2015) *Strategic Human Resource Management,* 4th Edition. Mason, OH: South-Western Centage Learning.

5 U.S. Bureau of Labor Statistics (2014) Union Members 2013, http://www.bls.gov/news.release/union2.nr0.htm. Retrieved February, 2014.

6 Hill, C. (2013) "Unionizing nonprofits." *East Bay Express,* August 7, 2013, http://www.eastbayexpress.com/oakland/unionizing-nonprofits/Content?oid=3675593. Retrieved January, 2014.

7 Peters, J. B., & Masaoka, J. (2000) "A house divided: How nonprofits experience union drives," *Nonprofit Management & Leadership,* 10(3): 305–317.

8 The UK Department for Business, Innovation & Skills (n.d.) Trade Union Membership 2012: Statistical Bulletin, https://www.gov.uk/government/uploads/system/uploads/attachment_data/file/299291/bis-13-p77-trade-union-membership-2012-corrrection.pdf. Retrieved January, 2014.

9 Cunningham, I. (2000) "Prospects for union growth in the UK voluntary sector: The impact of the Employment Relations Act 1999," *Industrial Relations Journal,* 31(3): 192–205; Cunningham, I. (2008) "Mobilising workers within interorganisational relationships in the UK voluntary sector," *Industrial Relations Journal,* 39(3): 191–211.

10 Employment and Social Development Canada (n.d.) "Work—unionization rates." http://www4.hrsdc.gc.ca/.3ndic.1t.4r@-eng.jsp?iid=17. Retrieved December, 2013.

11 Galarneau, D., & Sohn, T. (2013) "Long term trends in unionization," Statistics Canada, Catalogue no. 75-006-X. http://www.statcan.gc.ca/pub/75-006-x/2013001/article/11878-eng.htm#a6. Retrieved January, 2014.

12 McMullen, K., & Brisbois, R. (2003) *Coping with Change: Human Resource Management in Canada's Non-Profit Sector (No. 4).* Ottawa: Canadian Policy Research Networks.

13 Akingbola, K. (2005) "Unionization and non-profit organizations," in K. S. Devine & J. Grenier (Eds.), *Reformulating Industrial Relations in Liberal Market Economies.* Ontario: Captus University Publications.

14 Baines, D. (2010) "In a different way: Social unionism in the nonprofit social services—an Australian/Canadian Comparison," *Labor Studies Journal,* 35(4): 480–502; Akingbola, "Unionization and non-profit organizations."

15 Examples of union-partnership agreements in the US and the UK, respectively, are cited in Cohen, R. (2013) "Unions and the nonprofit workforce: A few considerations," *Nonprofit Quarterly,* August 8, 2013, and Cunningham (2008) "Mobilising workers within interorganisational relationships in the UK voluntary sector," *Industrial Relations Journal* 39(3): 191–211.

16 Freeman, R. B., & Medoff, J. L. (1984) *What Do Unions Do?* New York: Basic Books.

17 Baines, D. (2010) "In a different way: Social unionism in the nonprofit social services."

18 Akingbola, "Unionization and non-profit organizations."

19 Hallock, K. F. (2002) "Managerial pay and governance in American nonprofits," *Industrial Relations,* 41: 411–428.

20 Cunningham, I. (2008) "Mobilising workers within interorganisational relationships in the UK voluntary sector," *Industrial Relations Journal,* 39(3): 191–211.

21 Pynes, J. E. (1997) "The anticipated growth of nonprofit unionism," *Nonprofit Management & Leadership,* 7(4): 355–371.

22 Peters & Masaoka, "A house divided."

23 Akingbola, "Unionization and non-profit organizations."

24 Baines, D. (2010) "In a different way: Social unionism in the nonprofit social services."

25 Ibid.

26 National Labor Relations Board. National Labor Relations Act, http://www.nlrb.gov/resources/national-labor-relations-act. Retrieved December, 2013.

27 Carter, D., England, G., Etherington, B., & Trudeau, G. (2004) "Labour law in Canada," pp. 11-16, in Labour Law Casebook Group (Eds.), *Labour and Employment Law: Cases Materials, and Commentary*, 7th Edition. Toronto: Irwin Law.

28 National Labor Relations Board (2012) *National Labor Relations Board Annual Report*. Washington, DC.

29 National Labor Relations Board. NRLB Process http://www.nlrb.gov/resources/nlrb-process.

30 The National Archives. Employment Relations Act 1999, http://www.legislation.gov.uk/ukpga/1999/26/notes/division/2/1. Retrieved December, 2013.

31 Employment Relations Act, http://www.legislation.gov.uk/ukpga/1999/26/notes/contents.

32 Carter et al., "Labour law in Canada."

33 Ibid.

34 Hill, "Unionizing nonprofits"; Hemmings, M. (2011) " 'What problems you got?' Managerialisation and union organising in the voluntary sector," *Industrial Relations Journal*, 42(5): 473–485.

35 Cunningham, I. (2000) "Prospects for union growth in the UK voluntary sector: The impact of the Employment Relations Act 1999," *Industrial Relations Journal*, 31(3): 192–205.

36 Kimel, E. (2006) "Labour relations practices of nonprofits acting as for-profits: an explainable dissonance," *Just Labour*, 8 (Spring): 10–24.

37 Adams, R. (2004) "Industrial relations under liberal democracy: North America in comparative perspective," in Labour Law Casebook Group (Eds.), *Labour and Employment Law: Cases Materials, and Commentary*, 7th Edition. Toronto: Irwin Law.

38 Ibid.

39 Ibid.

40 National Labor Relations Board (1997) *Basic Guide to the National Labor Relations Act*. Washington, DC.

41 Freeman & Medoff, *What Do Unions Do?*

42 Hirsch, B.T. (Ed.) (1997) *Unionization and Economic Performance: Evidence on Productivity, Profits, Investment, and Growth*. Vancouver: The Fraser Institute.

43 Jalette, P. (1997) *The Impact of Human Resource Management and Industrial Relations Practices on the Organizational Performance of Credit Unions in Quebec* (Working Paper No. W-97-6E). Ottawa: HRDC Applied Research Branch.

44 Nolan, P., & O'Donnell, K. (Eds.) (2003) *Industrial Relations, HRM and Performance*, 2nd Edition. Malden, MA: Blackwell Publishing.

45 Rouse, W. B., & Morris, N. M. (1986) "On looking into the black box: Prospects and limits in the search for mental models," *Psychological Bulletin*, 100: 349–363.

11

VOLUNTEER MANAGEMENT IN STRATEGIC HUMAN RESOURCE MANAGEMENT

Learning Objectives

After studying this chapter, you should be able to:

1. Discuss what volunteers do.
2. Explain the importance of volunteers in nonprofits.
3. Describe volunteer employee partnership.
4. Outline strategies nonprofits can use to attract, recruit, and manage volunteers.

Volunteers Take Care of Business[1]

In the warmth of a rural community center on a cold blustery day, Alison McCaffree is reminded of the value of nonprofit partnerships. As executive director of Washington Nonprofits, Alison in Belfair, Washington, to kick off a Finance 101 training. She's standing in front of a packed room of nonprofit volunteer treasurers. Some have driven more than two hours, most have paid the $10 enrollment fee, and others needed a scholarship to participate. What made her pause was this: the event volunteers, knowing it would be chilly in the room, brought in their own space heaters from home. Alison explains, "I am reminded that our work goes beyond bringing needed resources to local communities. Our work involves building critical partnerships that allow these resources to make a difference within these communities. I didn't know this room was going to be cold, but by partnering with a local organization, things were taken care of, and we were comfortable. The environment was set so volunteers could learn how to help their organizations prosper."

Alison McCaffree Executive Director, Washington Nonprofits.
LeadOn 2013 Annual Report Independent Sector. https://www.
independentsector.org/uploads/About_IS/2013AnnualReport.pdf

Introduction

Volunteers are the backbone of nonprofit organizations. Hence, any text on human resources in nonprofits is incomplete without a discussion of volunteers. This chapter provides an overview of volunteer management in nonprofits. Consistent with other chapters in this book, the role of volunteers is discussed from the point of view of strategic human resource management (SHRM). Following an overview of the concept of volunteering and types of volunteers, the chapter discusses the strategies nonprofits can use to attract, recruit and manage volunteers. The chapter underlines the importance of volunteer employee partnership in SHRM in the nonprofit sector. It shows how the human capital of the nonprofit sector includes competencies of volunteers both in terms of SHRM and service delivery.

What Is Volunteering?

The opening case, which is an excerpt from the 2013 annual report of the Independent Sector, illustrates the many dimensions of the work, the essence, the partnership and the strategy that volunteers foster in nonprofits. Beyond the granular of management discourse, take a moment to think of people who are investing time, energy and money, and doing whatever it takes to make the outcome a success for clients, the organization and the society. In this example, the volunteer treasurers went the extra mile to ensure that the training was a realization for the nonprofits they were representing and the Washington Nonprofits organization which organized the training. The multifaceted angles in the case exemplify many of the characteristics that embody what volunteering is really about.

Volunteering is a multidimensional concept.[2] Volunteering is about *doing* for others, for the community, for the nation, for the environment, or simply acting on values that exemplify humanity. Thus volunteering entails giving meaning and giving back to benefit the perpetrator and the recipient, to reward individuals, groups and organizations.[3] According to the United Nations, volunteering "promotes social participation and active citizenship, and strengthens civil society. It can also help to maintain society's stability and cohesion . . . it is a plus for society, for it is a conduit for universal value in terms of human rights, democracy, combating racism, solidarity and sustainable development."[4] The term "volunteer" is generally used to describe a person who freely engages in an activity with no expectation of reward or remuneration.[5] This definition attempts to emphasize that to volunteer does not include what an individual is required to do so by law or public policy. It also excludes volunteering when there is remuneration or expectation of reward.

From the discussions above, volunteering encompasses elements of unpaid work, community service, civil society and change. While the fundamental characteristics of volunteering, such as work in service delivery, fundraising and governance, remain the same, much of what volunteers do and how they do it is changing.

Dimensions of Volunteering

To explain the forms and changing nature of volunteering, it is important to understand the dimensions highlighted in the definition. One often-cited study on the dimensions of volunteering is the work of Cnaan et al. Following an extensive review of the literature, they found that four dimensions underlie the concept of volunteering.[6] As shown in Box 11.1, first, the volunteer activity may not involve any form of coercion. It should be an activity that the individual voluntarily chooses to engage in. Second, there should be no remuneration, neither should any be expected. However, expenses may be reimbursed. Third, the context of volunteering may be formal or informal. Finally, there should be beneficiaries of volunteering. The beneficiaries may be others, family, friend or the individual.

BOX 11.1 DIMENSIONS OF VOLUNTEERING

- Free choice—is there is any form of coercion involved?
- Remuneration—is there monetary reward for the activity?
- Structure—whether the context of the activity is a formal or informal setting.
- Beneficiaries—who benefits from the activity?

Source: Cnaan, R. A., Handy, F., & Wadsworth, M. (1996). "Defining who is a volunteer: Conceptual and empirical considerations," *Nonprofit and Voluntary Sector Quarterly*, 25: 364–383.

Volunteering can also be classified in terms of the formality involved. Informal volunteering involves less codified work, structure and time, general ad hoc activities that take place in smaller organizations[7] such as self-help and neighborhood groups. Other studies have defined informal volunteering as activities completed outside of a formal organization.[8] Irrespective of how it is defined, many volunteers engage in informal activities without actually considering their role as volunteering, thus making it difficult to record such contributions for statistical purposes. Formal volunteering is more structured with job descriptions, and occurs in organizational settings.

Roles of Volunteers

Although the definitions are important to explain the concept of volunteering, they only emphasize the most commonly articulated view of volunteering. The definitions emphasize the altruistic role or dimension of volunteering. Altruism is the essence of what volunteers do. As noted in the dimensions above, volunteers engage in altruistic activities to help others. However, there are other important dimensions of what volunteers do and why they do it. People volunteer to fulfill a social obligation of promoting a good and worthy cause.[9] The motivation for participation could be related to social identity. In this regard, people desire to be recognized with a particular cause that is synonymous with a particular group. Also related to the altruistic and participation viewpoints of what volunteers do is interest in civil society. Many volunteers simply want to be active in creating a vibrant civil society, for example, by taking part in activities related to public advocacy, community development initiatives and commitment to social justice.

Perhaps the most important of the dimensions of volunteering from the perspective of SHRM is that it is a work activity. Beyond the altruistic, participation and civil society dimensions of what volunteers do, volunteering is also an important productive activity.[10] It is a work activity via which individuals contribute to the performance of organizations or individuals, or seek to enhance their own performance.[11] The work perspective includes the instrumental explanation of volunteering which notes that people may volunteer to acquire knowledge, skills and abilities.[12] Volunteer activities have been identified as a way of enhancing employment opportunities, career advancement or learning new skills.[13] For many new graduates and immigrants, volunteering is a way to acquire experience that benefits their job search.

The work activity perspective is even more evident in terms of the contribution made by volunteers to the performance of organizations. For many organizations, including those in the public sector and to some extent in the for-profit sector, volunteer labor is an invaluable component of their productive capacity. Across the US, government agencies at local, state and federal levels regularly engage volunteers in diverse areas such as public safety, cultural and arts programs, highway litter removal, youth development and veteran affairs.[14]

The altruistic, participation, civil society and work activity perspectives explain the important roles of volunteers. These perspectives indicate the different ways volunteering can benefit the individual, the organization and the society. Beyond these perspectives, research has also shown that volunteers drive organizational change in nonprofits.[15] The multifaceted roles of volunteers emphasize their diverse contributions to individuals and organizations.

Volunteering Change

Over the past three decades, volunteering has been undergoing major changes. One prominent change in volunteering has been the shift from what the literature has termed "classic volunteerism" to new volunteerism.[16] This change has been attributed to increased modernization and individualism, which have affected the structural and motivational bases of volunteering.[17] Research has surmised that the main differences between classic volunteerism and new volunteerism are in terms of the culture, choice of organization, choice of field of action, choice of activity, length and intensity of commitment, and relationship with the beneficiary.[18] New volunteers are more likely to participate in activities on a short-term or episodic basis.[19] They also tend to have weak ties with the organization, which suggests that they are interested in the mission of the organization but not necessarily in the affairs of organization. The research also emphasizes that new volunteerism tends to merge the personal choice of the volunteers with organizational needs.

In addition to the difference between classic volunteerism and new volunteerism, research has also explained that the changing nature of volunteering is an indication of the shift in the biographical frame of reference of individuals.[20] The researchers found that diverse cultural frames of reference appear to align with life cycle effects and processes of organizational socialization. This suggests that there are more variations in the nature of volunteering than presented in the one-dimensional classical and new volunteering framework. Hence, it could be misleading to classify volunteers under the broad categories of classical or new volunteering.

Apart from the broad changes in the nature of volunteering, other forms of volunteering are emerging in response to changing technology and the context of nonprofit organizations. Virtual volunteering is one such new area that is emerging primarily as a result of the advancement in information and communications technology. Virtual volunteering makes it possible for volunteers to work without being physically present in the organization or volunteer location.[21] Although promising, virtual volunteering is limited to specific types of work that can be completed at a distance using information technology, such as data entry, research on the web, technical support, etc.

Volunteers and Nonprofits

As discussed above, volunteers play different roles and contribute significantly to critical functions in society. However, it is in the nonprofit sector that the work activity perspective of volunteering is particularly invaluable. Volunteers contribute the critical knowledge, skills, abilities and experience that nonprofit organizations need to deliver services, to have governance, and to advocate for the causes that represent the brand proposition of that organization. Volunteering is one of the means of achieving the mission of the nonprofits. In most nonprofits, volunteers are the organization. If there are no volunteers, there is no mission.

Most nonprofits use volunteers in front line and administrative roles, in addition to those who are members of the board of directors.[22] This underlines the depth and range of the involvement of volunteers in the operation of nonprofits. It is irrefutable that volunteers offer nonprofits a number of important tangible and intangible benefits. Box 11.2 shows the benefits most nonprofits considered volunteers contributed to their operations.

BOX 11.2 BENEFITS VOLUNTEERS CONTRIBUTE TO NONPROFITS

- Increases in the quality of services or programs you provide.
- Cost savings to your organization.
- Increased public support for your programs, or improved community relations.
- Services or levels of service you otherwise could not provide.
- More detailed attention to the people you serve.
- Access to specialized skills possessed by volunteers.

Source: Hager, M. A. (2004) *Volunteer Management Capacity in America's Charities and Congregations: A Briefing Report*. Washington, DC: Urban Institute.

However, as there are benefits, there are also costs to the organization that are related to the use of volunteers. Moreover, these costs and benefits may contribute to the extent to which nonprofits use volunteers. Research has shed some light on the question of costs and benefits. First, research has found that as the costs associated with volunteer use increase, nonprofits will tend to use fewer volunteers.[23] The reasoning here is that although nonprofits may have access to unlimited volunteers, they would curtail their use of volunteers if the costs increase. Second, further research has shown that even when costs increase, nonprofits may still use more volunteers because of the indirect benefits of volunteer participation.[24] As noted above, the overall benefits of volunteering extend beyond the individual and the organization to the society. The literature suggests that it is equally important to understand the problems and issues that come with volunteer use, such as lack of training and high turnover.[25] To better understand the full picture, nonprofits must consider all the costs and benefits, including time and in-kind donations, provided the organization is not able to operate without these resources.

Monetary Value

For a number of years now, researchers have proposed formulae to calculate the value of volunteer time. The result is that there is annual value of volunteer time based on relevant hourly earnings and accounting standards. In the US,

TABLE 11.1 2012 Value of Volunteer Time

Beverly Bootstraps, Beverly	Youth Outreach Services, Chicago
$493,000	$116,071

the independent sector estimated value of volunteer time per hour in 2013 was $22.55 per hour and $22.14 in 2012. Along the same line, 64.5 million volunteers contributed 7.9 billion hours of service worth a total market value of $175 billion in 2012.[26]

To operationalize the monetary value of volunteer contribution, many nonprofits now include the total number of hours and the monetary value of volunteer hours in their annual report. Table 11.1 provides the total value of volunteer time in two nonprofits as reported in their annual reports.

Documenting and reporting the monetary value of volunteer time is important to nonprofits from several perspectives. At the least, the information will help the organization to accurately account for the labor of volunteers. Internally, such information is useful for resource allocation in the organization and is particularly critical for program planning and strategic planning. It could also be valuable in funding applications, regardless of whether funders consider the information as a condition for funding. In this respect, it adds value to the legitimacy of the nonprofit.[27] On the whole, the information is an important input for SHRM in nonprofits.

Volunteers and SHRM

In conjunction with employees, volunteers are the source of the human capital—the economic value of competencies, knowledge, skills and talents—of nonprofit organizations.[28] In nonprofit HRM, volunteers are the collective talent that defines the core capabilities nonprofits deploy to deliver services, to advocate for social justice, and to operationalize the mission of the organization. Volunteers do not only understand the mission and values of a nonprofit, they also actualize the value proposition of the organization. They inform and represent the social good the organization has articulated in its mission statement. Hence, they are also a critical nexus in the foundation and enhancement of the social capital of the organization. Together, these points highlight the need for volunteer management to be an integral SHRM function in nonprofits. As a result, most of the HR practices covered in this book are equally applicable to volunteers, especially in the area of recruitment, training and performance management.

However, there are major challenges that affect the current state of volunteer management that are important to review from an SHRM viewpoint. The major challenges can be classified into three broad categories: environment, resource and management challenges.

Environment Challenges

The environment challenges are related to the external factors that influence the operations of nonprofits discussed in Chapter 3. The two main environment factors shaping the nature of volunteering in nonprofits are (a) contract funding or purchaser provider relations, and (b) the accountability requirements from funders. Contracting has accentuated the need for professionalization of the roles and jobs in nonprofits. On the one hand, this has often increased replacement of volunteers with professional employees to perform the highly technical roles in many of the services downloaded by the government to the nonprofit sector.[29] On the other hand, the old and new volunteer roles require specific skills. This means that nonprofits must target recruiting volunteers with those skills and not just people who are willing to help out. To illustrate this point, Box 11.3 shows the list of specific roles posted on the website of the Alzheimer's & Dementia Alliance of Wisconsin.

BOX 11.3 ALZHEIMER'S AND DEMENTIA ALLIANCE OF WISCONSIN

Sampling of volunteer responsibilities (but not limited to):

- helpline volunteer
- client follow-up
- computer database work
- answer phones (reception)
- co-facilitate a support group
- make community presentations for the Speaker's Bureau
- transport members to support groups
- filing/copying/folding
- stuff envelopes, help with mailings
- manage the lending library
- bookkeeping responsibilities
- write thank you letters
- order pamphlets and resource materials
- maintain mailing lists
- update community service information
- assist with Alzheimer's awareness events
- staff health fairs
- assist at special events
- serve on Alzheimer's Walk Committee (one committee in each county we hold a walk in)
- serve on Education Committee

(continued)

(continued)

- serve on An Evening to Remember Committee
- serve on Million Dollar Shootout Committee
- serve on Legal and Financial Planning Committee
- serve on Public Policy Committee.

Source: Alzheimer's and Dementia Alliance of Wisconsin, http://www.alzwisc.org/About%20us.htm.

On the accountability front, volunteer board members must contend with different and stringent requirements. At the operations and governance levels, nonprofits must overcome the challenges of recruiting volunteers with the right skills and experience. All in all, the environment challenges are defining the knowledge and skills as well as the roles of volunteers in nonprofits.

Resource Challenges

The resource challenges are the manifestation of the very limited financial resources of most nonprofits. Although volunteers are the source of the human capital the organization needs to deliver services, to have governance oversight, and in some cases to manage the operations, many nonprofits do not have a volunteer management staff or department.[30] It is not uncommon for volunteers not to have a designated staff support. This lack of support for volunteers impacts the ability of the organization to manage volunteers, including training and performance management. Also, it means there is no opportunity to align volunteer management with SHRM practices.

Management Challenges

The third category of challenges is related to the inability of management to effectively manage the challenges outlined above. Although managers acknowledge the challenges, except for large nonprofits, they appear not to be adopting volunteer management practices to mitigate their impact.[31] In fact, the study found that most nonprofit managers do not adopt volunteer management practices that support volunteers. Box 11.4 outlines the major gaps in the nonprofit management practices. Also, there is the issue of the perception of volunteers and their contribution to the organization. It has been suggested that volunteer work is still considered as nice but not necessary work.[32] It is possible that this perception of volunteer work could be a factor in management decisions about how to support volunteer management and resource allocation to it. When managers consider a role to be relevant but not critical, especially in the context of tight resources, they are not likely to invest the resources of the organization in the role.

**BOX 11.4 GAPS IN VOLUNTEER MANAGEMENT
PRACTICES**

- not matching volunteers' skills with assignments
- failing to recognize volunteers' contributions
- not measuring the value of volunteers
- failing to train and invest in volunteers and staff
- failing to provide strong leadership

Source: Eisner, D., Grimm Jr., R. T., Maynard, S., & Washburn, S. (2009) "The new volunteer workforce," *Stanford Social Innovation Review*, Winter 2009.

In addition to the broad categories of challenges, there are also the more regular issues of communication, poor habits of some volunteers, and the recognition of volunteers. Although these are not major challenges, they are standard volunteer management issues that a typical nonprofit should be prepared to manage. From the orientation of new volunteers to daily operations, communication between volunteers, employees and the organization is a challenge that effective volunteer management can address. Managing volunteers with poor habits is simply an everyday management issue. Similarly, recognition is an issue that can easily fall through the cracks at the expense of volunteer retention.

Strategic Volunteer Management Model

Volunteers are invaluable and, together with employees, are the critical human resources of nonprofit organizations. The need to attract, retain and motivate volunteers is central to the performance of nonprofits. Following from the strategic importance of volunteers and the challenges examined above, nonprofits must develop and implement systems and processes that combine the needs of the organizations, the challenges, the opportunities and the support that would help to recruit, retain and motivate volunteers. Nonprofit organizations must consider and adopt an integrative strategy that aligns volunteer management practices.

Figure 11.1 presents a strategic volunteer management model that could provide nonprofit managers with a framework for aligning and managing the challenges, opportunities and organizational dynamics of volunteers. The model employs a strategic nonprofit human resource management (SNHRM) approach by emphasizing the link between the internal and external environment of the organization, the vertical alignment between nonprofit strategy and volunteer management, and the horizontal alignment between volunteer management practices. The need for managers to be more strategic in volunteer management, in

FIGURE 11.1 Strategic Volunteer Management Model

how they deploy the skills of volunteers in the context ⟨ the challenges and opportunities in the sector, is evident in research.

There are three levels that represent the phases of alignment in the model:

- *Environment, mission, and strategy*: The outermost circle includes the analysis of the external environment for forces that impact the organization. This level of the model will help the organization to determine the specific challenges that could affect the strategy and volunteer management in the organization. These factors must be monitored and analyzed regularly to determine the impact on volunteers. Similarly, the mission of the organization must be explained in terms of the programs, the services and the clients. The non-profit strategy must determine the roles and responsibilities of volunteers in the organization. It must also underlie the volunteer management practices.
- *Volunteer management practices and SHRM*: The outer circle includes the major volunteer management practices such as recruitment, training and recognition. It is important that these practices must be aligned with the nonprofit strategy. For example, the knowledge and skills that are required to achieve the strategic goals

of the organization should inform the skills emphasized in recruitment. They should also determine the primary training needs of the organization. At this level, all volunteer activities and outcomes should be informed by the strategic direction and organization priorities of the nonprofit. The second level must also align specific volunteer management practices such as recruitment, performance management and training. For example, once volunteers are recruited, their skills should determine the roles and responsibilities they are assigned in the organization. Also, volunteer management must be formulated and implemented within the broader SHRM functions. At the minimum, this involves the analysis of volunteer roles in relation to employee roles and the workflow processes between volunteers and employees, if applicable. Nonprofits should also analyze how volunteers and employees work together, and provide guidelines to facilitate processes and address issues. Feedback and recognition are core practices in volunteer management. Hence, it is important for nonprofits to implement an appraisal/feedback system for volunteers. A formal recognition program that incorporates informal and on-the-spot recognition should be implemented.

- *Effective volunteer management*: The center circle represents the impact and outcome of volunteer management. By aligning the nonprofit strategy with the volunteer management practices, the organization is positioned to address the challenges affecting volunteers and adapt to change in volunteering. At the operational level, it helps the organization to develop volunteer work roles that actually meet the needs of the organization. The alignment will also help the organization to develop and implement training and provide resources and critical support to volunteers. The goal is to showcase the outcome of the implementation of the volunteer management practices.

Employee Volunteer Partnership

It is not uncommon for nonprofits to commence operations with only volunteers and gradually integrate paid employees as they evolve in their organizational life cycle.[33] While the degree of the partnership between employees and volunteers varies in nonprofits,[34] the environment of HRM is characterized by unique dynamics as a result of the partnership. When it comes to attitude towards work, research indicates that employees are not fundamentally different from volunteers.[35] The research suggests that when employees and volunteers work together in the same location, perform similar work, and are subject to similar work rules, procedures, contracts, expectations, discipline and evaluations, they are likely to have similar job attitudes in terms of affective commitment, psychological contract and organizational justice.

Beyond the work attitude, there are two major factors to highlight in SHRM in relation to employee/volunteer partnership. First, employees and volunteers interchange roles and responsibilities. Some of the tasks performed by employees and volunteers are interchangeable.[36] In other words, employees can do some of the jobs of volunteers and vice versa. The second factor is that there is evidence that employees are replacing volunteers due to increased professionalization of non-profits, especially in response to change in funding.[37] Many funding applications now require nonprofits to recruit employees with specific knowledge and skills to provide the service the funding will support. These two factors indicate two sides of the SHRM in nonprofits in terms of employee/volunteer partnership. On the one hand, the collaboration between employees and volunteers provides a rich source of human capital for nonprofits to draw upon in order to achieve their organizational goals. The combination of employee and volunteer skills provides diversity of talent for the organization[38] and facilitates coproduction of organizational output.[39] On the other hand, it portends a complex working relationship between employees and volunteers that may threaten employee morale. Employees may feel vulnerable that volunteers could provide unpaid labor that would threaten their jobs or other terms of their employment. In fact, research suggests that nonprofits that engage volunteers tend to pay lower wages than other nonprofit organizations.[40]

However, the benefits of employee/volunteer partnership significantly outweigh the concerns about the impact on the jobs and terms of employment of employees. The professionalization trend suggests that employee/volunteer partnership must be leveraged as an integral component of volunteer management model and SHRM in nonprofits. The three levels of alignment emphasized in the volunteer management model are enhanced with an emphasis on volunteer management partnership. Box 11.5 shows the examples of practices the American Cancer Society is using to foster employee/volunteer partnership.

BOX 11.5 EMPLOYEE/VOLUNTEER PARTNERSHIP AT AMERICAN CANCER SOCIETY

- Respects and cares for volunteers in the same manner that the organization cares for its own staff.
- Staff and volunteers participate together in orientation and training classes.
- Work together on important projects such as creating curriculum, delivering quality of life programs to cancer patients and their families, and serving as community health liaisons.
- ACS expects staff to recruit and work with community volunteers, and it enforces this through performance reviews that measure volunteer engagement.

Source: Adapted from Eisner, D., Grimm Jr., R. T., Maynard, S., & Washburn, S. (2009) Copyright © *Stanford Social Innovation Review*. Reproduced in *Managing Human Resources for Nonprofits* with permission. Text originally appeared in "The New Volunteer Work Force," winter 2009. *Stanford Social Innovation Review*. Available online at http://www.ssireview.org/articles/entry/the_new_volunteer_workforce.

Summary

Volunteer management is critical to the organizational effectiveness of nonprofits. The ability of a nonprofit to actualize its mission and deliver services is significantly dependent on the volunteers who serve on the frontline, in management and in governance roles. The recruitment, retention and engagement of volunteers are undoubtedly top-of-mind issues for managers in nonprofits. Some of the related and constant questions that managers must grapple with include:

- How do nonprofit managers understand the challenges and emerging issues in volunteering?
- What are the knowledge and skills that volunteers can contribute to the organization?
- How best can the organization deploy the human and social capital volunteers contribute to the organization?
- How does the organization effectively manage and support volunteers?
- What is the monetary and non-monetary value of the human and social capital that volunteers contribute to the organization?

This chapter provides a brief overview of how some of these questions have been addressed in the literature. It also offers a model to provide a guideline for nonprofit managers on the relevant factors, practices and processes that would facilitate effective volunteer management. The chapter is not intended to be exhaustive, as the topic of volunteer management is extensive and complex, and cannot be covered entirely in one chapter. It provides a brief introduction to the key concepts and issues as well as the importance of volunteer management as a SHRM function in nonprofits.

In conclusion, through the link of volunteer management to SHRM, the chapter emphasizes that nonprofit managers must embrace the idea that it is a critical component of strategic management in their organization. Volunteer resource is part of the core resources the organization needs to achieve any form of competitive advantage in the constantly changing nonprofit environment. The value of the knowledge, skills and abilities that volunteers contribute is one of the few ingredients available to nonprofits to enhance their adaptive capabilities. The strategic perspective must underlie volunteer management if the organization is to reap the true value of volunteers as a key resource for sustainable competitive advantage.

Discussion Questions

The questions that nonprofit managers must consider are relevant to understand the importance of volunteers in nonprofits.

1. How do nonprofit managers understand the challenges and emerging issues in volunteering?
2. What are the knowledge and skills that volunteers can contribute to the organization?
3. How best can the organization deploy the human and social capital volunteers contribute to the organization?
4. How does the organization effectively manage and support volunteers?
5. What is the monetary and non-monetary value of the human and social capital that volunteers contribute to the organization?

Notes

1 The excerpt is from Vital Voices, Alison McCaffree Executive Director, Washington Nonprofits. In LeadOn 2013 Annual Report, Independent Sector, Washington, DC.
2 Akingbola, K. Duguid, F., & Viveros, M. (2013) "Learning and knowledge transfer in volunteering: Exploring the experience of red cross volunteers," in D. Schugurensky, K. Mundel, & F. Duguid (Eds.), *Volunteer Work, Informal Learning and Social Action.* Rotterdam: Sense Publishers.
3 Brudney, J. L. (Ed.) "Emerging areas of volunteering," *ARNOVA Occasional Paper Series,* 1(2): 7–12.
4 United Nations Volunteers (2001) "A turning point for volunteers," in United Nations Volunteers (Ed.) *Proceedings of Discussions of the UN General Assembly Debate on Government and United Nations System Support for Volunteering* (pp. 10, 18). New York: United Nations Volunteers.
5 Meinhard, A. (2006) "Managing the human dimension in nonprofit organizations: Paid staff and volunteers," in V. Murray (Ed.), *Management of Nonprofit and Charitable Organizations in Canada* (pp. 387–428). Markham, ON: LexisNexis Canada.
6 Cnaan, R. A., Handy, F., & Wadsworth, M. (1996) "Defining who is a volunteer: Conceptual and empirical considerations," *Nonprofit and Voluntary Sector Quarterly,* 25: 364–383.
7 Anheier, H., Hollerweger, E., Badelt, C., & Kendall, J. (2003) *Work in the Nonprofit Sector: Forms, Patterns and Methodologies.* Geneva: International Labour Organization.
8 Hall, M., McKeown, L., & Roberts, K. (2001) *Caring Canadians, Involved Canadians: Highlights from the 2000 National Survey of Giving, Volunteering and Participating.* Ottawa: Statistics Canada.
9 Basok, T., Ilcan, S., & Malesevic, B. (2002) *Volunteerism and Social Justice in Community Agencies.* Toronto: Canadian Centre for Philanthropy.
10 Gomez, R., & Gunderson, M. (2003) "Volunteer activity and the demands for work and family," *Relation Industrielles/Industrial Relations,* 58(4): 573–589.
11 Day, K., & Devlin, R. A. (1998) "The payoff to work without pay: Volunteer work as an investment in human capital," *Canadian Journal of Economics,* 31: 1179–1191.
12 Akingbola, Duguid, & Viveros, "Learning and knowledge transfer in volunteering."
13 Gomez & Gunderson, "Volunteer activity and the demands for work and family."
14 Rehnborg, S. J. (2005) "Government volunteerism in the new millennium," in J. L. Brudney (Ed.), "Emerging areas of volunteering," *ARNOVA Occasional Paper Series,* 1(2): 93–112.

15 McDonald, C., & Warburton, J. (2003) "Stability and change in nonprofit organizations: The volunteer contribution," *Voluntas: International Journal of Voluntary and Nonprofit Organizations*, 14(4): 381–399.

16 MacDuff, N. (2005) "Societal changes and the rise of the episodic volunteer," in J. L. Brudney (Ed.), "Emerging areas of volunteering," *ARNOVA Occasional Paper Series*, 1(2): 49–62.

17 Hustinx, L., & Lammertyn, F. (2004) "The cultural bases of volunteering: Understanding and predicting attitudinal differences between Flemish Red Cross volunteers," *Nonprofit and Voluntary Sector Quarterly*, 33(4): 548–584.

18 Hustinix, L. (2001) "Internationalization and new style of youth volunteering: An empirical exploration," *Voluntary Action*, 3(2): 57–76.

19 Ibid.

20 Hustinx & Lammertyn, "The cultural bases of volunteering."

21 Murray, V. & Harrison, Y. (2005) "Virtual volunteering," in J. L. Brudney (Ed.), "Emerging areas of volunteering," *ARNOVA Occasional Paper Series*, 1(2): 31–48.

22 Hager, M. A. (2004) "Volunteer management capacity in America's charities and congregations: A briefing report," Washington, DC: The Urban Institute, http://www.urban.org/UploadedPDF/410963_VolunteerManagment.pdf. Retrieved December, 2013.

23 Emanuele, R. (1996) "Is there a (downward sloping) demand curve for volunteer labour?" *Annals of Public and Cooperative Economics*, 67: 193–208.

24 Handy, F., & Brudney, J. (2007) "When to use volunteer labor resources? An organizational analysis for nonprofit management," *Vrijwillige Inzet Onderzocht (VIO, Netherlands)*, 4: 91–100.

25 Handy, F., & Mook, L. (2011) "Volunteering and volunteers: Benefit cost analyses," *Research on Social Work Practice,* 21(4): 412–420.

26 Corporation for National and Community Service (2012) *Research Brief: Volunteering in America Research Highlights*.

27 Brudney, J. L., & Meijs, L. C. P. M. (2009) "It ain't natural: Toward a new (natural) resource conceptualization for volunteer management," *Nonprofit and Voluntary Sector Quarterly*, 38: 564–581.

28 Hall, M. H., Andrukow, A., & Associates. (2003) *The Capacity to Serve: A Qualitative Study of the Challenges Facing Canada's Nonprofit and Voluntary Organizations*. Toronto: Canadian Centre for Philanthropy.

29 Brock, K. L. (2000) "Sustaining a Relationship: Insights from Canada on Linking the Government and Third sector." Paper presented at the International Society for Third Sector Research (ISTR), Dublin.

30 Hager, "Volunteer management capacity in America's charities and congregations."

31 Ibid.

32 Eisner, D., Grimm Jr., R. T., Maynard, S., & Washburn, S. (2009). "The new volunteer workforce," *Stanford Social Innovation Review*, Winter 2009.

33 Anheier, Hollerweger, Badelt, & Kendall, *Work in the Nonprofit Sector*.

34 Handy, F., & Brudney, J. L. (2007) "When to use volunteer labour resources? An organizational analysis for nonprofit management," *Vrijwillige Inzet Onderzocht (VIO, Netherlands) Jaargang*, 4: 91–100.

35 Liao-Troth, M. A. (2001) "Attitude differences between paid workers and volunteers," *Nonprofit Management and Leadership*, 11(4): 423–442.

36 Handy, F., Mook, L., & Quarter, J. (2008) "The interchangeability of paid staff and volunteers in nonprofit organizations," *Nonprofit and Voluntary Sector Quarterly*, 37(1): 76–92.

37 Akingbola, K. (2004) "Staffing, retention and government funding," *Nonprofit Management & Leadership*, 14(4): 453–465.

38 Hartenian, L. S. (2007) "Nonprofit agency dependence on direct service and indirect support volunteers: An empirical investigation," *Nonprofit Management & Leadership*, 17(3): 319–334.

39 Ibid.

40 Pennerstorfer, A., & Trukeschitz, B. (2012) "Voluntary contributions and wages in non-profit organizations," *Nonprofit Management & Leadership*, 23(2): 181–191.

12

CHANGE MANAGEMENT IN NONPROFITS

Learning Objectives

After studying this chapter, you should be able to:

1. Discuss the concepts of organizational change.
2. Understand drivers of change and uncertainty in nonprofits.
3. Illustrate change management approaches in nonprofits.
4. Explain the role of SHRM in nonprofit change management.

Adapting to Change[1]

The American Red Cross (ARC) began consolidating affiliates around the nation in response to a $200-million operating deficit, and before the depths of the 2008 recession struck. The ARC today has 550 chapters connected to 1,200 offices, compared with approximately 700 chapters four years ago. "Much of our effort has been focused on consolidating support services and back-office functions . . . where we found a great deal of duplication in our chapters," said spokesman Roger Lowe. He added that the number of Red Cross offices is roughly equal to the number of chapters a decade ago.

United Way affiliates have merged in recent years to increase efficiency. For smaller affiliates, mergers sometimes took place to maintain a presence in a particular service area, according to United Way Worldwide spokesman Bill Meierling. There were about 60 affiliates in 2008, but now there are roughly 30. Four more mergers of United Way affiliates went into effect this summer, including seven affiliates in the Philadelphia and southern New Jersey area, Michigan, Florida and Wisconsin.[2]

Introduction

Change is everywhere in nonprofits. As illustrated in the excerpt above, both the American Red Cross and the United Way affiliates implemented change in response to different factors in their operating environment. In fact, the content of this book up to this chapter has been essentially about the various manifestations, dimensions and dynamics of change and its implications for SHRM in nonprofits. This chapter adds to the change theme by briefly examining change management in nonprofits. It provides an overview of the concept of change management followed by a review of the drivers of change in nonprofit organizations. The chapter also discusses the strategic choices of nonprofits in a continuously changing environment.

Organizational Change

The notion of change is a common theme in everyday life. In the political sphere, elections are won and lost on the basis of change. Economists describe the goods and services we are likely to purchase by trending change in consumption patterns. Technology continues to revolutionize many aspects of daily living, especially the way we interact. Changes in social values and community needs are key drivers of the size and scope of nonprofit organizations; we will return to this topic later in the chapter. Essentially, change is everywhere in society, in all institutions in society including organizations. This ubiquitous nature of change is an important foundation in our attempt to understand the concept. However, it only gives us a glimpse into the preponderance of change. The reason for this is simple: change is complex.[3]

Organizational change is about movement, innovation and adapting. It is about movement from the past to the present point, and from the present to a future point in the life of an organization. Change is also about innovation to respond to emerging needs in the community or in the market. Change as innovation could create a need in the community or the market. Moreover, organizational change could simply be about adapting to realign a process or component of an organization.

Perhaps a couple of definitions would encapsulate this narrative and summarize what we refer to as organizational change in this chapter. Organizational change can be defined *as a planned alteration of organizational components to improve the effectiveness of the organization.*[4] This definition emphasizes that the organization is made up of components. The key components are mission, strategy, system, process and, of course, people. A change in the general or competitive environment often requires one or more of these components to be realigned to enhance organizational effectiveness.

Another definition emphasizes the critical role of managers in organizational change. It defines managing organizational change as a way of addressing *the issue of moving an organization or a system from point A to point B in the most effective and efficient manner.*[5] An important assumption in this delineation of managing change is that it assumes that a manager or change agent can accurately envision where point B is and the direction needed to get to it. In effect, a manager can analyze the factors in the general and competitive environment to formulate and implement a strategic change. An extension of managing change is creating the enabling environment and adaptive capacity for the organization to change.[6] The elements emphasized in these definitions capture the description of change as a phenomenon of time involving three elements: identity (what something is and becomes); the process of transformation; and people.[7] Managing organizational change means facilitating how these elements interact through change strategies.

As a phenomenon of time, organizational change is a process and not a state. It generally involves some form of transaction, transition and transformation, most of which are defined by the context of the organization. Hence, change is a multifaceted concept that is characterized by different but complementary elements.[8] The multifaceted nature of change means that there is a chance that any discussion of the concept might overlook one or more aspects of the process. However, if these different aspects are combined, a comprehensive understanding of the nature of change can be achieved.[9] Managers must be aware of the multifaceted nature of change in order to understand it. They must not only respond to the factors driving the movement of the organization from point A to point B, they must manage the change, and position the organization to better adapt to change, otherwise the organization may not survive. It is this action of managers that underlies and defines organizational change.

Although the main impetus for change management is the fear that inaction could affect the survival of the organization, change efforts have been remarkably unsuccessful. Leading change theorists and researchers have repeatedly found that most change initiatives or programs fail. Since the 1990s, it has been consistently reported that up to 80 percent of change initiatives do not succeed.[10] While there is limited research on the outcome of change initiatives in nonprofits, findings from research on hospitals, many of which are nonprofits, suggest that change efforts may not fare better in the sector.[11] Regardless of the pervasive failure of change initiatives, the appetite for change management among managers is inescapable.[12] Managers engage in change to meet specific objectives.

The objectives of managers can be explained from two perspectives: the economic and the organizational learning perspectives.[13] According to the economic perspective, managers deploy change management in order to continue to achieve better organizational performance that will help to deliver value for shareholders in terms of share price, earnings and dividends. For nonprofits, the economic value delivered by the organization is in terms of the economic activities they generate. Examples of the economic value of nonprofits include the value of volunteer and paid labor and the market value of goods and services purchased and provided by each nonprofit.[14] This social economy paradigm emphasizes that nonprofits deliver economic value to a wide-ranging list of stakeholders. As a result, from a change angle, nonprofit managers deploy change management initiatives to deliver organizational performance that ensures that there is economic value for stakeholders. Regardless of the sector, this economic perspective suggests that managers may use a top-down approach and emphasize structure and systems.

The organizational learning perspective emphasizes that the adaptive capacity of the organization is the primary goal that underlies why managers continue to deploy change management. From this perspective, the need to deliver value to shareholders or stakeholders is important; however, the way it is achieved is different. This approach to change management builds the employees' competencies and, through it, develops the organization's capabilities. The end result is that the organization will develop the adaptive capacity to position itself and respond to change.

In this approach to change, managers are more likely to elicit employee participation, influence their attitude and behavior, and work to build the organization's culture.

There is no doubt that change is a reality in organizations. Ignoring change is not an option because it is a constant in the life of the organization.[15] Hence, managers must continuously position the organization not only to respond to change but also to be able to forecast the direction of change and to be agile enough to maximize the opportunities that change offers and mitigate the threats it brings. These change management skills are core to the effectiveness of managers. A first step in building the change management skills of managers is to understand the key elements of change. In addition to the overview we have discussed, two such elements are the general environment factors that are driving change and the general types of change

Drivers of Change

Many of the general and competitive environment factors that we discussed in Chapter 3 are part of the important drivers of change in organizations in general. The trend in and the direction of the external environment are the prime forces that define the need of the organization to change. Although the internal factors in the organization can play a significant role in driving change, often they coalesce with external factors or result from the impact of the external environment. Nevertheless, both factors in the internal and external environment define why change is necessary.[16] A review of some of the external and internal environment factors is presented in this section.

External Environment Factors

Government Legislation and Policy

Throughout this book, we have emphasized the close relationship between nonprofits and government as a key factor in SHRM and specific HR practices in the sector. Hence, it is not a surprise to identify government as a major driver of change in nonprofits. The role of government in driving change in nonprofits is multifaceted. However, for the purpose of this chapter, the impact of the relationship on change can be explained using three overlapping elements: funding, measure of performance and accountability.

The *funding* relationship between nonprofits and the government means that a change in government policy and priorities could drive a need for change in nonprofits. Since many nonprofits depend significantly on government funding, the impact of government funding on change in nonprofits has been very evident in research.[17] For example, a study by the Urban Institute found that 82 percent of nonprofits in the study introduced change in response to decreases in local, state and federal government funding.[18] Some of the change initiatives adopted include reduced services and revised employee compensation and benefits.

Nonprofit-government relations also drive change in terms of the *measures of performance* adopted by nonprofits. Specifically, the impact of government and the politics of the day have come to dictate the types of performance measures nonprofits are required to use for reporting.[19] The performance measures required by government drive nonprofit managers to adopt change in what and how they measure performance of the organization. The change necessitated by the performance measures required in government is cascaded through the systems and processes including the HR practices of the organization. Once performance measures are defined, HR practices such as performance management are redefined to align employee performance with organizational performance.

Accountability is another strand of the impact of government on change in nonprofits. The accountability requirement is directly tied to performance measures and outcomes of the organization. As nonprofits strive to meet the performance expectations of the government contracts, the related reporting requirements drive change in the administrative system designed to support the operations of the organization. A change in performance measures could drive a corresponding change in accountability and the administrative system.

These three elements provide an insight into how governments drive change in nonprofits. Evidently, there are other elements of the government-nonprofit relationship that contribute to change in the sector. Although there is a significant body of research that has found that nonprofits are forced to adopt different forms of strategic change in order to have access to government funding, or manage the impact of the funding, some of this research may not expressly use the terms "change strategy" or "change management." Regardless of the perspective, what is important to surmise is that government is an important source of change in nonprofits. Government also plays into most of the other general and competitive environment factors that drive change in nonprofits.

Economy

The state of the economy creates the need for change in nonprofits on multiple levels. The economy affects the tax revenue of the government, earnings of corporations, and disposable income of people in society. On the one hand, the sources of revenue of nonprofits are directly impacted by the state of the economy. Most often, any downturn in one or more of the sources of revenue means there could be a threat not only to the cash flow of a nonprofit but the survival of the organization. In this circumstance, change is inevitable. For example, the impact of the 2008 recession forced many nonprofits to introduce different change initiatives, including fundraising strategies, in order to adapt to the emerging challenges in their operating environment.[20] On the other hand, a downturn in the economy tends to increase the demand for the services of nonprofits. Since economic downturns such as a recession often affect the most vulnerable in society, the demand for the services of nonprofits is increased and exacerbates the need for government funding.[21] In essence, the economy drives change in nonprofits in terms of strategy and operations including funding, philanthropy and services.

Competition

Whether it is acknowledged or not in public perception, there is competition in nonprofits.[22] Competition for funding, to deliver services, for donations, and even in advocacy are the hallmarks of the nonprofit operating environment. In fact, the level of competition has significantly intensified over the past decades.[23] Moreover, it has been suggested that competition could enhance the quality of governance of nonprofits.[24] The result is that nonprofit managers must continue to adopt and implement change in strategies to gain competitive advantage. The impact of competition on change in nonprofits is particularly important in terms of how the organization deploys its most important asset, human resources. Beyond strategies, change is also necessary in the systems and processes of the organization in order to create efficiencies.

Demographic Change and Community Needs

Demographic factors influence the mission of nonprofits. Factors such as age, level of education, income level, where people live, the family status of the people, and diversity impact the demand for the services of nonprofits. Demographic factors also determine the human resources available to nonprofits for service delivery, management and governance. As noted in Chapter 3, the impact of an aging population is a good example of a demographic factor that is driving change in nonprofits. Demographic change means nonprofits must assess the viability of current services and the need to develop new services. It also means re-evaluating the strategy of the organization. The need to develop and implement change initiatives to maximize the opportunities and mitigate the challenges of the aging population is a strategic imperative for nonprofits.[25]

Moreover, nonprofits are products of the shared values and problem-solving needs of the society.[26] Hence, as the values and problem-solving needs of society evolve, the change is reflected in the services and activities of nonprofits. It is not uncommon for nonprofits to develop change initiatives to leverage the emerging community needs, including the funding and revenue opportunities that are available as a result of the social trends.

Technology

Although it is less emphasized in research about change in nonprofits, technology is a potential driver of change in the sector. At a minimum, technology could impact the internal systems and processes of a nonprofit organization. The way nonprofits deliver services and use social media in fundraising, volunteer recruitment and advocacy are a few examples of how technology could drive significant change in nonprofits. Box 12.1 presents an example of how a nonprofit used technology to drive change in its operations. The article was retrieved from the website of the Nonprofit Technology Network, a membership organization of nonprofit technology professionals. The fact that the organization exists is a testament to the importance of technology in driving change in nonprofits.

BOX 12.1 EXAMPLE OF TECHNOLOGY DRIVING CHANGE IN NONPROFITS

For instance, the International Rescue Committee (IRC), a global humanitarian aid, relief, and development nongovernmental organization, needed to develop a new emergency response portal that's easily accessible from laptops online or offline. Leveraging a cloud platform API, the IRC was able to help field workers in disaster relief situations access manuals, procedures, and templates while directly in the middle of a crisis.

Source: Appleton, Karen (2014) "Modernizing nonprofits with cloud technology for good," http://www.nten.org/articles/2014/modernizing-nonprofits-with-cloud-technology-for-good. First published in NTEN Connect Newsletter (http://www.nten.org), March 2014, CC BY-SA 3.0 (http://creativecommon.org/licenses/by-sa/3.0/).

Management Fashion

Similar to organizations in the business and the public sectors, nonprofits could adopt change initiatives that have been implemented successfully in other organizations within and outside the sector. Nonprofits routinely adopt management concepts and practices developed in for-profit business organizations.[27] In fact, in addition to adopting specific management practices used by successful organizations to gain social legitimacy,[28] nonprofits adopt high performance work practices used in other nonprofits.[29] This practice of imitating management practices used in other organizations that are deemed to be successful or legitimate is known as *mimetic isomorphism.*[30] Evidence of its use has been found in nonprofits.[31] The change initiative adopted in a nonprofit could therefore be the result of similar initiatives that have been adopted by successful organizations in the nonprofit, for-profit and public sectors.

The external environment factors reviewed in this section are some of the key drivers of change in nonprofits. Directly and indirectly, the economic, community, demographic and other factors related to government/political forces are the reasons why nonprofits introduce change initiatives. Although technology appears to be less of a factor in major change, it is expected that nonprofits will adopt more change as a result of technology as they grow in size and scope.

Internal Environment Factors

Research appears to suggest that to a lesser extent than the external factors discussed above, internal environment factors contribute to the need to consider and implement change initiatives in nonprofits. It is possible that even when an internal factor is the key driver for change, the underlying factor for this change could be traced to the external environment. Basically, the need to realign the organization with the challenges, opportunities and threats in the external environment could be the root cause or driver of change initiatives spearheaded by internal environment factors or players in nonprofits. Nonetheless, some examples of the internal environment factors that drive change in nonprofits are worth mentioning.

Internal Stakeholders

The internal stakeholders of nonprofits, from employees to frontline and governance volunteers, have their own expectations of the mission, values, goals and activities the organization should emphasize. Similar to the impact of the external stakeholders such as the government and the community, these expectations are relative and open to the interpretation of the respective stakeholder. As noted in nonprofit research, the diversity and heterogeneity of expectations and goals suggest that the performance of nonprofits is susceptible to the perception of stakeholders.[32] The activities nonprofits engage in, how the activities are coordinated and integrated, and the measures of performance used to evaluate the outcome may be viewed differently by different stakeholders.

In effect, the characteristics of stakeholders, their collective orientation, and the goals they want the organization to emphasize are important factors not only in the strategy the organization adopts but also in the systems and processes that evolve to manage the operations.[33] The dynamics in terms of the importance of internal stakeholders is a factor in the change initiatives adopted in nonprofits. The interactions and processes in the internal environment underlie the decision about change. The intentions, choices and actions of the internal stakeholders are reflected in change and the strategies adopted to manage change.

Moreover, since employees and volunteers are attracted to nonprofits because of the mission and values of the organization, the imperative for change for them must be consistent with the mission and values they signed up for. Employees, in particular, have been noted to be more susceptible to conflict in terms of competing values and expectations. Employee may experience job dissatisfaction if they perceive that their organization is not achieving the public good that attracted them.[34] For change to be supported by employees, it must at least align with their expectations of the organization.

Management Factors

Closely related to the importance of internal stakeholders are management related factors that are generally part of the responsibilities or characteristics of managers of the organization. One such management factor is the *strategic choices* managers make on behalf of the organization. Managers make critical decisions that influence whether and how the organization will grow. Managers manage people, facilitate the interactions with the external stakeholders, and allocate resources based on their strategic choice.

The strategic choices are related to the *organizational life cycle*. As organizations navigate the stages of their life cycle, managers must manage the opportunities, threats and challenges in the internal and external environment.[35] The need for resources and capabilities reflect the life cycle stage of the organization. Strategic choices about *growth, stability* and the *structure* of the organization are necessary to enable the organization to align itself with the forces of its life cycle stage. Different organizations experience passages through life cycle stages differently. Hence managers are likely to interpret the opportunities, challenges and threats that are related to the organization's life cycle stage differently (Table 12.1).

TABLE 12.1 Organizational Life Cycle Stage and Needs

Life Cycle Stage	Critical Needs
Start-up Stage	Start-up funds, cash flow, and customer acceptance
Emerging Growth Stage	Stabilizing production and service reliability, matching demand increases, maintaining cash flow, and formalizing organizational structure
Mature Stage	No critical needs, strong cash flows, positive leadership image, overconfidence, due to excess cash and the absence of critical needs, resource allocation decisions are likely to be framed from a gain domain.
Decline/ Transition Stage	Strategies such as mergers, downsizing, and layoffs to ensure organizational survival. Also Technical efficiency to develop new products.

Source: This summary is based on Jawahar, M., & McLaughlin, G. L. (2001) "Toward a descriptive stakeholder theory: an organizational life cycle approach," *The Academy of Management Review*, 26(3): 397–414.

Together, management factors in terms of strategic choices about growth and how managers navigate life cycle stage issues are major drivers of change. The strategic choices and the type of leadership deployed to manage life cycle stage opportunities and threats could drive change in strategic goals, SHRM and the systems and processes in the organization. In nonprofits, the management factors could also include leadership orientation or position on advocacy to drive change that are aligned with the mission of the organization.

Model of Change

Many of the theories and models of change can be traced to the work of Kurt Lewin. Lewin stressed the need to understand the system as a whole, including the context and the components of the system.[36] To recognize and manage change, Lewin emphasized that it is important to understand the complex interplay between the environment factors such as the ones discussed above and personal psychological factors.[37] As a result, each change situation is different and depends on the challenges, players and culture of the organization.

Lewin proposed a three-step model of change:

$$Unfreeze \longrightarrow Change \longrightarrow Refreeze$$

Unfreezing involves the disrupting of the status quo that exists in the system. It means that the fundamental assumptions and practices of the system players must be called to question in order to make a case for the need for change.[38] Unfreezing is a prerequisite for change. For example, government contract funding has been a major factor in the unfreezing of the status quo in the nonprofit operating environment. Nonprofit managers have had to emphasize its impact and use it to introduce the disruption to the status quo. The old system of relationship with the government was not working; therefore, there was a need for change. The change is the determination and formulation of a specific change initiative for the organization. It is at this stage that the options for change are considered and change is implemented. During the refreezing phase, the organization institutionalizes the change. The new system, structure and behaviors are reinforced as the new way of doing business in the organization. Lewis emphasized that it is critical to involve people who are gatekeepers of the system in order for change to succeed.

Nature and Types of Change

Before providing an overview of the types of change, it is important to consider some of the assumptions about the *nature of change*. To answer the question "what is the nature of change," Poole[39] reviewed three conceptualizations of the nature of change. These assumptions about the nature of change provide a good foundation for understanding the types of change.

Poole noted that Bennis[40] explained change in terms of the difference between theories of change and theories changing. Theories of change are focused on how organizations change and the factors that contributed to the change while the theories of changing are concerned about how change can be instituted and managed in organizations.[41] An important factor in this conceptualization of change is the role of people in terms of whether the change is planned or unplanned.

Drawing on the conceptualization of change by Weick and Quinn,[42] Poole also noted that change can be explained as either episodic or continuous change. *Episodic change* is infrequent, discontinuous and intentional, while *continuous change* is ongoing, evolving and cumulative.[43] Episodic change is likely to occur at periodic intervals influenced by change in the external or internal environment. Continuous change involves emerging practices and process updates. The emphasis of this conceptualization is the character of change. It highlights the dimensions of change.

From another conceptualization, change is seen as the result of the mechanisms that make it happen.[44] In this explanation, based on the work of Van de Ven and Poole, four ideal types of processes through which change can come about are presented. The ideal types or models are *life-cycle, teleological, dialectical* and *evolutionary*.[45] *Life cycle* is focused on the key stages that the organization must pass through. These are the sequence of prescribed life cycle stages discussed in this chapter. *Teleological* is based on the sequence of goal formulation, implementation, evaluation and modification. The sequence of change is recurrent and discontinuous. *Dialectical* is based on the synthesis that results from opposing thesis and antithesis. Change is characterized by consensus that results from initial differences in opinion and conflict. The *evolutionary* model involves a natural selection process among competitors. It incorporates repetitive sequence of variation, selection and retention among entities.

These three conceptualizations explain change from different angles. Very importantly they overlap and can fit into each other. For the purpose of this chapter, the conceptualizations present different ways of categorizing change and lay the foundation for the types of change. Next, we review the general types of change.

Types of Organizational Change

An extensive list of types of change has been proposed in the change management literature. One common typology of change is the difference between episodic and continuous change that was reviewed in the discussion about conceptualization of change earlier. Another one is based on the work of Nadler and Tushman.[46] They develop a matrix that distinguishes between incremental

TABLE 12.2 Types of Organizational Change

	Incremental	*Discontinuous*
Anticipatory	**Tuning**	**Reorientation**
	Adjustment	Major change
	Improvement	Positioning entire organization
	Internal alignment	Frame bending
	Components or sub-systems	
Reactive	**Adaptation**	**Recreation**
	Internal alignment	Reevaluate whole organization
	External event	Rapid system–wide change
		Frame breaking

Source: Nadler, D. A., & M. L. Tushman (1995) "Type of organizational change: From incremental improvement to discontinuous transformation," in D. A. Nadler, R. B. Shaw & A. E. Walton (Eds.), *Discontinuous Change: Leading Organizational Transformation* (pp. 14–33). San Francisco: Jossey-Bass.

and discontinuous change as well as anticipatory and reactive change to differentiate between four types of change: *tuning, reorientation, adaptation* and *recreation* (see Table 12.2).

Tuning involves incremental improvements and modifications that are designed to help the organization to withstand anticipated change in the external environment. Generally, the goal of the change is the internal alignment between individual components or sub-systems of the organization. Hence, there is no urgent need for the change. For example, a nonprofit may revise its volunteer recruitment process as part of improvement in volunteer management.

Adaptation involves an incremental change that results from the organization's reaction to specific change driver(s) in the external environment. The change ensures that the organization keeps up with the environment or faces the consequence of inaction. In Box 12.2, the change at Amnesty International UK included some elements of adaptation in terms of the need to adapt to technological change.

Reorientation is a type of anticipatory and discontinuous strategic change that is characterized by a focus on the major components of the organization. It involves frame-bending, in the sense that the goal is to change core elements such as the culture, values, strategy and structure of the organization. The anticipatory nature of the change means that it is implemented in advance of predicted major competitive pressure, crisis or change in the environment. Thus, the process of time enables the organization to absorb the effects of the implementation of the change without breaking. Since employees and stakeholders may not see the immediate need for the change, the role of senior management to create a sense of urgency about the change is important. Apart from the technological factor noted in the change at Amnesty International UK in Box 12.2, the change appears to be consistent with a reorientation type of change.

BOX 12.2 TYPE OF CHANGE AT AMNESTY INTERNATIONAL UK

At Amnesty International UK, change was imperative. The UK arm of the global nonprofit that work to *protect men, women and children wherever justice, freedom, truth and dignity are denied* needed to implement a change. The drivers of the change include concerns about long-term viability and a wish to invest heavily in Asia coupled with climate of austerity and technological changes. However, the organization was mindful of cutting jobs in core services and had a preference for the greater safety of taking small steps.

To move forward, Amnesty appeared to have adopted to manage the change in a very open manner. They worked with the union and engaged stakeholders in the change process.

Source: Adapted from Gotham, Peter (2013) "Amnesty's open approach to change is commendable," *Third Sector*, February 26, 2013.

Recreation is a reactive change that is implemented in response to a significant crisis. In this type of change, the need is to re-evaluate the whole organization, including its core values. The focus is on frame-breaking because it involves reassessing and, if necessary, the discarding and replacement of the elements of the organization. Since the situation is unanticipated and sudden, the goal is to achieve rapid system-wide change in all components of the organization. The desperation of the crisis situation means there is generally no time to experiment with alternatives. The opening case on the change at American Red Cross and the United Way illustrates the kind of crisis that could lead to *recreation*. Moreover, research and reports on the survival of nonprofits highlight why *recreation* type of change has been evident in the sector. For example, research has found that nonprofits that are not quickly adapting to change in funding by using more strategies to attract funders and use less diversified income were less likely to survive.[47]

Nonprofit Change Strategies and HRM

Nonprofits have adopted varied strategies to adapt to and manage the impact of the change drivers that we have discussed in this chapter. Although these adaptive strategies could vary based on the size and scope of the organization, research has found consistent patterns in the use of some specific change initiatives. One research found that social service nonprofits adopted four main change strategies to adapt to change the funding challenges: (1) pursuing strategic expansion;

(2) developing business management techniques; (3) stepping up boundary-spanning activities; and (4) maintaining public service character through commercialization—that is, using the autonomy resulting from revenue-generating services to develop services required by low-paying clients.[48] The research noted that expansion through introduction of new services and populations was one of the most common adaptation strategies.

A more recent research found that the size of the organization predicted four of the five change strategies that human service nonprofits are likely to use when faced with economic uncertainty: (1) adding new programs, (2) discontinuing existing programs or reducing staff, (3) starting joint programs, (4) increasing earned income, and (5) starting or expanding advocacy involvement.[49] The research found that starting joint programs was predicted by having a strategic plan and not reporting funding to be a future challenges. The findings provide evidence that size and the access to resources that come with size could impact the ability of a nonprofit to implement a change strategy. This could explain previous research that found that nonprofits tend to focus on change strategies that contribute to increased revenue rather than a cost containment strategy when they need to manage the impact of government funding.[50] The focus on revenue is important to enable nonprofits to build a resource capacity that enhances their ability to adapt to change.

The research findings on the change initiatives that nonprofits adopt emphasize the importance of HR practices in the adaptive strategies of nonprofits. Generally, HR is critical to change strategies in nonprofits at two levels: HR as a change strategy and as a factor in a change strategy.

HR as a Change Strategy

Nonprofit research has found that a number of ific HR practices have been implemented as part of the change strategies of iizations in the sector. First, nonprofits have introduced or enhanced the trai   ; they provide to employees to ensure that they have the competencies requi   by the organization to adapt to change. The deployment of training is explici   a strategy to meet the operational need for diverse competencies with a fo   on immediate organizational goals as well as to provide employees with the s   lls and to foster behaviors that are needed to adapt to change.[51] This explains w   nonprofit research has underscored the importance of training in the sector.[52]

Second, enhanced opportunity for employee involvement in decision-making has also been highlighted as a distinct HR practice that nonprofits have adopted in change management. A study found that employee participation initiatives were deployed as adaptive strategies in addition to the introduction of new processes and technology.[53] In another study, a nonprofit organization adopted an employee involvement model in order to use it as a key HR initiative to facilitate skills and learning and coach managers about the drivers of the social business of the organization.[54] The thinking here was that when employees are involved in decision-making, the organization will be better able to determine the knowledge and skills required to meet the changing needs on the frontline as well as link managers to the frontline seamlessly. Along the same lines, the example of Amnesty International UK discussed above also highlighted that the organization used employee and stakeholder involvement in the change process.

Third, although it is not a specific HR initiative, retention has been emphasized as an essential component of the adaptive strategies of some nonprofits.[55] As an outcome of the HR practices of an organization, retention helps a nonprofit to maintain and deploy the knowledge, skills and behavior of employees to adapt to change. A high level of turnover is a challenge not only to the knowledge and skills that will facilitate change but also to the culture, strategy and structure of the nonprofit. It is difficult to institutionalize new systems and processes in situation of low retention.

HR as a Factor in Change Strategies

From this perspective, HR practices are considered and implemented as key components of the specific change initiatives nonprofits have adopted. In many cases, the role and importance of HR practices as a factor in the change initiative nonprofits have adopted is in addition to specific HR practices the organization has adopted. For example, a nonprofit could emphasize training as key change management initiative and also have compensation as a subcomponent in its change strategy of adding new programs. Although not specific, the research noted above appears to suggest that nonprofits have combined distinct HR practices developed as change initiatives with HR practices that are developed to support major change strategies of the organization.

In terms of specific change initiatives that nonprofits adopt, HR practices are important to the outcome of any such initiative. On the front end, research has found that HR issues relating to employees and volunteers are a major barrier to change in nonprofits.[56] The specific HR issues that were highlighted are recruitment, training and the difficult responsibility of managing the obligations of employment law. The challenges were accentuated by lack of resources, a problem that is common in most nonprofit organizations.

Box 12.3 provides an example of organizational change at Family Services, Inc. in North Carolina. The change initiatives include a new strategic vision and plan and program partnership with three local nonprofits. One HR initiative, the introduction of a cross functional team, is part of the major change strategies of the organization. In addition, HR practices are integral to the key change initiatives.

BOX 12.3 CHANGE AND HRM AT FAMILY SERVICES, INC.

Family Services, Inc. is a nonprofit organization that provides a range of services including counseling, education, intervention, and advocacy. The mission of the nearly 110-year North Carolina nonprofit is to promote the school readiness of children, the well-being of adults and families, and the safety of those in the community impacted by domestic violence and sexual assault. Revenue in 2012 was about $5 million.

Change Initiatives: New strategic vision and action plan. Project with three local nonprofits to provide family therapy, relationship skills training, parenting education and support, financial education and coaching, and job training and employment services. Less silos in three divisions. Creation of staff cross functional teams.

Performance: Change in progress.

HRM

Staff participation in developing new strategic vision and action

Use of cross functional teams

Redeployment of staff

Specialized staffing

Source: Adapted from Schaefer, C. (2014) "Human services groups collaborate to survive," *The NonProfit Times,* March 14, 2014.

The development of the new strategic vision and action plan of Family Services, Inc. has included employee participation in the process. The organization noted that staff redeployment and specialized staffing could be part of the change relating to the program partnership with three local nonprofits.

The point to emphasize here is that HRM is critical in the effectiveness of change management. Regardless of whether specific HR practices are used as a change initiative or HR is acknowledged as a factor in the change strategies deployed by a nonprofit, HR practices can impact the outcome of change initiatives. This was evident in one study that noted that insufficient attention to HRM issues such as communication and involvement strategies, training, job design and reporting structures could undermine the process of change management.[57] Box 12.4 shows some of the general HR consequences of change.

BOX 12.4 EXAMPLES OF HR CONSEQUENCES OF CHANGE

- recruitment of new employees
- new or enhanced training
- employees gain new skills
- employees develop new behaviours
- employees form new internal network
- employee layoff
- employee turnover
- volunteer turnover
- recruitment of new volunteers
- stress and burnout among employees
- increased employee/volunteer interchangeability
- revised job profiles for volunteers
- improved employee and volunteer engagement
- new organizational culture and values.

To recap, HRM comprises HR philosophy, practices and policies aimed at attracting, motivating and retaining employees required by the organization to achieve its strategic goals. Employee behavior including motivation and commitment and their knowledge and skills are fundamental to organizational performance. Therefore, the role of HR is to facilitate the behavior, knowledge and skills required to achieve the performance goals of the organization. However, there is change, and change is difficult. Organizations need to change in order to adapt to the opportunities and threats in the external environment. To do this, organizational change generally requires employees to change their behavior and acquire new knowledge and skills. As a result, organizational change requires HRM in order to be effective. HRM is the key ingredient for the effectiveness of many organizational change initiatives. Nonprofit SHRM stresses the alignment of strategy with how nonprofits attract, recruit, deploy, motivate and retain employees to respond to change in the operating environment. The role, choices and impact of people are the defining elements of change management.

Summary

The question of change management is a particular reality that nonprofits cannot afford to ignore. Change in the external and internal environment is part and parcel of the operational dynamics of providing social goods and services, managing systems and processes, and ensuring there is governance. In change management, HRM is front and center. Change management needs HRM to be effective and to institutionalize new culture and values. Change has implications for HRM. This is the focus of this chapter. After introducing change and reviewing relevant elements of change, the chapter offers a brief insight into change management in nonprofits. The chapter also discusses the strategic choices nonprofits are deploying to adapt to a continuously changing environment. It also highlights how change and HRM are related, especially in terms outcomes of change management.

Discussion Questions

1. Consider a nonprofit organization that you know has implemented a change initiative. What are the major factors that necessitated the change?
2. Stakeholders play an important role in the operations of nonprofits. How can nonprofits ensure that the perspective of stakeholders is taken into account when major strategic change occurs in an organization?
3. Think of a major organizational change that you have experienced or know about in a nonprofit. What were the steps in the change process?
4. Nonprofit managers must prepare their organization to be positioned to adapt to change. What are some of the ways in which managers can facilitate change readiness?

Notes

1 The excerpt is from Hrywna, M. (2012) "Me   ke   ors open, refocuses management," *The Nonprofit Times*, http://ww   no   ttimes.com/news-articles/ mergers-keep-doors-open-refocuses-manage   . Ret   ved December, 2013.
2 Ibid.
3 Harvey, T. R. (1995) "Change checklist," in (ist for Change: A Pragmatic Approach to Creating and Controlling Change* (pp. 53–90). L   ster   chnomic Publishing.
4 Cawsey, T. F., & Deszca, G. (2007). *Toolkit for   aniz   nal Change*. Los Angeles: Sage Publications.
5 Zimmerman, B. J. (1993) "Strategic control: mar   ing change or managing changeability," Proceedings of The Chaos Network, 1993 Con   rence, St. Paul, MN, pp. 55–60.
6 Ibid.
7 Morgan, M., & Sturdy, A. (2000) "The soc   approach to organizational change," in *Beyond Organizational Change: Structure, D   urse and Power in UK Financial Services* (pp. 3–40). New York: St. Martin's Press.
8 Poole, M. S. (2004) "Central issues in the study of change and innovation," in M. S. Poole & A. H. Van de Ven (Eds.), *Handbook of Organizational Change and Innovation* (pp. 3–31). Oxford: Oxford University Press.
9 Harvey, T. R. (1995) "Change checklist."

10 Beer, M., Eisenstat, R. A., & Spector, B. A. (1990) *Why Change Programs Don't Produce Change*. Cambridge, MA: Harvard Business Review Press; Kotter, John. (1995) "Leading change: Why transformation efforts fail," *Harvard Business Review*, March–April; Knodel, T. (2004) "Preparing the organizational 'soil' for measurable and sustainable change: business value management and project governance," *Journal of Change Management*, 4(1): 45–62.

11 Clinton, O., Longenecker, C. O., & Longenecker, P. D. (2014) "Why hospital improvement efforts fail: A view from the front line," *Journal of Healthcare Management*, 59(2): 147–157.

12 Palmer, I., Dunford, R., & Akin, G. (2006) *Managing Organizational Change: A Multi Perspective Approach*. Toronto: McGraw-Hill Irwin.

13 Beer, M., & Nohria, N. (2000) "Cracking the code of change," *Harvard Business Review*, May–June, 78(3): 133–141.

14 Quarter, J., Mook, L., & Armstrong, A. (2009) *Understanding the Social Economy: A Canadian Perspective*. Toronto: University of Toronto Press; Quarter, J., Mook, L., & Richmond, B. J. (2003) *What Counts: Social Accounting for Non-Profits and Cooperatives*. Upper Saddle River, NJ: Prentice-Hall.

15 Vales, E. (2007) "Employees CAN make a difference! Involving employees in change at Allstate Insurance," *Organization Development Journal*, 25(4): 27–31.

16 Pettigrew, A. (1987) "Context and action in the transformation of the firm," *Journal of Management Studies*, 24(6): 649–670.

17 Smith, R., & Lipsky, M. (1993) *Nonprofits for Hire: The Welfare State in the Age of Contracting*. Cambridge, MA: Harvard University Press; Salamon, L. M., Geller, S. L., & Spence, K. L. (2009) *Impact of the 2007–2009 Economic Recession on Nonprofit Organizations*. Baltimore, MD: Johns Hopkins Center for Civil Society Studies.

18 Boris, E. T., de Leon, E., Roeger, K. L., & Nikolova, M. (2010) *Human Service Nonprofits and Government Collaboration. Findings from the 2010 National Survey of Nonprofit Government Contracting and Grants*. The Urban Institute, http://www.urban.org/uploadedpdf/412228-nonprofit-government-contracting.pdf. Retrieved December, 2013.

19 Alexander, J., Brudney, J., & Yang, K. (2010) "Introduction to the symposium: Accountability and performance measurement: the evolving role of nonprofits in the hollow state," *Nonprofit Management and Leadership*, 39(4): 565–570.

20 Hall, H. (2009) "Half of charity campaigns plan to extend the length of the drive, survey finds," *Chronicle of Philanthropy*, March 31, 2009, http://philanthropy.com/blogs/conference/half-of-charity-campaigns-plan-to-extend-the-length-of-the-drive-survey-finds/10505.

21 Cho, S., & Gillespie, D. F. (2006) "A conceptual model exploring the dynamics of government-nonprofit service delivery," *Nonprofit and Voluntary Sector Quarterly*, 35(3): 493–509.

22 Castaneda, M. A., Garen, J., & Thornton, J. (2008) "Competition, contractibility, and the market for donors to nonprofits," *Journal of Law, Economics, and Organization*, 24(1): 215–246.

23 Chetkovich, C., & Frumkin, P. (2003) "Balancing margin and mission: Nonprofit competition in charitable versus fee-based programs," *Administration & Society*, 35(5): 564–596.

24 Glaeser, E. L. (2003) "Introduction," in *The Governance of Not-for-Profit Organizations*. Chicago: University of Chicago Press.

25 Espy, Siri N. (1992) "The aging of America: Implications for nonprofit planning," *Nonprofit World* 10(2) (Mar/Apr): 31.

26 Smith & Lipsky, *Nonprofits for Hire*; Salamon, Geller, & Spence, *Impact of the 2007–2009 Economic Recession on Nonprofit Organizations*.

27 Salipante, P. E., & Golden-Biddle, K. (1995) "Managing traditionality and strategic change in nonprofit organizations," *Nonprofit Management & Leadership*, 6(1): 3–20.

28 DiMaggio, P. J., & Powell, W. W. (1983) "The iron cage revisited: Institutional isomorphism and collective rationality in organizational fields," *American Sociological Review*, 48(2): 147–160.

29 Kalleberg, A. L., Marden, P., Reynolds, J., & Knoke, D. (2006) "Beyond profit! Sectoral difference in high-performance work practices," *Work and Occupations*, 33(3): 271–302.

30 DiMaggio & Powell, "The iron cage revisited."

31 Kalleberg, Marden, Reynolds, & Knoke, "Beyond profit!"

32 Herman, R. D., & Renz, D. O. (2004) "Investigating the relation between good management, financial outcomes and stakeholder judgement of effectiveness in donative and commercial nonprofit organizations." Paper presented at the annual conference of the Association for Research on Nonprofit Organizations and Voluntary Action, Los Angeles.

33 Akingbola, K. (2012) "A model of strategic nonprofit human resource management," *Voluntas: International Journal of Voluntary and Nonprofit Organizations*, 24(1): 214–240.

34 Kim, S. (2005) "Three big management challenges in nonprofit human services agencies," *International Review of Public Administration*, 10(1): 85–93.

35 Jawahar, M., & McLaughlin, G. L. (2001) "Toward a descriptive stakeholder theory: an organizational life cycle approach," *The Academy of Management Review*, 26(3): 397–414.

36 Cawsey & Deszca, *Toolkit for Organizational Change*.

37 Scott, B. B. (2009) "Organization development primer: Change management, Kurt Lewin and beyond," IRC Article Series. Kingston, ON: Queen's University IRC.

38 Cawsey & Deszca, *Toolkit for Organizational Change*.

39 Poole, M. S. (2004) "Central issues in the study of change and innovation," in M. S. Poole & A. H. Van de Ven, (Eds.), *Handbook of Organizational Change and Innovation* (pp. 3–31). Oxford: Oxford University Press.

40 Bennis, W. (1966) *Changing Organizations*. New York: McGraw Hill.

41 Ibid.

42 Weick, K. E., & Quinn, R. E. (1999) "Organizational change and development," *Annual Review of Psychology*, 50: 361–386.

43 Ibid.

44 Van de Ven, A. H., & Poole, M. S. (1995) "Explaining development and change in organizations," *Academy of Management Review*, 10(3): 510–540.

45 Ibid.

46 Nadler, D. A., & Tushman, M. L. (1995) "Type of organizational change: From incremental improvement to discontinuous transformation," in D. A. Nadler, R. B. Shaw & A. E. Walton (Eds.), *Discontinuous Change: Leading Organizational Transformation* (pp. 14–33). San Francisco: Jossey-Bass.

47 Bielefeld, W. (1994) "What affects nonprofit survival?" *Nonprofit Management & Leadership*, 5(1): 19–36.

48 Alexander, J. (2000) "Adaptive strategies of nonprofit human service organizations in the era of devolution and new public management," *Nonprofit Management & Leadership* 10(3): 287–303.

49 Mosley, J. E., Maronick, M. P., & Katz, H. (2012) "How organizational characteristics affect the adaptive tactics used by human service nonprofit managers confronting financial uncertainty," *Nonprofit Management & Leadership*, 22(3): 281–303.

50 Foster, M. K. & Meinhard, A. (2002) "A contingency view of the responses of voluntary social service organizations in Ontario to government cutbacks," *Canadian Journal of Administrative Sciences*, 19(1): 27–41.

51 Akingbola, K. (2013) "Contingency, fit and flexibility of HRM in nonprofit organizations," *Employee Relations*, 35(5): 479–494.

52 Parry, E., Kelliher, C., Mills, T., & Tyson, S. (2005) "Comparing HRM in the voluntary and public sectors," *Personnel Review*, 34(5): 588–602.

53 Durst, S. L., Newell. C. (2001) "The who, why and how of reinvention in nonprofit organizations," *Nonprofit Management & Leadership,* 11(4): 1443–1457.

54 Akingbola, "Contingency, fit and flexibility of HRM in nonprofit organizations."

55 Alexander, "Adaptive strategies of nonprofit human service organizations in the era of devolution and new public management."

56 Hay, G. K., Beattie, R. S., Livingstone, R., & Munro, P. (2001) "Change, HRM and the voluntary sector," *Employee Relations*, 23(3): 240–255.

57 Ibid.

13

METRICS AND HUMAN RESOURCE MANAGEMENT IN NONPROFITS

Learning Objectives

After studying this chapter, you should be able to:

1. Explain what metrics are about.
2. Discuss why metrics are important.
3. Provide examples of the importance of metrics in HRM.
4. Illustrates the role of metrics in SHRM in nonprofits.

Metrics Driving the Mission at Friendship ub Charter School[1]

The Friendship Collegiate Academy is a unique school i   shington, DC. The school has a near perfect graduation rate and college acceptance rate f   duating seniors. Since it opened in 1997 in a former public school building overrun by dru   ilers, the school has transformed the lives of its mostly low-income students—around 65 p   t of Friendship students qualify as low income. Friendship Collegiate Academy is one of i   charter schools of the Friendship Public Charter School (Friendship). Friendship manages to   hools in the Baltimore and DC area. The mission of the publicly funded nonprofit is to pre   e students to become ethical, literate, well-rounded and self-sufficient citizens by providing   world-class education that motivates students to reach high academic standards, enjoy lear   ng, achieve success and contribute actively to their communities. One of the key ingredients in the success of Friendship is metrics. Friendship created opportunities for the use of metrics to improve student outcomes, drive performance management for teachers and administrative staff and organizational accountability to its multiple stakeholders. According to Friendship COO Patricia Brantley, "We use the data as the common driver of urgency for leadership and urgency for management."

Introduction

The chapter provides a very brief overview of why nonprofit organizations should pay attention metrics in HRM. The question of metrics or measures of performance in general is of particular importance in nonprofits. Although one cannot conclusively say that the level of importance of metrics in the sector has been extended to HRM, there are undoubtable rationales for examining metrics and HRM in nonprofits. The chapter introduces metrics and analytics, and considers why the use of metrics is important in nonprofit HRM. To provide a background, the chapter starts off with an overview of organizational effectiveness in nonprofits.

Organizational Effectiveness

What is organizational effectiveness in nonprofits? This is one of the central questions that defines the sector and is a logical starting point of any discussion about the use of metrics in nonprofits. In other words, what tells stakeholders that a nonprofit is performing? As discussed in previous chapters, one major characteristic that defines nonprofits is the absence or, more appropriately, the elusiveness of a universally accepted measure of organizational performance.[2] In fact, nonprofit research has shown us that while the "bottom line" is important, financial results are not the primary emphasis of a non-profit organization.[3] Put simply, financial results cannot be used as an indicator of the effectiveness of a nonprofit organization. So, if not financial result, what is the primary indicator of the effectiveness of a nonprofit?

The answer is the mission. Both academic and practitioner literature have pointed to the mission of each organization as perhaps the only indicator of the performance of a nonprofit. Indeed, it is argued that the essential indicator of performance is the extent to which nonprofits achieve their mission.[4] While there appears to be a consensus on the pre-eminence of the mission as the primary indicator of the performance of a nonprofit, there are still questions about effectiveness in general.

As a result, nonprofit literature has continued to explore perspectives for assessing the effectiveness of nonprofits. One study proposed a multidimensional and integrated model of nonprofit organizational effectiveness that distinguishes between management and program outcomes and highlights interrelationships in the dimensions.[5] Building on their 1999 article, Herman and Renz[6] examined nonprofit research and organizational effectiveness literature to propose nine theses on effectiveness in nonprofit organizations (see Box 13.1). The theses encapsulate the key elements and many of the critical issues in the conceptualization of the organizational effectiveness in nonprofits.

Regardless of the different perspectives, one consensus in the literature is that nonprofit effectiveness is multidimensional and social in nature.[7] The multidimensional indicators of effectiveness further heighten the importance of stakeholders and the external environment. The importance and expectations of stakeholders directly translate into the key elements of the multidimensional performance indicators in nonprofits.

BOX 13.1 THESES ON NONPROFIT EFFECTIVENESS

1. Nonprofit organizational effectiveness is always a matter of comparison
2. Nonprofit organizational effectiveness is multidimensional
3. Boards of directors make a difference in the effectiveness of NPOs, but how they do this is not clear
4. The more effective NPOs are more likely to use correct management practices
5. Nonprofit organizational effectiveness is a social construction
6. It is unlikely that there are any universally applicable "best practices" that can be prescribed for all NPO boards and management
7. Responsiveness is a useful overarching criterion for resolving the challenge of differing judgments of NPO effectiveness by different stakeholder groups
8. It is useful to differentiate among different types of nonprofit organizations in assessing the merits of different approaches to understanding nonprofit effectiveness
9. Level of analysis makes a difference in understanding effectiveness, and it is important to differentiate effectiveness at program, organization, and network levels.

Source: Herman, R. D., & Renz, D. O. (2008) "Advancing nonprofit organizational effectiveness research and theory: Nine theses," *Nonprofit Management & Leadership*, 18: 399–415.

Measures of Performance in Nonprofits

From the literature, it is clear that the mission is the fundamental driver of measures of performance in nonprofits. However, there are still questions. If the mission is the core indicator of the performance of nonprofits and if the effectiveness that is defined by the mission is multidimensional and social in nature, what are the actual measures that should be considered to meet the expectations of stakeholder? Although the recent manifestations of this question do often and rightly suggest that the demand for accountability is one of the primary reasons for the emphasis on performance measures in the sector, nonprofits are not strangers to performance measures. Nonprofits have been documenting and counting outcomes since the early years of the settlement house movement in the US[8] and the Bureau of the Poor in the French colony of Quebec before it was part of Canada.[9] What is different is the shift in metrics of performance and the players influencing what to measure.[10] Although significant, the shift reflects the nature of change in the environment of nonprofits.

Consistent with the shift in the environment, what nonprofits measure to indicate organizational effectiveness and performance has been influenced by different perspectives. Generally, the measures of performance have varied over time to include measures of inputs, revenue, number of employees and output (mainly in terms of number of clients).[11] However, in recent years, the measures of performance have focused more on outcomes.[12] Outcome measures of performance are generally quantitative and consider the impact of the services on the client of the organization.[13] For some nonprofits, the impact can also be qualitative. Impact can be explained as the tangible value that the services of the nonprofits have contributed to the well-being of their clients. To determine the impact on clients, nonprofits need to know the condition or state of the attribute their services will add value to before and after clients receive the services or intervention.[14] The quantitative and tangible qualitative value of the services of nonprofits is extensive. The specific measures of performance that are adopted are relative to the services and context of a nonprofit including funders and clients.

It is important to emphasize that many of the outcomes and activities of nonprofit organizations are complex and difficult to measure. In some cases, it is simply impractical to quantify the outcome of a nonprofit. In addition, outcomes are subjected to the perception of stakeholders, which are often divergent. Hence, there are questions on whether measures are flawed and whether they reflect the actual indicators of the value provided by nonprofits or the judgment of the stakeholders who developed the measures.[15] Nonetheless, one cannot disagree with the need to measure the outcome and, by extension, the performance of nonprofits.

This need to manage and measure outcomes provides the basis for the use of metrics in nonprofits. The requirement to have information for the purpose of accountability to funders is an important part of the rationale. Nonprofits must understand the state, direction and the impact of the organization at all times. The information tools to navigate the continuous change in the environment, to position the organization in order to be able to mitigate threats and maximize opportunities, and to really deliver value to stakeholders are within the realms of metrics. The perspective of using metrics to measure nonprofit outcomes dictates not only the need for metrics in the core systems, processes and interactions of the organization, including HRM, but also the integration of the metrics that are collected for decision-making.

Metrics and Analytics

From the preceding discussion, one can surmise that *metrics* are measures or indicators of the outcomes and activities of organizations. For the purpose of this book, metrics are measures of the activities and outcomes of nonprofit organizations. Although metrics provide information or data on various components of the activities of an organization, the general goal for developing and implementing metrics is to measure efficiency and effectiveness. Most nonprofits track their activities and performance by metrics. It could be as simple as the number of clients, the number of volunteers, total revenue or sources of funding over a period of time. Two examples of metrics that are tracked by Charity Navigator, the nonprofit rating agency that examines and rates the performance of charities in the United States, concern two broad areas: financial health and accountability and transparency (Box 13.2).

BOX 13.2 EXAMPLES OF METRICS

Program Expenses:

This measure reflects what percentage of its total budget a charity spends on the programs and services it exists to deliver. Dividing a charity's program expenses by its total functional expenses yields this percentage.

Key Staff Listed:

It is important for donors and other stakeholders to know who runs the organization day-to-day. Charity Navigator does not cross-check the leadership listed on the website with that reported on the Form 990 because the latter often isn't available until more than a year after the charity's fiscal year ends. In that time, the charity's leadership may have changed and the charity typically reflects those more recent changes on the website. In other words, since the Form 990 isn't especially timely, it cannot be used to verify the leadership information published on the charity's site.

Source: Charity Navigator, http://www.charitynavigator.org/index.cfm?bay=studies. metro.main.

It is valuable to develop and collect metrics on the activities and performance of the organization. However, metrics are of little value if the organization cannot or does not use the information they provide to facilitate decision-making process. It is worse still if a nonprofit organization invests scarce resources to collect metrics that it cannot utilize to facilitate operations and influence the strategic direction of the organization.

One of the ways an organization can effectively use metrics it has collected is through analytics. In simple terms, when managers and employees review and analyze the metrics they have collected for the purpose of decision-making, they are generally undertaking analytics. Analytics can be used to improve the quality of metrics an organization collects. Analytics has been defined as:

> The use of data and related insights developed through applied analytics disciplines (for example, statistical, contextual, quantitative, predictive, cognitive and other models) to drive fact-based planning, decisions, execution, management, measurement and learning.
>
> Analytics may be descriptive, predictive or prescriptive.[16]

Although small nonprofits may lack the financial resources to create metrics and use analytics at the same level at which large nonprofits and for-profit businesses deploy the tools, there are still significant benefits to be gained from deploying small-scale analytics. Some basic insight in this regard may be of help to such organizations. In a joint study by *MIT Sloan Management Review* and the IBM Institute of Business Value, the research partnership found that organizations typically need to master three competencies in order to achieve analytics sophistication: (1) information management, (2) analytics skills and tools, and (3) data-oriented culture.[17] Based on these findings they developed the capabilities required to achieve each of the competencies (see Table 13.1).

It can be seen from Table 13.1 that the competencies are applicable to both large and small nonprofits. By developing these competencies, nonprofits can use analytics to drive the mission of the organization. With a directed focus on the critical performance drivers within the organization, analytics will help to emphasize the descriptive and predictive levels of analysis of the metrics that contribute to the outcomes of the organization including financial and human

TABLE 13.1 Organizations Must Master Three Analytics Competencies to Achieve Competitive Advantage

Manage the Data	*Understand the Data*	*Act on the Data*
Information management	**Analytics skills and tools**	**Data-oriented culture**
Solid information foundation	Skills developed as a core discipline	Fact-driven leadership
Standardized data management practices	Enabled by a robust set of tools and solutions	Analytics used as a strategic asset
Insights accessible and available	Develop action-oriented insights	Strategy and operations guided by insights

Source: The New Intelligent Enterprise, a joint *MIT Sloan Management Review* and IBM Institute of Business Value analytics research partnership. Cited in Kiron, D., Shockley, R., Kruschwitz, N., Finch, G., & Haydock, M. (2011) "Analytics: The widening divide. How companies are achieving competitive advantage through analytics," IBM Institute for Business Value & *MIT Sloan Management Review*.

resources metrics.[18] Senior leaders and managers can leverage analytics to learn how to figure out the pulse points in their organization.

HR Metrics and Nonprofits

To discuss the importance of HR metrics in nonprofits, it is relevant to briefly recap the critical role of employees and volunteers in these organizations. As noted repeatedly in this book, employees and volunteers are arguably the most important factors in the ability of a nonprofit to achieve its mission. Employees and volunteers are the source of the human capital a nonprofit requires to develop and deliver services, to manage the operations of the organization and to provide governance for effective oversight in the organization. Their knowledge, skills and abilities are the core competencies that shape the competitiveness of nonprofits. Consequently, as noted in Chapter 4, the performance goals of nonprofits simply cannot happen without competent and committed employees and volunteers. Moreover, and again as noted previously, nonprofit employees tend to have a different type of relationship with the organization than employees in other sectors. This portends a different level of "fit" between the organization's human capital, strategy and the environment.[19] SHRM and specific HR practices are essential not only as strategies to gain competitive advantage but also serve to enable nonprofit-specific activities such as advocacy and community engagement.

With this background in mind, one can posit that the need to deploy the human capital of employees and volunteers in nonprofits is inextricably linked to metrics. Many of the critical questions that determine the metrics nonprofits should focus on are directly or indirectly related to employees and volunteers. For example, one of the typical opening questions in developing metrics is, *what metrics do we need to be successful in delivering our critical goals?* This question leads on to a number of follow-up questions such as what knowledge and skills are available in the organization and which skills should be targeted in recruitment.

Why Use HR Metrics

Integrating HRM with metrics in nonprofits offers a number of benefits to the organization (Box 13.3). It enables the nonprofit to manage and translate the unique challenges that are reflected in their HR practices into metrics and helps the nonprofit to determine the emerging HR metrics that the organization must adopt to track and support organizational goals. Consistent with a survey report in *HR Focus*,[20] the other benefits of HR metrics include the abilities to monitor the achievements, failures and progress of specific initiatives, to compare performance with other organizations, and to gather information for return on investment (ROI). HR metrics can also be used to address performance management, recruitment and retention efforts.

Following from the importance of HRM in organizational metrics, nonprofit manages should consider adopting the following process to better align HRM to strategic goals and gain support in the formulation and use of HR metrics.

BOX 13.3 HOW TO GAIN SUPPORT FOR HR METRICS

1. involve HR in the development of overall business strategy;
2. enlist leaders outside of HR to help develop and back metrics;
3. collaborate with business managers to ensure metrics link to business unit strategic goals;
4. focus more attention on links between people measures and intermediate performance drivers (e.g., customer satisfaction, innovation, engagement);
5. increase manager acceptance through training programs and concrete action plans; and
6. work with HR to simplify metric and automate data collection.

Source: Gates, S. (2002) *Value at Work: The Risks and Opportunities of Human Capital Measurement and Reporting.* New York: The Conference Board.

What to Measure

Although most of the HR practices in a nonprofit would theoretically benefit if metrics were created and used to measure performance or progress, it is not practical or cost-effective to measure too many metrics. Irrespective of the sector, many of the measures used as metrics in HR are consistent. From the brief discussion about HR metrics in Chapter 4, some of the common types of metrics used to measure HR performance and outcomes include turnover rate, cost per hire, absenteeism, demographic metrics, training costs, and vacancy rate. Table 13.2 re-presents the 23 key HR metrics used by the HR Metrics Service which is a joint service of three Canadian provincial Human Resources Professional Associations (British Colombia, Manitoba and Ontario).[21] Each measure is categorized into metric categories such as compensation, productivity and HR efficiency. In nonprofits, these metrics would provide opportunities for the organization to link HR strategies and practices with organizational goals. As noted above, the metrics are also useful as benchmarks to compare performance among nonprofit organizations.

The survey by *HR Focus*[22] found that most HR professionals indicated that the typical HR activities that were measured with metrics included: employee skills, employee attitudes toward job/organization, recruiting, hiring, onboarding, turnover, training use, training return on investment (ROI), promotions and the

TABLE 13.2 Key HR Metrics*

Metric Name	Metric Category
Labor Cost per FTE	Compensation
Labor Cost Revenue Percent	Compensation
Labor Cost Expense Percent	Compensation
HR FTE Ratio	HR Efficiency
HR Costs per Employee	HR Efficiency
HR Costs per FTE	HR Efficiency
Absenteeism Rate	Productivity
Human Capital Return on Investment	Productivity
Revenue Per FTE	Productivity
Profit Per FTE	Productivity
Vacancy Rate	Recruitment
1st Year Resignation Rate	Recruitment
Turnover	Retention
Voluntary Turnover Rate	Retention
Involuntary Turnover Rate	Retention
Resignation Rate	Retention
Cost of Voluntary Turnover	Retention
Retirement Rate	Retention
Average Retirement Rate	Retention
Average length of Service	Workforce Demographics
Average Age	Workforce Demographics
Union Percentage	Workforce Demographics
Promotion Rate	Workforce Demographics

*HR Metrics Service. A joint service of BC HRMA, HRMAM & 1   A.

use of HR consultants. The important point is to d   nine what to measure with metrics based on the goals of the activity or proce:

Summary

The mission is the benchmark for organizational effect veness in nonprofits. The chapter reviews the intersection of HRM and metrics in nonprofits. Specifically, it provides a brief overview of why nonprofit organizations should pay attention to HR metrics. At the time of writing this chapter, research on HR metrics in nonprofits is scarce. However, available research that is not specifically about nonprofits suggests that many organizations are experiencing major issues with the development and use of appropriate HR metrics.[23] The issues range from a lack of understanding of theoretical models, measures and the application of measurements. Rather than cast a shadow on the need for nonprofit managers to use HR metrics for the benefits of their organizations, these challenges highlight barriers the organization needs to overcome in order to reap the reward of HR metrics in the sector. As organizations that are well attuned to metrics imposed by funders, developing and implementing HR metrics aligned with organizational goals can help to predict and prescribe trends and outcomes that would help to mitigate threat and maximize opportunities.

Discussion Questions

As a group, use the following questions to determine the metrics a nonprofit organization may need:[24]

1. What outcomes do we want to achieve?
2. What services must we provide to promote and achieve those outcomes?
3. What resources do we need to provide those services?
4. What are key metrics we need to measure to monitor progress and outcomes?

Notes

1 Adapted from Morino, M. (2011) *Leap of Reason: Managing Outcomes in an Era of Scarcity*. Washington, DC: Venture Philanthropy Partners; Hardman, Jesse (2012) "How a D.C. High School Football Team Beat All Odds," http://keepingscore.blogs. time.com/2012/12/05/how-a-d-c-high-school-football-team-beat-all-odds/. Retrieved December 5, 2012.

2 Herman, R. D., & Renz, D. O. (2004) "Investigating the relation between good management, financial outcomes and stakeholder judgement of effectiveness in donative and commercial nonprofit organizations," Los Angeles, CA: Association for Research on Nonprofit Organizations and Voluntary Action.

3 McFarlan, W. (1999, November/December) "Don't assume the shoe fits," *Harvard Business Review*. http://hbr.org/1999/11/dont-assume-theshoe-fits/ar/1.

4 Moore, M. (2000) "Managing for value: Organizational strategy in for-profit, non-profit, and governmental organizations," *Nonprofit and Voluntary Sector Quarterly*, 29: 183–208.

5 Sowa, J., Selden, S. C., & Sandfort, J. (2004) "No longer unmeasurable? A multi-dimensional integrated model of nonprofit organizational effectiveness," *Nonprofit and Voluntary Sector Quarterly*, 33: 711–728.

6 Herman, R. D., & Renz, D. O. (2008) "Advancing nonprofit organizational effectiveness research and theory: Nine theses," *Nonprofit Management & Leadership*, 18: 399–415.

7 Herman, R. D., & Renz, D. O. (1999) "Theses on nonprofit organizational effectiveness," *Nonprofit and Voluntary Sector Quarterly*, 23(2): 107–126.

8 Alexander, J., Brudney, J. L., & Yang, K. (2010) "Introduction to the symposium: Accountability and performance measurement: The evolving role of nonprofits in the hollow state," *Nonprofit and Voluntary Sector Quarterly*, 39(4): 565–570.

9 Martin, S. (1985) *An Essential Grace*. Toronto: McCllelland and Stewart.

10 Barman, E. (2007) "What is the bottom line for nonprofit organizations? A history of measurement in the British voluntary sector," *Voluntas: International Journal of Voluntary and Nonprofit Organizations*, 18: 101–115.

11 LeRoux, K., & Wright, N. S. (2010) "Does performance measurement improve strategic decision making? Findings from a national survey of nonprofit social service agencies," *Nonprofit and Voluntary Sector Quarterly*, 39(4): 571–587.

12 Herman & Renz, "Theses on nonprofit organizational effectiveness."

13 Speckbacker, G. (2003) "The economics of performance management in nonprofit organizations," *Nonprofit Management and Leadership*, 13(3): 267–281.

14 Herman & Renz, "Theses on nonprofit organizational effectiveness"; MacIndoe, H. & Barman, E. (2012) "How organizational stakeholders shape performance measurement

in nonprofits: Exploring a multidimensional measure," *Nonprofit and Voluntary Sector Quarterly*, 42(4): 716–738.

15 Hager, M. A., & Flack, T. (2004). *The Pros and Cons of Financial Efficiency Standards* (Nonprofit Overhead Cost Project). Washington, DC: Urban Institute Center on Nonprofits and Philanthropy and Indiana University Center on Philanthropy; Mitchell, G. E. (2012) "The construct of organizational effectiveness: Perspectives from leaders of international nonprofits in the United States," *Nonprofit and Voluntary Sector Quarterly*, 42(2): 324–345.

16 Messatfa, H., Reyes, L., & Schroeck, M. (2011) "The power of analytics for the public sector Building analytics competency to accelerate outcomes," Somers, NY: IBM Global Services, http://www-304.ibm.com/easyaccess/fileserve?contentid=219184. Retrieved October, 2012.

17 Kiron, D., Shockley, R., Kruschwitz, N., Finch, G., & Haydock, M. (2011) "Analytics: The widening divide. How companies are achieving competitive advantage through analytics," IBM Institute for Business Value & MIT Sloan Management Review.

18 Adams, J. & Klein, J. (2011) "Business intelligence and analytics in health care - a primer, 2011," The Advisory Board Company: Washington, DC. http://www.advisory.com/Research/Health-Care-IT-Advisor/Research-Notes/2011/Business-Intelligence-and-Analytics-in-Health-Care.

19 Akingbola, K. (2012) "Context and nonprofit human resource management," *Administration and Society*, 45(8): 974–1004.

20 HR Focus (2010) "Special report on HR metrics. Survey looks at reasons for using metrics, functions most measured," Supplement to *HR Focus*, The Bureau of National Affairs.

21 HR Metrics Service. A joint service of BC HRMA, HRMAM & HRPA http://www.hrpa.ca/Pages/HRMetricsService.aspx

22 HR Focus (2010) "Special report on HR metrics."

23 Tootell, B., Blackler, M., Toulson, P., & Dewe, P. (2009) "Metrics: HRM's Holy Grail? A New Zealand case study," *Human Resource Management Journal*, 19(4): 375–392.

24 Adapted from Dawson, T. (2013) "Simplify your process with a dashboard approach," *Texas CEO Magazine,* August 23, 2013. http://texasceomagazine.com/departments/meaningful-metrics-for-the-nonprofit-organization/.

INDEX